QUANTUM APPROACH
TO INFORMATICS

Motto

Whatever is investigated by human reason commonly also contains falsehood, and this derives partly from the weak judgement of our intellect and partly from the admixtures of pictures. Consequently many, who remain unaware of the power of visualization, will doubt such things that have been most truly demonstrated. This is the case especially because each one having a reputation as a wise man teaches his own version of the creed. In addition, many truths that are taken to be demonstrated also encompass something false, something which has not been truly demonstrated but rather is claimed on the basis of some probable or contrived argument, which is nevertheless taken to be a valid demonstration.

Thomas of Aquinas
1224–1274

QUANTUM APPROACH TO INFORMATICS

Stig Stenholm

KTH, Stockholm, Sweden
and HUT, Espoo, Finland

Kalle-Antti Suominen

University of Turku, Finland

A JOHN WILEY & SONS, INC., PUBLICATION

Library of Congress Cataloging-in-Publication Data:

Stenholm, Stig.
    Quantum approach to informatics / Stig Stenholm, Kalle-Antti Suominen.
      p. cm.
    Includes bibliographical references and index.
    ISBN-13 978-0-471-73610-3
    ISBN-10 0-471-73610-4
    1. Quantum theory—Mathematics. 2. Computer science—Mathematics. 3. Quantum computers. I. Suominen, Kalle-Antti, 1964–II. Title.
    QC174.17.M35S74 2005
    530.12—dc22

                          2005042842

CONTENTS

PREFACE

To see the world as a web of information is a recent view. Humanity has contemplated the source and character of our knowledge since the dawn of time, but the present technologically oriented civilization demands a more concrete concept. Knowledge has been replaced by information. The information has to be carried by physical objects, and these are described by the theories of physics. Thus, we have to develop a theory for information coded in physical objects.

Long ago, scientists developed formal descriptions of classical information transfer and its manipulation. Only recently, however, have we encountered the information capacity carried by quantum entities. The quantum theory of information, communication, and computing is rather recent. It has grown and matured at a surprising speed. Many discussions of physical observations and quantum measurements are today phrased in terms of information-theoretic concepts. Thus, there is a need to educate students in this thinking but also a need for established researchers to get acquainted with the new way of thinking provoked by the informational aspects of physics. The present book is written to fulfill this need. We consider our readership to be mainly physicists who want to absorb the basics of quantum information within the quantum mechanical framework with which they are familiar. For people who wish to work seriously on the topic or who have a nonphysicist background, many alternative sources are already available.

We regard this book as a contribution to the theory and applications of quantum physics. However, most scientists working with applied quantum theory lack knowledge of classical information theory. Consequently, we introduce the basic ideas from information theory on which the quantum developments are to be built. On the other hand, standard courses in quantum mechanics do not necessarily cover those aspects most significant for the processing of quantum information. Thus, we present the fundamentals of quantum theory as an introduction to the information discussion. Here we need to explore the actual process of quantum observations in more detail than is usually contained in standard textbooks. The material is not really new, but it acquires novel significance in the present context. Armed with this knowledge, we are prepared to develop the theory of information processing and computing in the quantum domain.

We present the basic ideas of quantum information through an introduction to its basic concepts and methods. It should be useful as the material for a one-semester course of quantum information. The book requires some prior knowledge of quantum theory; thus, it is a text aimed primarily at physicists. This prerequisite should not exceed that given in the standard courses at most universities. The book may, however, be used to indicate to information theorists which parts of quantum theory they need to learn in order to work in this new field; to them the task may not be too arduous. It is our hope that we may introduce the field to a broad range of readers. These may be approaching the text either out of curiosity or in order to be able to proceed to more advanced material.

The presentation aims at neither completeness nor formal rigor. We present the necessary quantum concepts in their simplest forms and introduce ideas by concrete examples. These are presented in such detail that the reader should be able to work through all exercises. Thus, we teach general principles by example rather than by formal demonstrations and general theorems. Many aspects of information theory, classical as well as quantum, can be the subject of formal proofs. For these we refer the reader to the literature.

The references we give are only a small part of the rapidly growing literature in this field. We offer primarily reviews or monographs to set the stage of the action. In addition, we give specific references to particular results treated in the text. The development of the field is too rapid for the reference list to be complete and up to date. We do believe, however, that having mastered the material in this book, the reader can utilize the literature to penetrate any chosen aspect further. In addition, there are comprehensive monographs covering the scope of the field much more completely than we do.

After a brief introduction to set the scene, in Chapter 2 we present the formalism and structure of quantum theory in a form needed for the rest of the book. In addition to a summary of the theory, we introduce some concepts and methods that emerge from this approach. Many of these aspects are treated in further detail in other works, to which we refer. This chapter is central to an understanding of later applications; the basic theme of the book is methods and meanings of quantum manipulations.

Chapter 3 covers the application of information concepts to quantum physics. We summarize briefly the results of information theory and then implement them on quantum systems. No prior knowledge of information theory is assumed. The many quantum results presented in the literature are elucidated by a few central examples. Of particular interest is the possibility to detect and identify information coded in quantum states. The special character of quantum uncertainties makes this problem different from the corresponding classical problem in noisy transmission channels.

In Chapter 4 we take up the highly topical field of quantum information processing and computing. Most of the material in this chapter is independent of Chapter 3 and can be approached directly after Chapter 2. We do not assume any prior knowledge of computer science; however, those who want to pursue such problems further need more classical background material than we can present here. The text first summarizes the classical approach to data processing and the abstract concept of classical computation. The results are then implemented on quantum systems, and the concept of a quantum computing element, a gate, is introduced. The treatment indicates how quantum gates can be utilized to realize quantum algorithms by combining gates into circuits. As an application, the by-now canonical integer factoring problem is discussed in some detail. We review its origin in methods of classical secret communication and briefly present the method to speed up the factoring on a quantum computer. This solution initiated the present lively interest in quantum computing. We also briefly introduce the sources and character of computing errors and the possibilities for correcting them by quantum means. To conclude the chapter, the energy aspects of quantum computing are briefly introduced.

Finally, in Chapter 5 we present some aspects of the physical realizations of quantum computing circuits. This chapter is rather sketchy, for two reasons: The material covers a broad range of physical phenomena and we can treat their necessary background only briefly. Second, the field is evolving rapidly, so whatever we write here is going to be obsolete in a very brief time. Thus, we begin the chapter by summarizing general considerations concerning possible realizations. We subsequently present the physics behind the most promising systems at the time of writing. The technical details and up-to-date achievements must be learned from more complete presentations than the present one.

We have not inserted detailed references into the text of the book. This would only interrupt the flow of the argument and be useless at a first reading. Instead, we have collected all references into a section at the end of each chapter. In this way we can comment briefly on the contents and significance of the various sources. This is intended to help the reader find a reference dealing with just the specific problem for which he or she requires additional information. We also give the necessary credits to material taken directly from specific publications.

Acknowledgments

We are very grateful to Rainer Blatt and Anton Zeilinger for permission to present images obtained by their experimental research groups. We have, over the years, benefited from discussions with too many persons to mention them all here. A selected list is, however, as follows: Erika Andersson, Adriano Barenco, Steve Barnett, Ingemar Bengtsson, Rainer Blatt, Sam Braunstein, Časlav Brukner, Dagmar Bruss, Vladimír Bužek, John Calsamiglia, Ignacio Cirac, David DiVincenzo,

Joe Eberly, Göran Einarsson, Artur Ekert, Barry Garraway, Florian Haug, David Haviland, Peter Knight, Pekka Lahti, Maciej Lewenstein, Göran Lindblad, Norbert Lütkenhaus, Chiara Macchiavello, Harri Mäkelä, Klaus Mølmer, Massimo Palma, Sorin Paraoanu, Jukka Pekola, Jyrki Piilo, Martin Plenio, Anna Sanpera, Päivi Törmä, Vlatko Vedral, Martin Wilkens, Anton Zeilinger, and Peter Zoller.

STIG STENHOLM
KALLE-ANTTI SUOMINEN

Stockholm, Sweden
Turku, Finland
December 2004

CHAPTER 1

INTRODUCTION

1.1 BACKGROUND

Quantum mechanics arose from the need to understand the thermal properties of radiation and the discrete spectral features of atoms. From this developed the present understanding of the nonclassical behavior of the fundamental units of matter and radiation. Quantum theory has turned out to be the most universally successful theory of physics. From its start in atomic spectroscopy, it has developed to predict structures of molecules, nuclei, and even the large-scale structures of the universe.

Much of our electronics industry today utilizes quantum phenomena in an essential manner. Without the understanding offered by quantum theory, our ability to build integrated circuits and communication devices would not have emerged. In these areas the basic theoretical progress took place in the middle of the twentieth century; the engineers who plan electronics devices need hardly worry about the problems still lingering on our interpretation of quantum theory.

Despite all its successes, quantum theory is more a set of recipes than a well-formed theory. Even if we master quantum theory in practical applications, we do not really comprehend its basic structure as a probabilistic theory with its associated highly nonclassical and nonlocal correlations. The rather strange role of an observer and the very act of measurements give an uneasy feeling that the theory is not closed. Over the decades, this feeling was put forward by many eminent physicists, including some of the very founders of the theory.

Quantum Approach to Informatics, by Stig Stenholm and Kalle-Antti Suominen
Copyright © 2005 John Wiley & Sons, Inc.

Quantum measurements have always been concerned with information transfer; the object under investigation is supposed to give up knowledge about some of its properties to a measuring device that is eventually read by an observer. Thus, even the very act of physical measurement can be regarded as an information transfer between nature and the scientist. The transmitting method is the totality of our laws of physics, with quantum theory being one eminent member.

But humans want to perform many other information-processing operations than observations. We want to communicate at arbitrary distances and process data to analyze them or obtain answers to well-posed mathematical queries. In some investigations in theoretical physics, we want to use computing devices to simulate natural phenomena. All this has to take place in media consisting of physical objects. These thus have to carry the necessary information, manipulate it, and inform the operator about the outcome. All information processing is to take place in a material medium.

The question arises: How does quantum mechanics affect all this? Richard Feynman was a pioneer in suggesting that the optimal way to model a quantum process would be to simulate it with an appropriate other quantum process. But quantum components are widely different from classical ones, and thus the understanding of their operation becomes an investigation into the scope and limit of quantum mechanics as we know it.

Quantum systems carry a character of wholeness, which is lacking in classical systems. If we interfere with one part of a system, this may have important consequences for the other parts. Thus, one cannot do onto quantum systems all one can do onto classical ones. This has been utilized in communication with quantum systems; if a photon is absorbed by a receiver, it is not available for any intruder.

On the other hand, quantum systems can do more things simultaneously than classical objects can. The well-known two-slit experiment shows interference between particle paths going different ways to their ultimate absorption; no classical particle can do that. This offers a possibility to let quantum systems perform all desired calculations in parallel, which has been found to speed up certain algorithmic processes beyond what classical computers can achieve. Thus, the idea of a quantum computer was born.

Over all such new applications falls the shadow of quantum measurements. The proper introduction of an observer and the processes he or she is able to effect play an important role in all quantum information-processing methods. Thus, we need to understand the fundamental structure of quantum theory at its deepest level. We must realize all the possibilities that the theory offers, but also be aware of the limitations imposed by quantum measurements. Recent developments in quantum information research can be seen as a thorough exploration of our basic understanding of the quantum theory of physical systems. Even if nothing else useful ever emerges from the effort, we may hope that it will result in a broader and deeper understanding of the theory.

Quantum technology is very much alive today. This is an interesting development, because there are no practically useful realizations available in the laboratories. All experimental setups are primitive and explorative. All practical rewards are far in the future. However, long before that, the field has reached a certain maturity. We are exploring the possible uses of generic quantum systems, which still are very far from practical materialization. This is new in quantum physics; so far it has been used primarily to analyze observed phenomena. Now we have reached the age of synthesis. Devices are planned and explored which today are far beyond our technical abilities. As to their eventual materialization, only the future can tell.

The popularity of the concept of information has inspired some researchers to claim that all our best descriptions of nature are based only on information retrieved from the observations; information theory lies behind all understanding. Sometimes an even wilder claim is made: The universe as we experience it is only a set of information carriers; its very existence is as information and nothing else. This is highly speculative; there is no empirical basis for such a claim. In fact, taken at face value, one may find it difficult to actually understand what this claim means. As physicists we believe in an independent reality, but quantum theory tells us that this is, in fact, weirder than we can imagine.

In this work we approach information transfer and manipulation as a branch of quantum physics. The basic facts of the fundamental theory are put forward in a form conducive to this end. We do not try to cover all the aspects of this rapidly developing field, but we present selected applications to illustrate how quantum mechanics is used in information physics. To make the presentation self-contained, we present such facts from classical information theory which are needed to comprehend the quantum application. The basic outlook is, however, that we are dealing with a branch of quantum physics. Thus, the progress in insight and understanding gained may turn out useful even if a technically successful quantum information machine is never to be built.

1.2 QUANTUM INFORMATION UNIT

Classical information is carried by numerical variables, which are in practice often reduced to the binary representation $\{0, 1\}$. A sequence $abcd$ of these correspond to the number

$$abcd \Leftrightarrow a \times 2^3 + b \times 2^2 + c \times 2 + d. \tag{1.1}$$

Each binary variable carries an amount of information called a *bit*; the number above thus carries 4 bits of information. This is a measure of the length of the string carrying the information, whereas the string can actually be used to name $2^4 = 16$ different numbers. From the point of view of information, the length of the string is interesting; it tells us how much space is required to hold the number. Hence the measure of information is often taken to be the length of this: in this case,

$$4 = \log_2 16 = \frac{\log 16}{\log 2}, \tag{1.2}$$

where "log" denotes the ordinary natural logarithm, based on Euler's number e. Using the logarithmic definition of information, we see that a single bit carries $\log_2 2 = 1$ (i.e., 1 bit of information).

In quantum mechanics, the simple two-level system based on the state space spanned by the basis vectors $\{|0\rangle, |1\rangle\}$ replaces the classical bit. Throughout this book we take Dirac's notation of bras and kets for granted. The basis states are assumed to be normalized and orthogonal with respect to the scalar product in the space

$$\langle k|n\rangle = \delta_{kn}. \tag{1.3}$$

We can represent a general state in this basis as

$$|\psi\rangle = c_0|0\rangle + c_1|1\rangle. \tag{1.4}$$

An alternative notation is the vector form

$$|\psi\rangle = c_0|0\rangle + c_1|1\rangle \Leftrightarrow \begin{bmatrix} c_0 \\ c_1 \end{bmatrix}. \tag{1.5}$$

For large state spaces the vector form (and the accompanying matrix notation for operators) becomes cumbersome, but for quantum information systems it provides a useful alternative to Dirac's notation.

The norm of the general state of a two-level system is given by

$$\| |\psi\rangle \|^2 \equiv \langle \psi|\psi\rangle = |c_0|^2 + |c_1|^2 = 1. \tag{1.6}$$

The two complex numbers $\{c_0, c_1\}$ have four real parameters; one of these is fixed by the normalization condition. We can write the state as

$$|\psi\rangle = e^{i\eta} \left(\cos\frac{\theta}{2}|0\rangle + e^{i\varphi} \sin\frac{\theta}{2}|1\rangle \right). \tag{1.7}$$

Usually, the overall (global) phase η lacks significance, and the state is thus determined by the two parameters $\{\theta, \varphi\}$. One should note, however, that when considering a larger system that consists of many such two-level systems, the phase relations between the two-level systems (given by η) are relevant.

The vector describing the state of a two-level quantum system carries the quantum analog of a bit; this is called a *qubit*. The qubit is a more general information carrier than the bit. Its use derives from a combination of quantum physics with ideas from classical information processing. The storing and processing of quantum information offers many exciting and novel features. Its practical utility and general properties are still only incompletely known.

If we choose to code some information in the coefficients $\{c_0, c_1\}$, we call this basis the *computational basis*. Choosing this, we have given up the well-known freedom to use an arbitrary basis in quantum mechanical calculations; the information is specifically carried in one basis only. We are, of course, free to redefine our computational basis at any time. Another very useful complementary basis is given by the states

$$|\psi_{\pm}\rangle = \frac{1}{\sqrt{2}} (|0\rangle \pm |1\rangle). \tag{1.8}$$

These are easily seen to be orthogonal, and in terms of the original basis states, we have

$$|\langle 0|\psi_{\pm}\rangle|^2 = |\langle 1|\psi_{\pm}\rangle|^2 = \frac{1}{2}. \tag{1.9}$$

Quantum mechanically, this tells us that when the system is in the states $|\psi_{\pm}\rangle$, there are equal probabilities that it will be found in any of the original basis states. The new states consequently carry no information about the occurrence of the original states. Performing a measurement, we will find that they occur with equal random probabilities.

In quantum physics a central role is played by linear transformations of the state vectors. These are given by the operators M, which appear as matrices if we use the vector notation for the amplitudes:

$$M|\psi\rangle \Leftrightarrow \begin{bmatrix} m_{00} & m_{01} \\ m_{10} & m_{11} \end{bmatrix} \begin{bmatrix} c_0 \\ c_1 \end{bmatrix}. \tag{1.10}$$

The matrix in Eq. (1.10) can be written in the form

$$M = \frac{m_{00} + m_{11}}{2} \begin{bmatrix} 1 & 0 \\ 0 & 1 \end{bmatrix} + \frac{m_{01} + m_{10}}{2} \begin{bmatrix} 0 & 1 \\ 1 & 0 \end{bmatrix}$$
$$+ i \frac{m_{01} - m_{10}}{2} \begin{bmatrix} 0 & -i \\ i & 0 \end{bmatrix} + \frac{m_{00} - m_{11}}{2} \begin{bmatrix} 1 & 0 \\ 0 & -1 \end{bmatrix}. \tag{1.11}$$

Here we have introduced the Pauli matrices

$$\sigma_1 = \begin{bmatrix} 0 & 1 \\ 1 & 0 \end{bmatrix},$$

$$\sigma_2 = \begin{bmatrix} 0 & -i \\ i & 0 \end{bmatrix}, \tag{1.12}$$

$$\sigma_3 = \begin{bmatrix} 1 & 0 \\ 0 & -1 \end{bmatrix}.$$

They are normally used to describe spin variables in quantum physics, but here we regard them as simple basis matrices for 2×2 matrix transformations. They obey the simple relations

$$\sigma_1 \sigma_2 - \sigma_2 \sigma_1 = 2i\sigma_3 \tag{1.13}$$

with cyclic permutations $1 \rightarrow 2 \rightarrow 3 \rightarrow 1$. We also have for any pair

$$\text{Tr}(\sigma_i \sigma_j) = 2\delta_{ij}, \tag{1.14}$$

where the notation $\text{Tr}(M)$ means the sum of the diagonal elements of a matrix M (i.e., its trace). Using these, we can write any matrix in the form

$$M = \frac{1}{2}\left(\text{Tr}(M) + \sum_{i=1}^{3} M_i \sigma_i\right), \tag{1.15}$$

with

$$M_i = \text{Tr}(\sigma_i M). \tag{1.16}$$

Note: In the quantum information literature, one often encounters the notation

$$\begin{aligned}
\sigma_1 &= X, \\
\sigma_2 &= Y, \\
\sigma_3 &= Z.
\end{aligned} \tag{1.17}$$

In this book we prefer, however, the Pauli notation, which is standard in quantum mechanics literature.

In telecommunications, light has a special role. Photons are natural carriers of quantum information. The orthogonal polarization states of a photon form a quantum mechanical two-level system, although technologically it is not necessarily the best option (e.g., in optical fibers, polarization states are extremely fragile). Another possibility is to consider the existence of the photon itself if we know that the photons are arriving at regular intervals. Recently, the orbital angular momentum carried by laser beams has emerged as yet another available degree of freedom at the level of single photons.

A photon is the bosonic quantum of the electromagnetic field. Its description follows from the fact that the theory of electromagnetic radiation can be cast in the form of an assembly of independent harmonic oscillators. The quantum theory of this system is well presented in most texts on quantum theory; here we refresh the reader's memory by summarizing the main parts of the argument. We return to this topic again in Sec. 5.3.1, where we consider field quantization in a cavity.

In suitably chosen units the Hamiltonian of one harmonic mode is given by

$$H = \frac{P^2}{2} + \frac{1}{2}\omega^2 Q^2, \tag{1.18}$$

where ω is the angular frequency of the mode. As P and Q are canonical variables, we perform the quantization by setting

$$[Q, P] \equiv QP - PQ = i\hbar. \tag{1.19}$$

If we define the operators

$$a = \sqrt{\frac{\omega}{2\hbar}} \left(Q + \frac{iP}{\omega} \right),$$

$$a^\dagger = \sqrt{\frac{\omega}{2\hbar}} \left(Q - \frac{iP}{\omega} \right),$$

(1.20)

we can then directly calculate

$$\left[a, a^\dagger \right] = aa^\dagger - a^\dagger a = 1.$$

(1.21)

This shows that the operators characterize bosons. We also obtain

$$aa^\dagger + a^\dagger a = \frac{2H}{\hbar\omega},$$

(1.22)

giving

$$H = \frac{\hbar\omega}{2} \left(aa^\dagger + a^\dagger a \right) = \hbar\omega \left(a^\dagger a + \frac{1}{2} \right).$$

(1.23)

We can now define the eigenstates $|n\rangle$ of the operator $N = a^\dagger a$, by requiring that

$$N|n\rangle = n|n\rangle.$$

(1.24)

Assuming the existence of a vacuum state $|0\rangle$ such that

$$a|0\rangle = 0,$$

(1.25)

we find that the eigenstates n have to be integers $\{0, 1, 2, \ldots\}$. These are taken to count the number of photons in the mode. From (1.21) we can prove that

$$a|n\rangle = \sqrt{n}|n - 1\rangle,$$

$$a^\dagger|n\rangle = \sqrt{(n + 1)}|n + 1\rangle.$$

(1.26)

This justifies calling a and $a^\dagger$ photon annihilation and creation operators, respectively. From (1.26) it follows that the eigenstates can be written as

$$|n\rangle = \frac{(a^\dagger)^n}{\sqrt{n!}}|0\rangle,$$

(1.27)

where the denominator is chosen to give normalized states. They are also easily seen to be orthogonal for different quantum numbers.

In optical physics there is one set of operators for each type of photon. Thus, the electromagnetic field is replaced by a set of boson excitation modes. This representation is particularly useful in the quantum mechanical description of optical devices.

Application: Beamsplitter A beamsplitter is an optical element with two inputs and two outputs (Fig. 1.1). We assume that the incoming signals are split equally between the outputs. If the state amplitudes coming in are a_1 and a_2, respectively, and the outputs are b_1 and b_2, respectively, the transformation between the inputs and the outputs can be written as

$$\begin{bmatrix} b_1 \\ b_2 \end{bmatrix} = \frac{1}{\sqrt{2}} \begin{bmatrix} 1 & i \\ i & 1 \end{bmatrix} \begin{bmatrix} a_1 \\ a_2 \end{bmatrix}. \tag{1.28}$$

This transformation is unitary, and we have the inverse transformation

$$\begin{bmatrix} a_1 \\ a_2 \end{bmatrix} = \frac{1}{\sqrt{2}} \begin{bmatrix} 1 & -i \\ -i & 1 \end{bmatrix} \begin{bmatrix} b_1 \\ b_2 \end{bmatrix}. \tag{1.29}$$

This guarantees that the state amplitude is conserved:

$$|b_1|^2 + |b_2|^2 = |a_1|^2 + |a_2|^2. \tag{1.30}$$

Classically, the same relation guarantees that the outgoing energy is equal to the incoming energy.

We have defined the beamsplitter transformation in a symmetric way. We can move the phases around by redefining the relative phase of incoming and/or outgoing state amplitudes, but for most applications the symmetric form is most advantageous.

The beamsplitter transformation (1.28) has been defined in terms of classical amplitudes impinging on the device. As this is a linear transformation of the signals, we may directly replace the amplitudes by the corresponding quantum operators. The symbols $\{a^\dagger, b^\dagger\}$ then become photon creation operators, and the

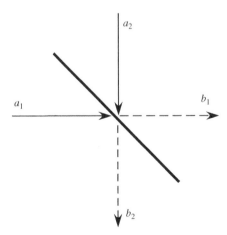

Figure 1.1 Beamsplitter with input amplitudes a_1, a_2 and output amplitudes b_1, b_2.

relations describe how incoming photons are transmitted into outgoing ones. This gives a convenient way to treat the properties of the device.

As an exercise, we calculate the output if one photon is impinging on the beamsplitter at each input port. Conveniently, we can replace the amplitudes in our description with the photon creation operators. Note that generally the photon vacuum is denoted with $|0\rangle$, which is not related to the quantum bit state $|0\rangle$ (unless we assign 0 to the detection of no photons). We have the input operators in terms of the output operators as

$$
\begin{aligned}
a_1^\dagger &= \frac{1}{\sqrt{2}} \left(b_1^\dagger + i b_2^\dagger \right), \\
a_2^\dagger &= \frac{1}{\sqrt{2}} \left(i b_1^\dagger + b_2^\dagger \right).
\end{aligned}
\tag{1.31}
$$

The input state is now given by

$$
\begin{aligned}
|\psi_{\text{in}}\rangle &= a_1^\dagger a_2^\dagger |0\rangle \\
&= \frac{i}{2} \left(b_1^{\dagger 2} + b_2^{\dagger 2} \right) |0\rangle \\
&= \frac{i}{\sqrt{2}} \left(|n_1 = 2, n_2 = 0\rangle + |n_1 = 0, n_2 = 2\rangle \right).
\end{aligned}
\tag{1.32}
$$

We thus find that both photons exit at the same output, and no coincidences can be observed between detectors in the two outputs. This is a manifestation of the bosonic character of the photons. Note that the original phase relation of the two photons plays no role; the incoming channels do not share the same state space (nor do the two output channels).

1.3   REPRESENTATION OF THE QUBIT

1.3.1   Bloch Sphere

From the representation (1.7) of the general quantum state $|\psi\rangle$ we define the quantities

$$
\begin{aligned}
u &\equiv \langle \psi | \sigma_1 | \psi \rangle = c_0^* c_1 + c_0 c_1^* = \sin\theta \cos\varphi, \\
v &\equiv \langle \psi | \sigma_2 | \psi \rangle = i \left(c_0 c_1^* - c_1 c_0^* \right) = \sin\theta \sin\varphi, \\
w &\equiv \langle \psi | \sigma_3 | \psi \rangle = c_0 c_0^* - c_1 c_1^* = \cos\theta.
\end{aligned}
\tag{1.33}
$$

From this we see that the real vector

$$
\vec{R} = \begin{bmatrix} \sin\theta \cos\varphi \\ \sin\theta \sin\varphi \\ \cos\theta \end{bmatrix}
\tag{1.34}
$$

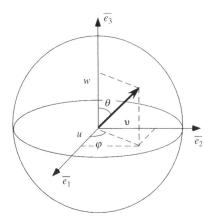

Figure 1.2   Bloch vector in the Bloch sphere and its parametrization with angles θ and φ.

is of unit length

$$\vec{R} \cdot \vec{R} = u^2 + v^2 + w^2 = 1. \tag{1.35}$$

It is a representation of the quantum state in a fictitious three-dimensional space, where u, v, and w are the coordinates along three axes represented by orthogonal unit vectors $\vec{e}_1$, $\vec{e}_2$, and $\vec{e}_3$ (Fig. 1.2). This is the Bloch vector. In fact, since $|\vec{R}| = 1$, the representation is reduced to defining a point on the surface of a unit sphere with angular coordinates (θ, φ). This unit sphere is called the *Bloch sphere*. The origin of the term is in nuclear magnetism, where by defining the quantum mechanical spin in this manner, one can identify the fictitious three-dimensional space with the actual three-dimensional space. This allows a simple description of the spin dynamics due to the coupling of the spin to the magnetic field (which is an object of the actual three-dimensional space).

For a given state, the vector $\vec{R}$ has the right number of real parameters to specify the state uniquely. The state $[1, 0]^{\mathrm{T}}$ is given by the "north pole," $w = 1$ ($\theta = 0$), and the state $[0, 1]^{\mathrm{T}}$ by the "south pole," $w = -1$ ($\theta = \pi$). States of the type

$$|\varphi\rangle = \frac{1}{\sqrt{2}} \left(|0\rangle + e^{i\varphi}|1\rangle \right) \tag{1.36}$$

lie along the "equator" [i.e., $\theta = \pi/2$, with φ as the angle in the $\vec{e}_1, \vec{e}_2$-plane, measured counterclockwise from the $\vec{e}_1$-axis (Fig. 1.2)]. In open quantum systems, probabilities are not necessarily normalized to unity, and the length of the Bloch vector becomes another variable, and the description of the two-level system is no longer limited to the surface of the Bloch sphere.

If we introduce the Pauli vector by setting

$$\vec{\sigma} = \begin{bmatrix} \sigma_1 \\ \sigma_2 \\ \sigma_3 \end{bmatrix}, \tag{1.37}$$

the quantum object called the *density matrix* can be written as

$$\rho \equiv \begin{bmatrix} c_0 c_0^* & c_0 c_1^* \\ c_1 c_0^* & c_1 c_1^* \end{bmatrix} = \frac{1}{2}\left(1 + \vec{R} \cdot \vec{\sigma}\right), \tag{1.38}$$

which is easily verified directly. The density matrix is going to play an essential role in our discussions.

1.3.2 Poincaré Sphere

There exists an alternative way to arrive at the representation of a quantum state as a sphere. We start from the state

$$|\psi\rangle = \begin{bmatrix} c_0 \\ c_1 \end{bmatrix} = c_0 \begin{bmatrix} 1 \\ z \end{bmatrix}, \tag{1.39}$$

where the complex number

$$z = \frac{c_1}{c_0} = e^{i\varphi} \tan\frac{\theta}{2} \tag{1.40}$$

can take any value in the complex plane. We then insert a three-dimensional sphere of unit radius centered at the origin in the plane. The axis orthogonal to the complex plane is designated the 3-axis, and the real and imaginary axes of the complex plane give the 1- and 2-axes, respectively (here we do not use unit vectors because they allude to a three-dimensional vector space).

We next perform a stereoscopic projection from the point z in the plane to the south pole of the sphere (Fig. 1.3). The point where the ray penetrates the sphere

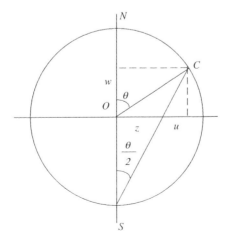

Figure 1.3 Poincaré sphere and its parametrization.

is taken to represent the state. It is obvious that this is a one-to-one mapping of the complex plane, and hence it represents all possible quantum states of a two-level system. The state $[1, 0]^T$ is given by the north pole ($|z| = 0$), and the state $[0, 1]^T$ by the south pole ($|z| = \infty$); this agrees with the situation for the Bloch sphere. Physicists use this sphere, called the *Poincaré sphere*, to describe the polarization states of light, but in mathematics it is known as the *Riemann sphere* and is used in complex analysis to map the surroundings of infinity into the surroundings of zero.

The Poincaré sphere turns out to be fully equivalent with the Bloch sphere of Sec. 1.3.1. To see this, we set $\varphi = 0$. From (1.40) this only rotates the complex plane; it contains no new information. From Fig. 1.3 we can see how the identification works: From the construction it follows that lengths OS and OC are equal to unity (i.e., of equal length), so $\angle SC$ must be equal to $\pi - \theta$, and thus $\angle NC$ is equal to θ. Therefore, the coordinates of point C must be $\sin\theta$ and $\cos\theta$ (i.e., the coordinates u and w of the corresponding point on the Bloch sphere). As we have $v = 0$, we see that this agrees with the result in (1.33).

The representation of a state on the Poincaré sphere is thus identical with the representation on the Bloch sphere. However, in addition, we have obtained the representation by z in the complex plane. Note that we have taken the south pole as a special point, whereas for the Riemann sphere one often uses the north pole and then defines $z = e^{i\varphi}\tan(\pi/4 + \theta/2)$, which is quite equivalent to our choice, Eq. (1.40).

Application: Photon Polarization   A quantum of the electromagnetic field, a photon, can have only two polarization states. This makes it an ideal object to use as a genuine two-state system. If we choose to describe the polarization state in the orthogonal basis formed by linear polarization states in the horizontal and vertical directions, we can set

$$| \updownarrow \rangle = \begin{bmatrix} 1 \\ 0 \end{bmatrix}; \quad | \leftrightarrow \rangle = \begin{bmatrix} 0 \\ 1 \end{bmatrix}. \tag{1.41}$$

We can also introduce orthogonal polarization states turned by an angle of $\pi/4$ in real space. These states are given by

$$| \nearrow \rangle = \frac{1}{\sqrt{2}} (| \updownarrow \rangle + | \leftrightarrow \rangle),$$

$$| \nwarrow \rangle = \frac{1}{\sqrt{2}} (| \updownarrow \rangle - | \leftrightarrow \rangle). \tag{1.42}$$

On the Bloch sphere these basis states are at an angle with respect to each other, which is given by

$$\cos\frac{\alpha}{2} = \langle \updownarrow | \nearrow \rangle = \frac{1}{\sqrt{2}}. \tag{1.43}$$

This yields $\alpha = \pi/2$. Since we have chosen our reference to be the north pole state, $\alpha = \theta$. Indeed, on the Bloch sphere (u, v, w) the coordinates of these new states are $(1, 0, 0)$ and $(-1, 0, 0)$. It is important to note that the Bloch vectors of two orthogonal states are always pointing in opposite directions.

We may also introduce circularly polarized states by setting

$$| \circlearrowleft \rangle = \frac{1}{\sqrt{2}} (| \updownarrow \rangle + i | \leftrightarrow \rangle),$$

$$| \circlearrowright \rangle = \frac{1}{\sqrt{2}} (| \updownarrow \rangle - i | \leftrightarrow \rangle). \tag{1.44}$$

A general photon state can be written as

$$|\psi\rangle = c_{\updownarrow} | \updownarrow \rangle + c_{\leftrightarrow} | \leftrightarrow \rangle = \begin{bmatrix} c_{\updownarrow} \\ c_{\leftrightarrow} \end{bmatrix}. \tag{1.45}$$

Polarization State of Photons The Poincaré sphere is used in a slightly different manner in describing the polarization state of electromagnetic fields, which we may interpret also as the polarization of the corresponding photons. We consider the propagation of a transverse wave in the z-direction. Without loss of generality, the components of the field can be written as

$$E_x = A_1 \cos \omega t,$$

$$E_y = A_2 \cos (\omega t + \delta). \tag{1.46}$$

In the phasor representation we write

$$\begin{bmatrix} E_x \\ E_y \end{bmatrix} = \mathrm{Re} \left(e^{i\omega t} \begin{bmatrix} \mathcal{E}_x \\ \mathcal{E}_y \end{bmatrix} \right) \equiv \mathrm{Re} \left(e^{i\omega t} \begin{bmatrix} A_1 \\ A_2 e^{i\delta} \end{bmatrix} \right). \tag{1.47}$$

From this we find that

$$\frac{\mathcal{E}_y}{\mathcal{E}_x} = \frac{A_2}{A_1} e^{i\delta}, \tag{1.48}$$

which shows that the phasors are separated by an angle δ in the complex plane.

If we choose $\delta = m\pi$, we find that $\mathcal{E}_y \propto \pm \mathcal{E}_x$, describing *linear polarization* of light. Choosing $\delta = \pm \pi/2$ and the amplitudes equal, $A_1 = A_2 = A$, we find the signals to be $90°$ out of phase with each other; this is *circular polarization*. The case $\delta > 0$ is defined as right-handed polarization, and we call the case $\delta < 0$ left-handed polarization.

Next we write

$$\frac{E_y}{A_2} = \cos \omega t \cos \delta - \sin \omega t \sin \delta$$

$$= \frac{E_x}{A_1} \cos \delta - \sin \omega t \sin \delta. \tag{1.49}$$

Squaring and eliminating the time variable, we find that

$$\left(\frac{E_y}{A_2} - \frac{E_x}{A_1} \cos \delta\right)^2 = \sin^2 \omega t \sin^2 \delta = \left(1 - \frac{E_x^2}{A_1^2}\right) \sin^2 \delta. \qquad (1.50)$$

This gives

$$\left(\frac{E_y}{A_2}\right)^2 + \left(\frac{E_x}{A_1}\right)^2 - \frac{2E_x E_y}{A_1 A_2} \cos \delta = \sin^2 \delta, \qquad (1.51)$$

which is clearly an ellipse. The handedness of polarization describes the direction of rotation of the field vector along the ellipse.

For linear polarization, $\delta = m\pi$, we find that

$$\left(\frac{E_x}{A_1} - (-1)^m \frac{E_y}{A_2}\right)^2 = 0; \qquad (1.52)$$

the ellipse degenerates into a line. For circular polarization, $\delta = \pm\pi/2$ gives

$$\left(\frac{E_y}{A_2}\right)^2 + \left(\frac{E_x}{A_1}\right)^2 = 1, \qquad (1.53)$$

which is indeed a circle for $A_1 = A_2$.

In the general case, (1.51) gives an ellipse. The main axes of this ellipse are rotated by an angle ψ with respect to the original x, y-axes (Fig. 1.4). To find ψ we first rotate the x, y-axes to new coordinates ξ, η by setting

$$E_x = \cos \psi E_\xi - \sin \psi E_\eta,$$
$$E_y = \sin \psi E_\xi + \cos \psi E_\eta. \qquad (1.54)$$

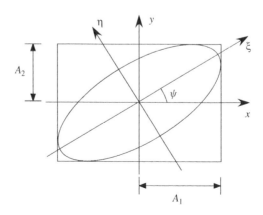

Figure 1.4   Polarization ellipse and rotated coordinate system.

Then we introduce this into (1.50) and demand that the coefficients of the cross terms $\propto E_\xi E_\eta$ vanish. This gives

$$-\frac{2\cos\psi\sin\psi}{A_1^2} + \frac{2\cos\psi\sin\psi}{A_2^2} - \frac{2\cos\delta}{A_1 A_2}\left(\cos^2\psi - \sin^2\psi\right) = 0. \qquad (1.55)$$

Introducing an auxiliary angle α by writing

$$\tan\alpha = \frac{A_2}{A_1}, \qquad (1.56)$$

we find from (1.55) that

$$\tan 2\psi = \frac{2A_1 A_2}{A_1^2 - A_2^2}\cos\delta = \tan 2\alpha\cos\delta. \qquad (1.57)$$

This defines the angle ψ of the elliptically polarized principal axes with respect to the x, y-coordinates.

The polarization state can also be described by the *Stokes parameters*. They are defined, using the Pauli matrices (1.12), by

$$s_1 = \begin{bmatrix} \mathcal{E}_x & \mathcal{E}_y e^{-i\delta} \end{bmatrix}\begin{bmatrix} 1 & 0 \\ 0 & -1 \end{bmatrix}\begin{bmatrix} \mathcal{E}_x \\ \mathcal{E}_y e^{i\delta} \end{bmatrix} = A_1^2 - A_2^2,$$

$$s_2 = \begin{bmatrix} \mathcal{E}_x & \mathcal{E}_y e^{-i\delta} \end{bmatrix}\begin{bmatrix} 0 & 1 \\ 1 & 0 \end{bmatrix}\begin{bmatrix} \mathcal{E}_x \\ \mathcal{E}_y e^{i\delta} \end{bmatrix} = 2A_1 A_2\cos\delta, \qquad (1.58)$$

$$s_3 = \begin{bmatrix} \mathcal{E}_x & \mathcal{E}_y e^{-i\delta} \end{bmatrix}\begin{bmatrix} 0 & -i \\ i & 0 \end{bmatrix}\begin{bmatrix} \mathcal{E}_x \\ \mathcal{E}_y e^{i\delta} \end{bmatrix} = 2A_1 A_2\sin\delta.$$

These form the components of a Stokes vector with the length

$$s^2 = s_1^2 + s_2^2 + s_3^2 = \left(A_1^2 + A_2^2\right)^2. \qquad (1.59)$$

This can be represented by a Poincaré sphere, which is, however, oriented differently from the Bloch sphere. It is easy to see how different polarization states are represented:

Circular polarization $\delta = \pm\pi/2$ is given by the vectors

$$\vec{s} = \{0, 0, \pm 2A^2\}. \qquad (1.60)$$

These are the north and south poles of the sphere. The linearly polarized states have the components

$$\vec{s} = \{A_1^2 - A_2^2, \pm 2A_1 A_2, 0\}. \qquad (1.61)$$

They are situated on the equator that separates the right-handed polarization states ($\delta > 0$) from the left-handed states ($\delta < 0$). All polarization states are represented by points on the sphere in a one-to-one mapping. It is easily seen that as in the case of the Bloch sphere, the mutually orthogonal states occupy opposite points on the surface.

If we represent the Stokes vector in polar coordinates, we write

$$s_1 = s \cos \theta \cos \varphi,$$
$$s_2 = s \cos \theta \sin \varphi, \tag{1.62}$$
$$s_3 = s \sin \theta.$$

From this we find the resulting angles,

$$\tan \varphi = \frac{s_2}{s_1} = \frac{2A_1 A_2}{A_1^2 - A_2^2} \cos \delta = \tan 2\alpha \cos \delta, \tag{1.63}$$

where (1.56) has been used. We thus find from (1.57) that $\varphi = 2\psi$, giving it a straightforward physical significance. We also find that

$$\sin \theta = \frac{s_3}{s} = \frac{2A_1 A_2}{A_1^2 + A_2^2} \sin \delta = \sin 2\alpha \sin \delta. \tag{1.64}$$

To determine the lengths of the principal axes of the rotated ellipse is too tedious to present here, but it turns out that their ratio is equal to $\pm \tan(\theta/2)$; thus, polarization ellipses of equal axis ratios but different rotation angles map to the latitudes of the sphere.

1.4   THE APPETIZER: SECURE COMMUNICATION

A frequently occurring communication situation is that a sender, A, usually called Alice, is transmitting a data stream to a receiver, B, usually called Bob. Without loss of generality, we can assume this to be a string of binary variables (i.e., zeros and ones). Let us assume that the communication between the two parties consists of a string of photons, and that the information resides in their polarization state. The advantage of using photons is that their character is to travel. In addition, they can only be observed by absorption; if B receives a photon, he knows that it has not been seen by anyone else.

Now there are two possible choices for the coding. We can use the vertical–horizontal coding or the rotated basis of (1.42). Thus, we define

Case	"0"	"1"
I	↕	↔
II	↗	↖

Now the procedure is as follows:

1. *A* sends a stream of photons encoding zeros and ones, but she chooses at random which polarization case carries the information.

2. *B* detects the photon stream with an arbitrary setting of his detection polarization. If he chooses the same as *A* chose, the outcome gives the bit encoded in the photon by *A*. If he chooses the wrong one, he gets a random result. *B* is, however, not yet in the position to know which observations carry the information and which are random only. A sequence of photons may be the following:

A:	↕	↗	↕	↔	↔	↖	↕	↖	↗	↔	↖	↗
	0	0	0	1	1	1	0	1	0	1	1	0
B:	↕	↗	↖	↔	↖	↖	↕	↖	↔	↔	↔	↗
	0̲	0̲	1	1̲	1	1̲	0̲	1̲	1	1̲	1	0̲

3. Now *A* calls up *B* on a public channel and states her choice of polarization coding, but of course not the bits encoded. At this point all measurements have been done, and the information offered cannot be used by any eavesdropper to influence the situation.

4. *B* now inspects his recorded data and selects those where he has used the same settings as *A*. For these photons he knows that his recorded values for the bits are the same as those encoded in them by *A*. Over the public channel he informs *A* for which photons the settings have been the same.

5. The procedure thus selects those bits framed in the table above; for these both *A* and *B* now know the values, assuming no transmission errors have occurred. In the present example the bit string selected is

$$00110110.$$

This is, of course, a totally random sequence, but it may be used directly to encode a message.

6. If an eavesdropper, usually called Eve, tries to intercept the message, she must capture and measure the photons during their transmission. But she must also choose the right polarization for the detection. If she does so, she gets the right answer and can retransmit a new photon of the right polarization state to *B*. But half the time, she chooses the wrong polarization, the answer she gets is nonsense, and if she transmits a new photon with the polarization she has observed, this will not carry any correlation with the one sent by *A*. Even with the same detection polarization as *A*, *B* will get the wrong answer in 50% of cases. *Note:* This rests on the fact that Eve cannot make an exact copy of the photon before she measures it; photons cannot be cloned.

7. To check whether an eavesdropper has intervened, the communicating parties can sacrifice some of their bits to determine if excessive errors have been introduced. This can be done simply by *B* publicly announcing the results for some of the bits supposed to be known to both parties. If these disagree in too many cases with those sent by *A*, the parties conclude that they have a leaky channel and have to start anew. Or alternatively, they must try to improve the security of their channel.

The communication protocol described above, called the *BB84 protocol* after its inventors, Bennett and Brassard, gave one of the first indications that quantum information carriers may offer substantial advantages. Later, the photon communication process has been the subject of much research. Improved protocols have been devised and techniques for eavesdropping have been developed and methods to detect them have been refined. The original simple version suffices, however, to give an idea of the possibilities offered by quantum information systems.

Example: Coding by Random Numbers If we want to send a string, 0110100 110 say, we may code it by adding, bit by bit, the random number generated by the procedure above. We get

$$0\ 1\ 1\ 0\ 1\ 0\ 0\ 1\ 1\ 0$$
$$0\ 0\ 1\ 1\ 0\ 1\ 1\ 0\ 1\ 0 \ .$$
$$0\ 1\ 0\ 1\ 1\ 1\ 1\ 1\ 0\ 0$$

The sender now transmits the bit string 0101111100 to the receiver, who also knows the random number. The original message can be recovered by bit-by-bit subtraction, or as is the case with binary arithmetic, by another addition. This follows from

$$0\ 0\ 1\ 1\ 0\ 1\ 1\ 0\ 1\ 0$$
$$0\ 1\ 0\ 1\ 1\ 1\ 1\ 1\ 0\ 0 \ .$$
$$0\ 1\ 1\ 0\ 1\ 0\ 0\ 1\ 1\ 0$$

The fact that the bottom line here agrees with the top line in the preceding array proves that the original message has been recovered.

The method with random numbers can be proved to be secure if the random encoding sequence is as long as the message and is used only once. This puts strong conditions on the ability to transmit code sequences securely between the parties. The quantum communication protocol offers a solution to this approach.

1.5 REFERENCES

To describe the world in terms of measured results has always been an integral part of quantum physics. Only recently, however, has it become fashionable to present these results in terms of information units. Classically, these are, of course, known as representable by binary bits, which carries over into the quantum description as qubits. Such an approach has been well documented in a number of monographs ([2], [17], and [72]) and in article collections such as [21]. The most general scope and prospect of this view are presented by Preskill in [84].

The quantum theory of the two-level system is the fundamental unit of quantum information. Its justification, presentation, and physical applications are discussed thoroughly by Allen and Eberly in [5], where the properties and applications of the Bloch vector are also presented in detail. The Riemann sphere is described in many books on complex analysis (e.g., by Silverman [91]). Use of the Poincaré sphere for polarization states of classical light is described in detail in a classic book by Born and Wolf [15].

The quantization of nonrelativistic electromagnetic fields is discussed in detail by Cohen-Tannoudji and co-workers in [29], and the photon states are also discussed in all basic treatises on quantum optics, such as the books by Loudon [62], Scully and Zubairy [88], and Walls and Milburn [102].

Even if there are many standard texts on quantum theory, they tend to concentrate on the manipulation techniques and leave out discussions on fundamentals. Some books, however, are more central to the interpretation than others (e.g., [50] and [78]). The mathematical formalism was introduced by von Neumann in 1931 [71], and the history of its interpretation is given in [51].

The secure communication system discussed here was introduced by Bennett and Brassard in 1984 [10] and is consequently called BB84. Later developments of quantum exchange of information are reviewed in [72] and [34]. The use of special quantum features to improve security has been presented by Ekert (see, e.g., [33]).

CHAPTER 2

QUANTUM THEORY

2.1 QUANTUM MECHANICS

2.1.1 Structure of Quantum Theory

The relation of quantum mechanics to physical reality is highly abstract and indirect. It does not give any intuitive image of the physical system but only provides a set of recipes to produce numbers that are predictions for the outcomes of experimental procedures. The theory has emerged from the treatment of experimental realities; the historical development is reviewed in many places.

In this book we do not follow the historical path to learn the theory; instead, we want to present it as an instrument to use in physical situations. As far as is possible, we avoid any too-specific interpretations; rather, we offer the results as concisely as we are able to. We present a sort of minimal interpretation of the apparatus provided by quantum theory. We do this partly because it avoids getting sidetracked by confusing arguments about interpretation and partly because the rapidly evolving field of quantum information casts a novel light on the standard procedures, and thus new interpretations may lurk just beyond the horizon. In this situation, any unnecessary attachment to views of the past may be a hindrance.

In many texts, the structure of quantum theory is presented as a formal axiomatic structure. Here we regard it, rather, as a toolbox providing instructions as to how to proceed in various situations. Hence, we do not formulate the

Quantum Approach to Informatics, by Stig Stenholm and Kalle-Antti Suominen
Copyright © 2005 John Wiley & Sons, Inc.

structure as axioms but rather as a set of rules agreed upon by the community. We start with

Rule 1: All possible information about an isolated physical system can be obtained from a state vector which is an element of a linear vector space.

If we denote these elements by $|\psi\rangle$, we conclude that if $|\psi_1\rangle$ and $|\psi_2\rangle$ represent possible states of a physical system, the superposition with complex coefficients

$$|\psi\rangle = c_1|\psi_1\rangle + c_2|\psi_2\rangle \tag{2.1}$$

represents another possible state. We also assume that the linear space is equipped with a scalar product, which we denote by

$$(\varphi, \psi) \equiv \langle\varphi|\psi\rangle = \langle\psi|\varphi\rangle^*. \tag{2.2}$$

To extract observable information from the quantum state, we need to relate it to measurement results. Later we expand on a detailed formulation of the process of quantum measurements, but here we give only the main rule of interpretation:

Rule 2: When we have a system in the state $|\psi\rangle$ and through some observation test whether it can be found in another state $|\varphi\rangle$, this will be found to occur with the probability

$$|\langle\varphi|\psi\rangle|^2 \geq 0. \tag{2.3}$$

Quantum theory is thus probabilistic; it predicts only statistical results and fails to assign definite values to observations except in special cases. In particular, if we ask for the system to be in its actual state, we expect this to be certain. Hence, we must have

$$\langle\psi|\psi\rangle = 1, \tag{2.4}$$

for all states $|\psi\rangle$. Quantum states are thus *normalized*.

If we choose to interrogate the quantum state with respect to an orthonormal basis $\{|\varphi_i\rangle\}$, we may expand the initial states in this basis:

$$|\psi\rangle = \sum_i c_i|\varphi_i\rangle. \tag{2.5}$$

Rule 2 then states that the probability of finding the system in the state $|\varphi_i\rangle$ is given by

$$|\langle\varphi_i|\psi\rangle|^2 = |c_i|^2. \tag{2.6}$$

As the states we use for this interrogation are orthonormal, $\langle\varphi_i|\varphi_j\rangle = \delta_{ij}$, their probabilities of occurrence are independent and the probability normalization gives

$$\sum_i |c_i|^2 = \sum_i \langle\psi|\varphi_i\rangle\langle\varphi_i|\psi\rangle = \langle\psi|\psi\rangle = 1. \tag{2.7}$$

The representability of any state in this basis is thus given by the *closure property*:

$$\sum_i |\varphi_i\rangle\langle\varphi_i| = 1. \tag{2.8}$$

The rules above suffice to relate the quantum state to observations carried out at a given instant of time. To describe time evolution, we have to provide a way to connect the quantum states at different times. We set down the rule:

Rule 3: When an isolated system evolves in time, its normalization is preserved and only the time interval $\{t, t_0\}$ and the initial state $|\psi(t_0)\rangle$ need to be given. The time evolution also preserves the linear superpositions.

From this it follows that we can write the connection between the two times in the form of a linear operator:

$$|\psi(t)\rangle = U(t, t_0)|\psi(t_0)\rangle. \tag{2.9}$$

It is obvious that we must have $U(t_0, t_0) = 1$, as no evolution has taken place. The probability interpretation presented above has to hold at all times, and hence the normalization of the quantum state has to be preserved:

$$\langle\psi(t)|\psi(t)\rangle = \langle\psi(t_0)|U^\dagger(t, t_0)U(t, t_0)|\psi(t_0)\rangle = \langle\psi(t_0)|\psi(t_0)\rangle. \tag{2.10}$$

This implies that

$$U^\dagger(t, t_0)U(t, t_0) = 1. \tag{2.11}$$

From a normalized state at time t we obtain the initial state by the relation

$$|\psi(t_0)\rangle = U^\dagger(t, t_0)|\psi(t)\rangle = U(t_0, t)|\psi(t)\rangle. \tag{2.12}$$

Thus, we must also have $U(t, t_0)U^\dagger(t, t_0) = 1$; the time evolution operator $U(t, t_0)$ is unitary. Because the time evolution depends only on the state at the initial time, two successive time steps must be equal to a single one, and we have the group property

$$U(t, t_0) = U(t, t_1)U(t_1, t_0), \tag{2.13}$$

for any time t_1 (not necessarily between the two endpoints of the time interval).

The time evolution operators are thus unitary and exemplify the mathematical concept of a group. These are briefly:

1. There exists a unit element $U(t_0, t_0)$.
2. Each element $U(t, t_0)$ has a unique inverse given by $U^\dagger(t, t_0)$.
3. A product of two elements is also an element of the group [cf. (2.13)].

Given any unitary operator $U(t, t_0)$, one can prove that there exists a hermitian operator H such that the evolution is represented by

$$U(t, t_0) = \exp[-iH(t - t_0)]. \qquad (2.14)$$

It is easily seen that this representation satisfies the requirements; that it is unique is a consequence of mathematical proof. It thus follows that

$$\frac{d}{dt} U(t, t_0) = -iHU(t, t_0). \qquad (2.15)$$

The form of the operator H can usually be obtained from its identification with the expression for classical energy; in systems having a classical limit one may show that H is to be proportional to the Hamilton function. Thus, when expressed in energy units, the operator is called the *Hamiltonian*. The state vector is then evolving according to the Schrödinger equation,

$$i\hbar \frac{d}{dt} |\psi(t)\rangle = H |\psi(t)\rangle, \qquad (2.16)$$

where $\hbar$ is Planck's constant. Solving this determines uniquely the time evolution of an isolated quantum system as soon as the Hamiltonian is known.

In the general argument above, we have assumed that the Hamiltonian is time independent. When the quantum system is driven by external fields, its parameters may acquire explicit dependence on time. Some of the results above then need reformulation; in particular, the result (2.14) requires a generalization.

Application: Quantum Two-Level System   The general time-independent Hamiltonian can be written in the form

$$H = \begin{bmatrix} E_1 & V \\ V & E_2 \end{bmatrix}, \qquad (2.17)$$

where, without lack of generality, we have assumed the off-diagonal elements to be real, $V^* = V$. We look for eigenfunctions of this operator in the form

$$|\psi\rangle = \begin{bmatrix} c_1 \\ c_2 \end{bmatrix}, \qquad (2.18)$$

and obtain the secular equation

$$\begin{vmatrix} E - E_1 & -V \\ -V & E - E_2 \end{vmatrix} = 0. \qquad (2.19)$$

We find the eigenvalues

$$E_\pm = \frac{E_1 + E_2}{2} \pm \frac{1}{2} \sqrt{(E_1 - E_2)^2 + 4V^2}, \qquad (2.20)$$

with the coefficients of the eigenstates corresponding to the eigenvalues given by

$$\left(\frac{c_1}{c_2}\right)_{\pm} = \frac{V}{E_{\pm} - E_1}. \tag{2.21}$$

The eigenstates are orthogonal $\langle +|-\rangle = 0$, and the time evolution of an arbitrary state is given by

$$
\begin{aligned}
|\psi(t)\rangle &= \exp\left(-i\frac{Ht}{\hbar}\right)(c_+|+\rangle + c_-|-\rangle) \\
&= \exp\left(-i\frac{E_+t}{\hbar}\right)c_+|+\rangle + \exp\left(-i\frac{E_-t}{\hbar}\right)c_-|-\rangle.
\end{aligned} \tag{2.22}
$$

We calculate the probability that we find the system in the state $|\psi(0)\rangle$,

$$|\langle\psi(0)|\psi(t)\rangle|^2 = \left|c_+^* c_+ \exp\left(-i\frac{E_+t}{\hbar}\right) + c_-^* c_- \exp\left(-i\frac{E_-t}{\hbar}\right)\right|^2, \tag{2.23}$$

which can be written as

$$
\begin{aligned}
|\langle\psi(0)|\psi(t)\rangle|^2 &= \left|c_+^* c_+ + c_-^* c_-\right|^2 - 2c_+^* c_+ c_-^* c_- (1 - \cos\Delta\Omega t) \\
&= 1 - 4c_+^* c_+ c_-^* c_- \sin^2\left(\frac{\Delta\Omega t}{2}\right),
\end{aligned} \tag{2.24}
$$

where we have defined the frequency splitting between the levels as

$$\Delta\Omega = \frac{E_+ - E_-}{\hbar} = \frac{\sqrt{(E_1 - E_2)^2 + 4V^2}}{\hbar}. \tag{2.25}$$

The second term in (2.24) indicates the interference of probability amplitudes which is so characteristic of quantum systems. The interference visibility is given by the prefactor $4c_+^* c_+ c_-^* c_-$; for an initially equal mixing of the states, $c_+ = c_- = 1/\sqrt{2}$, we find maximal visibility. If the initial state $|\psi(0)\rangle$ is an eigenstate of the Hamiltonian, no interferences develop.

Note: Because hermitian operators have orthogonal eigenfunctions, the energy eigenstates are orthogonal in the general case. Also, with degeneracy they can always be chosen orthogonal.

Our interpretation of the generator of time evolution, the Hamiltonian, as the quantum representation of the energy, opens the field for a more general statement about observations:

Rule 4: Physical entities that can be measured are represented by hermitian operators.

If a hermitian operator is denoted by A, we know that it has a spectral representation in terms of a complete set of orthogonal eigenstates $\{|\varphi_i\rangle\}$ with their corresponding real eigenvalues $\{a_i\}$:

$$A|\varphi_i\rangle = a_i|\varphi_i\rangle. \tag{2.26}$$

Utilizing these eigenelements, we can write the operator as

$$A = \sum_i |\varphi_i\rangle\, a_i\, \langle\varphi_i|. \tag{2.27}$$

The quantities $\Pi_i = |\varphi_i\rangle\langle\varphi_i|$ are the operators projecting onto the corresponding eigenstates, which follows from the relations

$$\Pi_i \Pi_j = \delta_{ij}\, \Pi_i. \tag{2.28}$$

If the eigenstates $\{|\varphi_i\rangle\}$ are used in the formulation of the measurement rule 2, we find the probability of the occurrence of the state $|\varphi_i\rangle$ to be

$$|\langle\varphi_i|\psi\rangle|^2 = \langle\psi|\Pi_i|\psi\rangle. \tag{2.29}$$

This is sometimes called a *projective measurement*. As the value of the operator A in the state $|\varphi_i\rangle$ is a_i, we find the mean value of such a series of measurements to be

$$\sum_i a_i|\langle\varphi_i|\psi\rangle|^2 = \langle\psi|\left(\sum_i |\varphi_i\rangle\, a_i\, \langle\varphi_i|\right)|\psi\rangle = \langle\psi|A|\psi\rangle. \tag{2.30}$$

In the same way, we can calculate the mean values of the higher powers of A. This serves to define all the statistical properties of the values observed for a given A. To obtain the full information, we do, however, need an infinite ensemble of identically prepared quantum systems, because an observation normally changes the state. In practice, a large number is judged sufficient. In particular, having access to only one system in a given state does not allow us to determine any of the properties of that state. We will see later that if we possess some prior knowledge, the situation is improved.

We thus see that any hermitian operator defines a complete set of eigenfunctions. If these can be used to define a measurement of the values of the operator, it is called an *observable*. An observable that is conserved (i.e., retains its values over time) has to commute with the Hamiltonian. This is seen from

$$\langle\psi(t)|A|\psi(t)\rangle = \langle\psi(0)|A(t)|\psi(0)\rangle, \tag{2.31}$$

where we have introduced the Heisenberg operator

$$A(t) = \exp\left(i\frac{Ht}{\hbar}\right) A \exp\left(-i\frac{Ht}{\hbar}\right). \tag{2.32}$$

Here we remind the reader of the two possible pictures: In the Heisenberg picture the time dependence lies in the operators, as above, whereas in the Schrödinger picture the state vectors are time dependent, as in Eq. (2.16). Equation (2.31) establishes the connection between these two pictures.

The expectation value (2.31) is independent of time if

$$\frac{d}{dt}A(t) = \frac{i}{\hbar}[HA(t) - A(t)H] \equiv \frac{i}{\hbar}[H, A(t)] = 0. \tag{2.33}$$

Thus, the operator A must commute with the Hamiltonian $[H, A] = 0$.

We have seen how quantum theory describes a physical system in terms of state vectors in a linear space. We still need to introduce a rule to combine different physical systems:

Rule 5: If two systems S_1 and S_2 are combined, their state space is the tensor product of the states of the individual systems.

Thus, if $\{|\varphi_i\rangle_1\}$ is a basis for system S_1 and $\{|\varphi_v\rangle_2\}$ is a basis for system S_2, the combined system has a basis set $\{|\varphi_i\rangle_1 \otimes |\varphi_v\rangle_2\}$. The general state in the combined space is thus

$$|\Psi\rangle_{12} = \sum_{i,v} C_{iv}|\varphi_i\rangle_1|\varphi_v\rangle_2. \tag{2.34}$$

If the coefficients C_{iv} are products $c_i * \eta_v$, the state factorizes as

$$|\Psi\rangle_{12} = |\Phi\rangle_1|\Xi\rangle_2, \tag{2.35}$$

where

$$|\Phi\rangle_1 = \sum_i c_i|\varphi_i\rangle_1; \quad |\Xi\rangle_2 = \sum_v \eta_v|\varphi_v\rangle_2, \tag{2.36}$$

and all joint probability statements referring separately to systems S_1 and S_2 become products. We do, however, have the more general situation where (2.34) does not factorize. Then we have correlations between observations on the two systems and the state is called *entangled*. This is an important concept in quantum information theory, and we will return to the properties of such states later.

If we have the system described by (2.34) in the special state

$$|\Psi\rangle_{12} = \sum_v C_v|\varphi_v\rangle_1|\varphi_v\rangle_2, \tag{2.37}$$

the two systems are strongly correlated, and this can be formulated as

Rule 6: If we test for the occurrence of the states $|\varphi_\alpha\rangle_1|\varphi_\beta\rangle_2$ in a system described by the state (2.37), we find the strong correlation

$$_{12}\langle\Psi|\varphi_\alpha\rangle_1|\varphi_\beta\rangle_2\ _2\langle\varphi_\beta|_1\langle\varphi_\alpha|\Psi\rangle_{12} = |C_\alpha|^2\delta_{\alpha\beta}. \tag{2.38}$$

This shows that the system cannot be observed to be in states with different values of α and β. As we have formulated this property in terms of orthogonal basis sets, it is independent of the order in which we perform observations on the two quantum systems; measurements on the two systems display strong correlations. If one of the sets, $\{|\varphi_i\rangle_1\}$ say, is not a basis, the observation on system S_2 induces the strong correlation of $|\varphi_\alpha\rangle_2$ with the state $|\varphi_\alpha\rangle_1$. In its turn, this state determines the outcomes of all later observations on the system S_1. This property is sometimes expressed as a reduction statement: When we have observed the system S_2 to be in the state $|\varphi_\alpha\rangle_2$, we will find system S_1 in the state $|\varphi_\alpha\rangle_1$. This property is, however, mainly a strong correlation between observations on the two systems, and no real action from one observation on the other system needs to be postulated.

We must note that the quantum correlations between the systems are exclusively correlations between probability statements about observations on the two systems. Thus, like all probability statements, they are independent of the spatial separation between them. If we learn about the state here and now, we must immediately adjust all other probability statements to confirm with this additional knowledge. The quantum theory is thus intrinsically a nonlocal theory, which is implicit in its probabilistic nature. Quantum correlations can occur over arbitrary distances.

Example: Singlet State of Two Spin-$\frac{1}{2}$ Particles   An entangled state between a pair of two-level systems is called a *singlet state* if it is of the form

$$|\psi_{\text{singlet}}\rangle = \frac{1}{\sqrt{2}} (|\uparrow\rangle_1 |\downarrow\rangle_2 - |\downarrow\rangle_1 |\uparrow\rangle_2)$$

$$= \frac{1}{\sqrt{2}} [|\uparrow\rangle_1, |\downarrow\rangle_1] \begin{bmatrix} 0 & 1 \\ -1 & 0 \end{bmatrix} \begin{bmatrix} |\uparrow\rangle_2 \\ |\downarrow\rangle_2 \end{bmatrix}. \tag{2.39}$$

We can rotate the spin vector by an arbitrary angle θ with the transformation

$$\begin{bmatrix} |\uparrow\rangle \\ |\downarrow\rangle \end{bmatrix} = \begin{bmatrix} \cos\theta & \sin\theta \\ -\sin\theta & \cos\theta \end{bmatrix} \begin{bmatrix} |+\rangle \\ |-\rangle \end{bmatrix}. \tag{2.40}$$

This transformation leaves the correlations in (2.39) unaffected because we have

$$\begin{bmatrix} \cos\theta & -\sin\theta \\ \sin\theta & \cos\theta \end{bmatrix} \begin{bmatrix} 0 & 1 \\ -1 & 0 \end{bmatrix} \begin{bmatrix} \cos\theta & \sin\theta \\ -\sin\theta & \cos\theta \end{bmatrix} = \begin{bmatrix} 0 & 1 \\ -1 & 0 \end{bmatrix}, \tag{2.41}$$

which gives

$$|\psi_{\text{singlet}}\rangle = \frac{1}{\sqrt{2}} (|+\rangle_1 |-\rangle_2 - |-\rangle_1 |+\rangle_2). \tag{2.42}$$

Thus, whichever spin direction is chosen for the observation, the values found in systems S_1 and S_2 are opposite. And this property will prevail however large the separation between the two systems and is also independent of the order of the measurements. Thus, it is clear that this type of measurement cannot carry any information between the two systems because neither observation can be considered to be the cause of the reduction of the state of the other system. Quantum correlations have no causal implications.

The singlet state is an example of an entangled state, and it is sometimes referred to as an EPR state, and the entangled systems form an EPR pair. States of this form were introduced into the discussion of quantum measurements by Einstein, Podolsky, and Rosen in 1935.

Remark: The term *entanglement* is in some sense relative to our description of the system. Namely, we have a system described by the set of observables $\{q_1, q_2, \ldots, q_N\}$. To ask about entanglement, we have to divide these into two groups, declared to be the systems A and B. We divide the set according to the scheme

$$\{q_1, q_2, \ldots, q_N\}_{AB} = \{q_1, q_2, \ldots, q_k\}_A \text{ and } \{q_{k+1}, \ldots, q_N\}_B. \qquad (2.43)$$

This choice is obviously not unique.

As an illustration we choose the ostensively entangled two-boson state

$$\frac{1}{2} \left(a^{\dagger 2} + b^{\dagger 2} \right) |0\rangle = \frac{1}{\sqrt{2}} \left(|n_a = 2; n_b = 0\rangle + |n_a = 0; n_b = 2\rangle \right). \qquad (2.44)$$

This could be the state of a correlated photon beam. However, if we let the state pass a beamsplitter, we find the new boson observables:

$$A^{\dagger} = \frac{1}{\sqrt{2}} \left(a^{\dagger} - i b^{\dagger} \right),$$
$$B^{\dagger} = \frac{1}{\sqrt{2}} \left(b^{\dagger} - i a^{\dagger} \right). \qquad (2.45)$$

These obviously satisfy the bosonic commutation relations and we find that

$$\frac{1}{2} \left(a^{\dagger 2} + b^{\dagger 2} \right) |0\rangle = i A^{\dagger} B^{\dagger} |0\rangle = i |n_A = 1, n_B = 1\rangle. \qquad (2.46)$$

This state is clearly of a product form and thus unentangled. The term *entanglement* thus refers to a certain division of the total state space.

If we want to avoid this ambiguity, we have to define entanglement in a more restricted way. We may, on the one hand, say that a state is entangled only if there is no division into A and B systems which allows it to be written as a product state. Alternatively, we may choose to say that a state is entangled only if the division into A and B refers to degrees of freedom that can be separated spatially into different locations. In the latter case the property of entanglement is closely related to the nonlocality of the quantum description of nature.

Example: Entanglement   We look at the textbook example of the wavefunction of the hydrogen atom. It consists of a product of the center of mass wavefunction $\varphi(R)$ and the state function depending on the distance between the proton and the electron $\psi(r)$. Expressing this in terms of the nuclear coordinate r_N and the electron coordinate r_e, we find the combined state

$$\Psi(r_N, r_e) = \varphi\left(\frac{M_N r_N + m_e r_e}{M_N + m_e}\right) \psi(r_e - r_N). \qquad (2.47)$$

Despite the original product state, in terms of the particle positions r_e and r_N, the state is highly entangled. In this case, of course, we can separate the coordinates so that the state is genuinely entangled.

2.1.2 Quantum Ensembles

Quantum mechanics assumes that an isolated system can be described by a state vector $|\Psi\rangle$; this is called a *pure state*. In the general case, the quantum properties must be described by a more general entity, the density operator or the corresponding matrix. In this case the system is said to be in a *mixed state*. Such a situation can be approached in two different ways.

Let us first consider a situation where we have an ensemble of quantum systems, where the state $|\psi_i\rangle$ occurs with frequency p_i. The average value of the quantum observable A is then given by

$$\langle A \rangle = \sum_i p_i \langle \psi_i | A | \psi_i \rangle \equiv \mathrm{Tr}(\rho A), \qquad (2.48)$$

where we have introduced the probabilistic density operator

$$\rho = \sum_i |\psi_i\rangle \, p_i \langle \psi_i|. \qquad (2.49)$$

Introducing an arbitrary basis $\{|\varphi_\mu\rangle\}$ we find from the expression

$$\langle A \rangle = \sum_{\mu, \nu} \langle \varphi_\mu | A | \varphi_\nu \rangle \langle \varphi_\nu | \rho | \varphi_\mu \rangle \qquad (2.50)$$

that the expression in Eq. (2.48) can be evaluated in any basis that is convenient. The density operator is seen to be an ensemble average over the state projectors

$$\rho = \overline{|\psi\rangle \langle \psi|}. \qquad (2.51)$$

Note: The states building up the density matrix need not be orthogonal nor complete. They may, for example, derive from a particle beam machine with limited control of the parameters. Then the states making up the ensemble are nearly the same; the uncertainty in the state preparation is, however, mirrored in the fact that we can describe the state with an ensemble only. As a consequence, there is no unique way to infer the ensemble from the density operator or its density matrix elements $\langle \varphi_\nu | \rho | \varphi_\mu \rangle$; many possible ensembles give rise to the same statistics of observed values. In the special case, however, when the states making up the ensemble are orthogonal, they are uniquely given; the representation (2.49) then gives the spectral decomposition of the hermitian operator ρ.

There is another representation of the density operator. We assume that the states making up the ensemble are picked from some set of states so that system number k is in the state $|\psi^{(k)}\rangle$, which characterizes N_k of the systems in the ensemble with $\sum_k N_k = N$. Thus, we have $p_i = N_i/N$ and we can replace the ensemble expression (2.49) by the sum

$$\rho = \frac{1}{N} \sum_k |\psi^{(k)}\rangle \langle \psi^{(k)}|; \tag{2.52}$$

note here that the sum goes over the various systems constituting the ensemble, in contrast to (2.49), where it goes over the various states. The ensemble described is, of course, the same.

From (2.49), we find that in case only one state occurs in the ensemble, $p_0 = 1$, and $p_i = 0$ $(i \neq 0)$, the density matrix becomes a projector,

$$\rho^2 = \rho. \tag{2.53}$$

This has been called a *pure state*. Then we have $\mathrm{Tr}\rho^2 = 1$, which may be used as a test for the lack of admixture of several states in the ensemble described by the density matrix. If several states are mixed in, we have

$$\mathrm{Tr}\rho^2 = \sum_{ij} p_i p_j \, \mathrm{Tr}\left(|\psi_i\rangle\langle\psi_i|\psi_j\rangle\langle\psi_j|\right)$$

$$= \sum_{ij} p_i p_j |\langle\psi_i|\psi_j\rangle|^2 \leq \sum_i p_i \sum_j p_j = 1. \tag{2.54}$$

We note that for orthogonal states the sum is directly $\sum_i p_i^2$, which obviously is less than 1. When the density matrix does not describe a pure state, the state has been called mixed. Given any density matrix, we can decide directly whether it is pure or mixed by evaluating $\mathrm{Tr}\rho^2$.

Example: Uniqueness of the Density Matrix   In an orthogonal basis, the density matrix is given by the expression

$$\rho = \sum_{i=1}^{3} |i\rangle p_i \langle i|. \tag{2.55}$$

We now define the states

$$|\Psi_1\rangle = \frac{1}{N_1\sqrt{2}}\left(\sin\theta\sqrt{p_1}|1\rangle + \sin\theta\sqrt{p_2}|2\rangle + \cos\theta\sqrt{p_3}|3\rangle\right),$$

$$|\Psi_2\rangle = \frac{1}{N_2\sqrt{2}}\left(\cos\theta\sqrt{p_1}|1\rangle - \cos\theta\sqrt{p_2}|2\rangle + \sin\theta\sqrt{p_3}|3\rangle\right),$$

$$|\Psi_3\rangle = \frac{1}{N_3\sqrt{2}}\left(\sin\theta\sqrt{p_1}|1\rangle - \sin\theta\sqrt{p_2}|2\rangle - \cos\theta\sqrt{p_3}|3\rangle\right),$$

$$|\Psi_4\rangle = \frac{1}{N_4\sqrt{2}}\left(\cos\theta\sqrt{p_1}|1\rangle + \cos\theta\sqrt{p_2}|2\rangle - \sin\theta\sqrt{p_3}|3\rangle\right),$$

$$(2.56)$$

where N_i is a normalization constant and θ is an arbitrary parameter. Evaluating the density matrix

$$\rho = \sum_{k=1}^{4} |\Psi_k\rangle N_k^2 \langle\Psi_k|, \tag{2.57}$$

we find that it equals the original density matrix, with the weight functions being

$$N_1^2 = N_3^2 = \frac{1}{2}(\sin^2\theta\, p_1 + \sin^2\theta\, p_2 + \cos^2\theta\, p_3),$$

$$N_2^2 = N_4^2 = \frac{1}{2}(\cos^2\theta\, p_1 + \cos^2\theta\, p_2 + \sin^2\theta\, p_3); \tag{2.58}$$

these are easily seen to add to unity.

Time Evolution   If the time evolution for all the states in the ensemble is determined by a single Hamiltonian H, all states evolve with the same Schrödinger equation, and we find from (2.51) the result

$$\rho(t) = \overline{\exp(-iHt/\hbar)|\psi\rangle\,\langle\psi|\exp(iHt/\hbar)}$$

$$= \exp(-iHt/\hbar)\overline{|\psi\rangle\,\langle\psi|}\exp(iHt/\hbar). \tag{2.59}$$

Consequently, for an ensemble evolving entirely because of a Hamiltonian, we find the equation of motion

$$i\hbar\frac{d}{dt}\rho(t) = [H, \rho(t)]. \tag{2.60}$$

As ρ describes the state of the ensemble, the time evolution is still in the Schrödinger picture, which is seen from the sign of the commutator on the right-hand side of (2.60).

There exists, however, another way to introduce the density operator in quantum mechanics. We consider two quantum systems, S and Σ, which are described by their basis systems, $\{|v_i\rangle\} \subset S$ and $\{|\varphi_\alpha\rangle\} \subset \Sigma$, respectively. The general state is then given by

$$|\Psi\rangle = \sum_{i,\alpha} C_{i\alpha}|v_i\rangle|\varphi_\alpha\rangle, \tag{2.61}$$

which is an example of an entangled state if the coefficients $C_{i\alpha}$ do not factorize. Such a state is normally prepared if the systems are allowed to interact; it is not possible to prepare it by local actions directed separately to the systems S and Σ. Thus, if these systems are separated in space, the entanglement must derive from some earlier period when they were allowed to interact. An equivalent method of preparing entangled states is to let them interact with a common third system. Nonlocal entanglement is thus a rather precious property, which is regarded as a fundamental resource in quantum information processing.

If we look at system Σ, we may ask which are the conditional states $|w\,[\varphi_\alpha]\rangle$ that according to Rule 6 are strongly conditioned on the observation of $|\varphi_\alpha\rangle$. We write the state (2.61) as

$$|\Psi\rangle = \sum_\alpha N_\alpha|w\,[\varphi_\alpha]\rangle|\varphi_\alpha\rangle, \tag{2.62}$$

where we have the normalized states

$$|w\,[\varphi_\alpha]\rangle = N_\alpha^{-1}\sum_i C_{i\alpha}|v_i\rangle,$$
$$N_\alpha^2 = \sum_i |C_{i\alpha}|^2. \tag{2.63}$$

So far our presentation has been symmetric with respect to systems S and Σ, but if we choose to perform a measurement on system Σ, an observation of state $|\varphi_\alpha\rangle$ will according to our Rule 6 imply that all later predictions on system S must be carried out assuming that this is in the correlated state $|w\,[\varphi_\alpha]\rangle$. From (2.62) we conclude that this occurs with the probability

$$P_\alpha = N_\alpha^2, \tag{2.64}$$

which according to (2.63) is correctly normalized:

$$\sum_\alpha P_\alpha = \sum_{\alpha,i} |C_{i\alpha}|^2 = 1. \tag{2.65}$$

If we carry out a large number of observations on system Σ, we build up an assembly of observations where state $|\varphi_\alpha\rangle$ appears with frequency N_α^2. After each such observation, any prediction made for system S must in each case be derived from the correlated state $|w\,[\varphi_\alpha]\rangle$. As this occurs with probability N_α^2, we must, after the observations, assign to system S the density operator

$$\rho_S = \sum_\alpha |w\,[\varphi_\alpha]\rangle N_\alpha^2 \langle w\,[\varphi_\alpha]\,|; \tag{2.66}$$

it is seen directly that this describes the measurement-induced ensemble correctly.

Another way to consider (2.66) is to form the *reduced density operator* by tracing out the dependence on the state describing Σ:

$$\rho_S = \mathrm{Tr}_\Sigma \rho = \sum_\alpha \langle \varphi_\alpha || \overline{\psi \rangle \langle \psi} || \varphi_\alpha \rangle, \tag{2.67}$$

which agrees with (2.66) when the state (2.62) is inserted. If we calculate the expectation values of an observable A_S in system S, we determine these from the reduced operator ρ_S because

$$\langle A_S \rangle = \mathrm{Tr}\,(A_S \rho) = \mathrm{Tr}_S \mathrm{Tr}_\Sigma\,(A_S \rho) = \mathrm{Tr}_S\,(A_S \rho_S)\,. \tag{2.68}$$

In the discussion on quantum measurements, it is often presented as the major problem that the observation forces the pure state (2.61) into the mixed state described by (2.66). From our present point of view this is simply a consistency criterion: If we assert that system Σ is such that its state can be determined experimentally, it follows that as a result of an ensemble of such observations, system S must necessarily be described by the state (2.66). No further mystery is involved. How the actual measurement is described is discussed in Sec. 2.3.

In general, the states $\{|w\,[\varphi_\alpha]\rangle\}$ are neither orthogonal nor complete. Next we ask when they form such a basis? This requires that we have

$$N_\alpha N_\beta \langle w\,[\varphi_\alpha]\,|w\,[\varphi_\beta]\rangle = \langle \Psi | \varphi_\alpha \rangle \left(\sum_i |v_i\rangle \langle v_i| \right) \langle \varphi_\beta | \Psi \rangle \Rightarrow N_\alpha^2 \delta_{\alpha\beta}. \tag{2.69}$$

Here we have introduced an arbitrary orthonormal basis $\{|v_i\rangle\}$. Multiplying (2.69) from the left by $|\varphi_\beta\rangle$ and summing over β, we obtain

$$\sum_i \langle v_i | \Psi \rangle \langle \Psi | v_i \rangle | \varphi_\alpha \rangle = \mathrm{Tr}_S\,(|\Psi\rangle\langle\Psi|)\,|\varphi_\alpha\rangle = N_\alpha^2 |\varphi_\alpha\rangle. \tag{2.70}$$

From (2.70) it follows that the states $|w\,[\varphi_\alpha]\rangle$ form an orthogonal set if the states $|\varphi_\alpha\rangle$ are chosen as the eigenstates of the reduced density operator:

$$\rho_\Sigma = \mathrm{Tr}_S\,(|\Psi\rangle\langle\Psi|)\,. \tag{2.71}$$

With this choice, the asymmetry between the systems disappears again; the basis states are also eigenstates of the operator ρ_S as seen from Eq. (2.62). The eigenvalues are in both systems given by N_α^2. In this situation the symmetric representation (2.62) is called the *Schmidt decomposition*, which always exists for any two entangled systems. For three or more systems, there exists no analogous simple symmetric expansion. We also note that the decomposition is not usually conserved during time evolution. A new decomposition is needed at each instant of time.

Note: If the two subsystems have different dimensionality, it follows that the Schmidt decomposition has got only as many terms as the lower one of the two dimensionalities.

We have derived the necessary condition for the states in the expansion to be orthogonal. The completeness is more complicated, but as both reduced density matrices are hermitian, we conclude that this problem is addressed in the mathematical theory of such operators.

Example: Schmidt Decomposition   We have a two-qubit state

$$|\Psi\rangle = \frac{1}{\sqrt{2}} \left(\sin\theta |00\rangle + \cos\theta |01\rangle + \cos\theta |10\rangle + \sin\theta |11\rangle \right). \tag{2.72}$$

The reduced density matrix becomes

$$\begin{aligned} \rho_1 &= \text{Tr}_2 |\Psi\rangle\langle\Psi| \\ &= {}_2\langle 0|\Psi\rangle\langle\Psi|0\rangle_2 + {}_2\langle 1|\Psi\rangle\langle\Psi|1\rangle_2. \end{aligned} \tag{2.73}$$

This gives

$$\rho_1 = \frac{1}{2} \begin{bmatrix} 1 & \sin 2\theta \\ \sin 2\theta & 1 \end{bmatrix} \tag{2.74}$$

with the eigenvalues

$$\lambda = \frac{1}{2} \left(1 \pm |\sin 2\theta| \right). \tag{2.75}$$

Calculating the corresponding eigenstates, we find the Schmidt decomposition

$$\begin{aligned} |\Psi\rangle &= \left(\frac{1}{\sqrt{2}} \right) \sqrt{1 + \sin 2\theta} \left(\frac{1}{\sqrt{2}} \right) \begin{bmatrix} 1 \\ 1 \end{bmatrix}_1 \otimes \left(\frac{1}{\sqrt{2}} \right) \begin{bmatrix} 1 \\ 1 \end{bmatrix}_2 \\ &+ \left(\frac{1}{\sqrt{2}} \right) \sqrt{1 - \sin 2\theta} \left(\frac{1}{\sqrt{2}} \right) \begin{bmatrix} 1 \\ -1 \end{bmatrix}_1 \otimes \left(\frac{1}{\sqrt{2}} \right) \begin{bmatrix} 1 \\ -1 \end{bmatrix}_2 \\ &= \left(\frac{\sqrt{1 + \sin 2\theta}}{2\sqrt{2}} \right) \left(|00\rangle + |01\rangle + |10\rangle + |11\rangle \right) \\ &+ \left(\frac{\sqrt{1 - \sin 2\theta}}{2\sqrt{2}} \right) \left(|00\rangle - |01\rangle - |10\rangle + |11\rangle \right). \end{aligned} \tag{2.76}$$

It is left as an exercise for the reader to show that assuming that $\theta \in [\pi/4, 3\pi/4]$, the state (2.76) equals the original state. How is the calculation changed for other values of θ?

We have seen that there are two essentially unrelated ways of introducing the density matrix; one relates to a preparation device which produces an ensemble, and the other to the fact that our system is part of a pure state but entangled with an unobserved part of the universe. We may, consequently, ask whether there are any physical implications that are different for the two cases. The answer is essentially that if we have no access to the information residing in the unobserved part of the universe, no observation carried out on the system we have access to can decide how the mixed state originated. If the system we observe became entangled with an environment very long ago, or the environment has been moved far away, all information residing in this environment has been lost and our only alternative for interpreting the density matrix is that it describes an ensemble of possible states. The considerations presented in connection with (2.66) to (2.68) indicate that if the observations had been carried out on the environment, we would, in fact, have created just the ensemble which we have to ascribe to the reduced density matrix. Thus, even if the mixed state derives from entanglement, the individual system under observation must be ascribed a pure state, but we must interpret this state as being sampled from the appropriate ensemble described by the density matrix in question. To assign the density matrix state to an individual quantum system suggests that in some way, it carries information about the ensemble from which it is sampled.

A central quantity in information processing is the entropy of a quantum system. Following von Neumann, we define the entropy of a quantum state as

$$S = -\text{Tr}\,(\rho \log \rho)\,. \tag{2.77}$$

This quantity is representation invariant, but for a pure state it is zero. As the entropy can be viewed as the capacity to carry information, the pure state can thus carry no information. This is a rather useless result, but the relative information carried by a subsystem with regard to the combined state is more illuminating. We define the entropy of a subsystem by using the reduced density operator

$$S_S = -\text{Tr}_S\,(\rho_S \log \rho_S) = -\text{Tr}_S\left[\text{Tr}_\Sigma \rho \log (\text{Tr}_\Sigma \rho)\right]. \tag{2.78}$$

This quantity is also representation independent, and from the Schmidt decomposition we obtain the expression

$$S_S = -\sum_\alpha N_\alpha^2 \log N_\alpha^2 = S_\Sigma, \tag{2.79}$$

where the second equality follows from the symmetry of the Schmidt decomposition. Thus, each subsystem carries the same amount of information capacity. If the systems are not entangled, the decomposition contains only one term, the state factorizes, and then both entropies are zero. The maximally entangled system with a state space of dimensionality D has all coefficients equal $N_\alpha^2 = N_\beta^2 = D^{-1}$ and carries the maximal entropy

$$S_S = S_\Sigma = \log D. \tag{2.80}$$

Purification Schmidt decomposition suggests a formal mathematical procedure by which we can represent a given density matrix ρ in terms of a pure state vector in an extended state space. This is a purely mathematical process, which, however, is useful in proving relations used in quantum information processing.

We use the fact that ρ is hermitian to express it in terms of an orthonormal set of states

$$\rho = \sum_k |\chi_k\rangle \chi_k \langle \chi_k|. \tag{2.81}$$

We now introduce a fictitious state space $\mathcal{H}$ with basis vectors $\{|k\rangle\}$ which has to be of the same dimensionality as the sum in (2.81). We now form the entangled state

$$|\Psi_{\text{ext}}\rangle = \sum_k \sqrt{\chi_k} |\chi_k\rangle |k\rangle. \tag{2.82}$$

If this is interpreted as the Schmidt decomposition of $|\Psi_{\text{ext}}\rangle$, it follows immediately that

$$\rho = \text{Tr}_\mathcal{H} \left(|\Psi_{\text{ext}}\rangle \langle \Psi_{\text{ext}}| \right). \tag{2.83}$$

As far as only physical properties of the original system are concerned, all results can be calculated from (2.82) as well as from (2.81).

Remark: In quantum information theory, the concept of entanglement is extended from the argument about pure states factoring. A quantum state is defined to be *entangled* if it cannot be expressed as an ensemble of factorizable states. Thus, an unentangled state can be written in the form

$$\rho = \sum_k p_k \rho_S^{(k)} \otimes \rho_\Sigma^{(k)}. \tag{2.84}$$

The justification for this definition is that a state of this form can be prepared locally in the two systems by mutual agreement between observers having access only to one subsystem each. Such procedures are called *local operations*. The mathematics of states like (2.84) is still rather incompletely known.

Test of Entanglement of Density Matrices If the density matrix is not of the form (2.84), it is termed *entangled*. Ideally, we should have a procedure to decide whether or not this is the case. Unfortunately, no such universal method has been found. A partial result is, however, based on the fact that if ρ is an acceptable density matrix, so is its transpose ρ^T. Because the two density matrices have the same secular equation, they have the same eigenvalues, which are positive and normalized to $\text{Tr}\rho = 1$.

If we look at the decomposition (2.84) taking the partial transpose on system 2, we should arrive at an acceptable density matrix for the combined systems. Note that to keep the notation unique, we always retain the order of the arguments inside a state vector: $|x\,y\rangle^{\dagger} = \langle x\,y|$. We illustrate the procedure by looking at two simple cases of 2×2 systems:

Look at the unentangled state of two systems:

$$\rho = \frac{1}{2} \left(|00\rangle\langle 00| + |11\rangle\langle 11| \right) . \tag{2.85}$$

In the basis given by

$$\mathcal{B} = \{ |00\rangle, |01\rangle, |10\rangle, |11\rangle \} , \tag{2.86}$$

this gives the matrix representation

$$\rho = \frac{1}{2} \begin{bmatrix} 1 & 0 & 0 & 0 \\ 0 & 0 & 0 & 0 \\ 0 & 0 & 0 & 0 \\ 0 & 0 & 0 & 1 \end{bmatrix} , \tag{2.87}$$

which clearly has nonnegative eigenvalues only. Taking the partial transpose is the transformation

$$\text{PT} : \begin{array}{l} |1\,x\rangle\langle 0\,y| \Rightarrow |0\,x\rangle\langle 1\,y| \\ |0\,x\rangle\langle 1\,y| \Rightarrow |1\,x\rangle\langle 0\,y| \end{array} \tag{2.88}$$

where $x, y \in \{0, 1\}$. Applying this to the state (2.85), we find the matrix

$$\rho^{\text{PT}} = \rho = \frac{1}{2} \begin{bmatrix} 1 & 0 & 0 & 0 \\ 0 & 0 & 0 & 0 \\ 0 & 0 & 0 & 0 \\ 0 & 0 & 0 & 1 \end{bmatrix} \tag{2.89}$$

This remains a nonnegative matrix, and we may thus confirm that the state is not entangled.

Alternatively, we look at the entangled quantum state

$$|\Psi\rangle = \frac{1}{\sqrt{2}} \left(|00\rangle + |11\rangle \right) . \tag{2.90}$$

This gives the density matrix

$$\rho = |\Psi\rangle\langle\Psi| = \frac{1}{2} \begin{bmatrix} 1 & 0 & 0 & 1 \\ 0 & 0 & 0 & 0 \\ 0 & 0 & 0 & 0 \\ 1 & 0 & 0 & 1 \end{bmatrix} . \tag{2.91}$$

This has got the eigenvalues $\{0, 0, 0, 1\}$, as it should. However, performing the partial transpose (2.88), we find the matrix

$$\rho^{\mathrm{PT}} = \frac{1}{2} \begin{bmatrix} 1 & 0 & 0 & 0 \\ 0 & 0 & 1 & 0 \\ 0 & 1 & 0 & 0 \\ 0 & 0 & 0 & 1 \end{bmatrix}, \tag{2.92}$$

which clearly displays one negative eigenvalue. The state considered must thus be entangled.

The criterion presented is, in general, a necessary one only; if the partial transpose is not positive, the density matrix state must be entangled. In two or three dimensions it has been shown to be sufficient, too, but in higher dimensions the issue is open.

2.2 NONLOCALITY OF QUANTUM MECHANICS

2.2.1 Nonsignaling by Quantum Observations

The fact that quantum correlations have strongly nonlocal implications evokes the question if they can be used to transmit meaningful signals instantaneously. If they can, this causes serious problems, because then quantum theory may allow signal transmission in violation of Einstein's theory of relativity. As nonrelativistic quantum theory as such does not know of any upper limit to velocities, such violation cannot be excluded on a priori grounds. Thus, it is comforting that we can show that no such transmission is possible as long as the two parties involved have access only to local operations acting within the state space of their respective systems.

Let two parties wanting to communicate be named A (called Alice) and B (called Bob). They have access to their respective parts of a correlated pair of quantum systems such that

$$\rho_{AB} \neq \rho_A \otimes \rho_B. \tag{2.93}$$

Party A selects a local operation from a set described by the unitary operations $\left\{ U_A^{(k)} : k = 1, 2, \ldots, N \right\}$. The resulting density operator is now

$$\rho_{AB}^{(k)} = U_A^{(k)} \rho_{AB} U_A^{(k)\dagger}. \tag{2.94}$$

We next pose the question whether B can determine which value k was chosen by A using only observations local to his system. Let an arbitrary observable in B's system be denoted by O_B. Its eigenstates are given by the corresponding spectral projectors Π_μ. If the observation of these can decide which operator $U_A^{(k)}$ A chose to apply, information can be transmitted instantaneously. It is almost obvious that this cannot be done, but the proof is simply

$$\langle \Pi_\mu \rangle = \mathrm{Tr}_{AB} \left(\Pi_\mu \rho_{AB}^{(k)} \right) = \mathrm{Tr}_B \left[\Pi_\mu \mathrm{Tr}_A \left(U_A^{(k)} \rho_{AB} U_A^{(k)\dagger} \right) \right]$$
$$= \mathrm{Tr}_B \left[\Pi_\mu \mathrm{Tr}_A \left(\rho_{AB} \right) \right]. \tag{2.95}$$

Thus, no local observation by B can depend on any local operation carried out by A. Only operations carried out in the combined state space of the two observers can be utilized to convey information. We thus need a Hamiltonian to couple the two systems, which then introduces the limitations of ordinary causality.

2.2.2 No Cloning of Quantum States

A classical system can be inspected at will and we can provide an arbitrary number of copies of it. In a quantum world, the situation is different. Having access to only one instance of a system in an arbitrary quantum state, we cannot copy it. This no-cloning possibility emerges from the following considerations.

We take two systems labeled by A and B and require a transformation of the type $|\varphi\rangle_A |0\rangle_B \Rightarrow |\varphi\rangle_A |\varphi\rangle_B$ for an arbitrary state $|\varphi\rangle_A$. Assume that this is accomplished by a unitary transformation

$$U_{AB} |\varphi\rangle_A |0\rangle_B = |\varphi\rangle_A |\varphi\rangle_B. \tag{2.96}$$

Take two different states $|\varphi_1\rangle_A$ and $|\varphi_2\rangle_A$. Applying the operator U_{AB} to both, we find the scalar product of the results to be

$$_A\langle \varphi_2 | \varphi_1 \rangle_{AB} \langle \varphi_2 | \varphi_1 \rangle_B = {}_A\langle \varphi_2 |_B \langle 0| U_{AB}^\dagger U_{AB} |0\rangle_B |\varphi_1\rangle_A$$
$$= {}_A\langle \varphi_2 | \varphi_1 \rangle_{AB} \langle 0|0 \rangle_B. \tag{2.97}$$

This shows that $_A\langle \varphi_2 | \varphi_1 \rangle_A$ has to be equal to unity or zero. In the former case the states are identical; in the latter they are part of a selected basis, and not arbitrary.

Another way to see that we cannot apply the cloning procedure to quantum states is based on the requirement for linear superposition of the states. To this end we consider a state

$$|\psi\rangle_A = c_1 |\varphi_1\rangle_A + c_2 |\varphi_2\rangle_A. \tag{2.98}$$

Applying the presumed cloning operation (2.96), we obtain

$$U_{AB} |\psi\rangle_A |0\rangle_B \Rightarrow c_1 |\varphi_1\rangle_A |\varphi_1\rangle_B + c_2 |\varphi_2\rangle_A |\varphi_2\rangle_B. \tag{2.99}$$

But this is not proper cloning, which should produce $|\psi\rangle_A |\psi\rangle_B$. Thus, the linearity of quantum mechanical operations prevents us from performing the cloning.

Note: If we choose a certain basis $\{|\varphi_\alpha\rangle\}$, we can always design a transformation cloning these basis states. But then the operation acts as in Eq. (2.99) and copies only the individual components. This does, however, provide a tool to create strongly entangled states.

The impossibility of cloning quantum states is an essential ingredient in the preservation of the integrity of quantum states. Usually, we cannot learn much about the state of a quantum system if we have access to only one copy; the statistical nature of quantum states prohibits this. However, if arbitrary cloning were possible, we could effect the transformation

$$|\varphi\rangle_A \prod_k |0\rangle_k \Rightarrow |\varphi\rangle_A \prod_k |\varphi\rangle_k, \qquad (2.100)$$

which provides an arbitrary number of copies of the state. From these we can extract all desired information about the original state. In this situation the difference between quantum systems and classical systems becomes blurred in an essential manner.

Quantum Copier   Even if we are not able to copy quantum states exactly, we may ask how well we can do with an arbitrary quantum state? We choose a basis set $\{|0\rangle, |1\rangle\}$ and start from a state in system 1:

$$|\varphi\rangle_1 = \alpha|0\rangle_1 + \beta|1\rangle_1. \qquad (2.101)$$

The state is taken to be normalized, $\alpha\alpha^* + \beta\beta^* = 1$. We want to transfer this state as faithfully as possible to system 2. To achieve this, we need to use an auxiliary system 3, which in this context usually is called an *ancilla*. We denote the states by the notation $|a\rangle_1|b\rangle_2|c\rangle_3 \equiv |a\,b\,c\rangle$. We assume that we manage to make a quantum transformation effecting the following mapping:

$$|0\rangle_1|0\rangle_2|0\rangle_3 \Rightarrow \sqrt{\frac{2}{3}}|000\rangle - \frac{1}{\sqrt{6}}\left(|011\rangle + |101\rangle\right),$$

$$|1\rangle_1|0\rangle_2|0\rangle_3 \Rightarrow -\sqrt{\frac{2}{3}}|111\rangle + \frac{1}{\sqrt{6}}\left(|010\rangle + |100\rangle\right). \qquad (2.102)$$

This transformation maps orthogonal states onto orthogonal states, and it can hence be realized by a unitary transformation.

We choose the initial state (2.101) and systems 2 and 3 in the state $|0\rangle_2|0\rangle_3$. Applying the transformation (2.102), we obtain the state

$$|\Psi\rangle_{123} = \sqrt{\frac{2}{3}}\left(\alpha|000\rangle - \beta|111\rangle\right) - \frac{\alpha}{\sqrt{6}}\left(|011\rangle + |101\rangle\right)$$

$$+ \frac{\beta}{\sqrt{6}}\left(|010\rangle + |100\rangle\right). \qquad (2.103)$$

We now calculate the reduced density matrices in systems 1 and 2 by tracing out the other degrees of freedom:

$$\rho_1 = \text{Tr}_{23}\rho,$$
$$\rho_2 = \text{Tr}_{13}\rho. \tag{2.104}$$

This one achieves most directly by forming $\rho = |\Psi\rangle_{123}\,_{123}\langle\Psi|$, and to obtain ρ_1 one identifies the terms containing

$$\{|0\rangle_2|0\rangle_3\,_3\langle0|_2\langle0|, \ |0\rangle_2|1\rangle_3\,_3\langle1|_2\langle0|, \ |1\rangle_2|0\rangle_3\,_3\langle0|_2\langle1|, \ |1\rangle_2|1\rangle_3\,_3\langle1|_2\langle1|\}$$

and combines the rest of the terms to obtain

$$\rho_1 = \rho_{\text{out}} = \frac{1}{6}\begin{bmatrix} 1 & 0 \\ 0 & 1 \end{bmatrix} + \frac{2}{3}\begin{bmatrix} \alpha\alpha^* & \alpha\beta^* \\ \beta\alpha^* & \beta\beta^* \end{bmatrix} = \frac{1}{6}\mathbf{1} + \frac{2}{3}\rho_{\text{in}}, \tag{2.105}$$

where ρ_{in} corresponds to the initial state (2.101). Carrying the corresponding tracing out of systems 1 and 3, we find for ρ_2 exactly the same expression as (2.105). Thus, both systems 1 and 2 retain the same information about the original state. To see how remarkable the expression (2.105) is, we write it as

$$\rho_{\text{out}} = \frac{5}{6}|\varphi\rangle\langle\varphi| + \frac{1}{6}(1 - |\varphi\rangle\langle\varphi|). \tag{2.106}$$

If we calculate how large the expectation value of the projector $|\varphi\rangle\langle\varphi|$ is, we find for an arbitrary state the value

$$\langle|\varphi\rangle\langle\varphi|\rangle = \langle\varphi|\rho_{\text{out}}|\varphi\rangle = \frac{5}{6}. \tag{2.107}$$

Thus, we have obtained a procedure, which retains information on the original state with probability 83% for any arbitrary input state, and this holds in both systems 1 and 2. The expectation value (2.107) is called the *fidelity*, which here achieves the high value of 5/6 in the copying process. It can be shown that this is the optimal value in the simple situation envisaged above.

From (2.105) it follows that the Bloch vector from Sec. 1.3.1 is transformed as

$$\vec{R}_{\text{out}} = \frac{2}{3}\vec{R}_{\text{in}}. \tag{2.108}$$

The normalization of the vector then becomes

$$\vec{R}_{\text{out}} \cdot \vec{R}_{\text{out}} = \frac{4}{9} < 1. \tag{2.109}$$

This multiplication of the Bloch vector by a constant *shrinking factor* indicates the loss of information in the copying process.

Exercise   Calculate the reduced density matrix in system 3.

2.2.3 Teleportation

We saw that a quantum state cannot be determined from a single entity, and it cannot be cloned to give another copy. The remarkable fact is, however, that if one party, A say, has access to this state, it can be transferred faithfully to the other party by the process called *teleportation*. Despite this fanciful name, of course, no material object is transferred. It is solely the quantum information encoded in the system that is transferred to another system, which may be situated at an entirely different location. This feat is accomplished because the two parties share a common resource; each has got access to a member of two maximally entangled systems.

We remind the reader that the Pauli operators can be written in the form

$$\sigma_1 = \begin{bmatrix} 0 & 1 \\ 1 & 0 \end{bmatrix}; \quad \sigma_2 = \begin{bmatrix} 0 & -i \\ i & 0 \end{bmatrix}; \quad \sigma_3 = \begin{bmatrix} 1 & 0 \\ 0 & -1 \end{bmatrix}. \tag{2.110}$$

We introduce an additional notation for the basis vectors in the two-level state space by setting

$$|+\rangle = \begin{bmatrix} 1 \\ 0 \end{bmatrix}; \quad |-\rangle = \begin{bmatrix} 0 \\ 1 \end{bmatrix}. \tag{2.111}$$

We now find that

$$\begin{aligned}
\sigma_1|+\rangle &= |-\rangle, \\
i\sigma_2|+\rangle &= -|-\rangle, \\
\sigma_3|+\rangle &= |+\rangle,
\end{aligned} \tag{2.112}$$

and similarly for applying the operators to $|-\rangle$. If we equip the Pauli operators with a superscript $\sigma^{(i)}$ when applied to system i, we conclude that this operation can be effected locally in the corresponding system. If we start by a maximally entangled state between two systems 2 and 3:

$$|\Psi_0\rangle_{23} = \frac{1}{\sqrt{2}} \left(|+\rangle_2|+\rangle_3 + |-\rangle_2|-\rangle_3 \right), \tag{2.113}$$

we can generate a set of orthogonal states by applying the Pauli operators locally in system 2; we obtain

$$|\Psi_1\rangle_{23} = \sigma_1^{(2)}|\Psi_0\rangle_{23} = \frac{1}{\sqrt{2}} \left(|-\rangle_2|+\rangle_3 + |+\rangle_2|-\rangle_3 \right),$$

$$|\Psi_2\rangle_{23} = i\sigma_2^{(2)}|\Psi_0\rangle_{23} = \frac{1}{\sqrt{2}} \left(|+\rangle_2|-\rangle_3 - |-\rangle_2|+\rangle_3 \right), \tag{2.114}$$

$$|\Psi_3\rangle_{23} = \sigma_3^{(2)}|\Psi_0\rangle_{23} = \frac{1}{\sqrt{2}} \left(|+\rangle_2|+\rangle_3 - |-\rangle_2|-\rangle_3 \right).$$

It is obvious that the states $\{|\Psi_i\rangle_{23}; i = 0, 1, 2, 3\}$ form a basis in the state space of systems 2 and 3; this is called a *Bell basis*. Conventionally, the Bell states have been labeled $\{\Phi^+, \Psi^+, \Psi^-, \Phi^-\}$, but here this notation is less convenient.

We now assume that the party A has got hold of a state

$$|\varphi\rangle_1 = \alpha|+\rangle_1 + \beta|-\rangle_1 = \begin{bmatrix} \alpha \\ \beta \end{bmatrix}_1. \tag{2.115}$$

In addition, A has access to system 2 in the entangled state $|\Psi_0\rangle_{23}$; the party B is assumed to access the system 3. The initial state is thus written as

$$|\Psi_{in}\rangle_{123} = |\varphi\rangle_1 |\Psi_0\rangle_{23}. \tag{2.116}$$

We now choose to reexpress this in terms of a Bell basis for the combined systems 1 and 2. We have

$$
\begin{aligned}
|+\rangle_1|+\rangle_2 &= \frac{1}{\sqrt{2}} \left(|\Psi_0\rangle_{12} + |\Psi_3\rangle_{12} \right), \\
|-\rangle_1|-\rangle_2 &= \frac{1}{\sqrt{2}} \left(|\Psi_0\rangle_{12} - |\Psi_3\rangle_{12} \right), \\
|-\rangle_1|+\rangle_2 &= \frac{1}{\sqrt{2}} \left(|\Psi_1\rangle_{12} - |\Psi_2\rangle_{12} \right), \\
|+\rangle_1|-\rangle_2 &= \frac{1}{\sqrt{2}} \left(|\Psi_1\rangle_{12} + |\Psi_2\rangle_{12} \right).
\end{aligned}
\tag{2.117}
$$

Introducing these relations into the state (2.116), we rewrite it as

$$
\begin{aligned}
|\Psi_{in}\rangle_{123} = \frac{1}{2} \Bigg\{ &|\Psi_0\rangle_{12} \begin{bmatrix} \alpha \\ \beta \end{bmatrix}_3 + |\Psi_1\rangle_{12} \begin{bmatrix} \beta \\ \alpha \end{bmatrix}_3 \\
&+ |\Psi_2\rangle_{12} \begin{bmatrix} -\beta \\ \alpha \end{bmatrix}_3 + |\Psi_3\rangle_{12} \begin{bmatrix} \alpha \\ -\beta \end{bmatrix}_3 \Bigg\}.
\end{aligned}
\tag{2.118}
$$

Having access to systems 1 and 2, A can now perform a projective measurement on the Bell states $|\Psi_i\rangle_{12}$, and depending on the outcome, B is left in possession of the corresponding conditional state according to the scheme

$$
\begin{aligned}
|\Psi_0\rangle_{12} &\Rightarrow \begin{bmatrix} \alpha \\ \beta \end{bmatrix}_3 = |\varphi\rangle_3, \\
|\Psi_1\rangle_{12} &\Rightarrow \begin{bmatrix} \beta \\ \alpha \end{bmatrix}_3 = \sigma_1^{(3)}|\varphi\rangle_3, \\
|\Psi_2\rangle_{12} &\Rightarrow \begin{bmatrix} -\beta \\ \alpha \end{bmatrix}_3 = -i\sigma_2^{(3)}|\varphi\rangle_3, \\
|\Psi_3\rangle_{12} &\Rightarrow \begin{bmatrix} \alpha \\ -\beta \end{bmatrix}_3 = \sigma_3^{(3)}|\varphi\rangle_3.
\end{aligned}
\tag{2.119}
$$

As the quantum information actually resides in the pair of complex numbers $\{\alpha, \beta\}$, the task is essentially completed. When A uses a classical communication line, a telephone, to tell B which Bell state was the outcome of the experiment, B immediately knows in which basis the quantum information is given. If it is necessary to actually reproduce the initial state, B can easily use a local operation to invert the operators $\{\sigma_1^{(3)}, i\sigma_2^{(3)}, \sigma_3^{(3)}\}$, which restores the state $|\varphi\rangle_3$ in the chosen basis. Thus, the quantum state has been faithfully transferred from A to B without either party being able to determine what the state is.

The information has, of course, been destroyed at the site of A. If this were not the case, cloning would be possible. The party A can, however, restore the entangled pair used to start with. This can be seen if we use relations (2.114) and (2.119) to write state (2.118) as

$$|\Psi_{in}\rangle_{123} = \frac{1}{2}\left(1 + \sigma_1^{(1)}\sigma_1^{(3)} + \sigma_2^{(1)}\sigma_2^{(3)} + \sigma_3^{(1)}\sigma_3^{(3)}\right)|\Psi_0\rangle_{12}\begin{bmatrix}\alpha \\ \beta\end{bmatrix}_3$$

$$= \frac{1}{2}\left(1 + \vec{\sigma}^{(1)} \cdot \vec{\sigma}^{(3)}\right)|\Psi_0\rangle_{12}|\varphi\rangle_3. \tag{2.120}$$

From this we can see that once the parties decide which operation is needed to restore the state $|\varphi\rangle_3$ at B's site, the same operation applied to system 1 at A's site will restore the entangled state $|\Psi_0\rangle_{12}$. By physically transporting system 2 to another location, we can then reuse the entanglement to effect a second teleportation. Thus, an initial two-system entanglement can be used for an arbitrary number of teleportation operations. The fact that one physical system transfer is necessary is natural; we cannot create entanglement locally, so such a transfer has to be performed even before the first teleportation could be attempted. The process can naturally be continued only as long as no irreversible processes destroy the entanglement.

The possibility of the information transfer in teleportation is already present in the initial state (2.118). Without any action of the two parties involved, the situation already prepared allows the potential assignment of the quantum information to either party. Only an action of party A makes the information actually accessible to party B. This is characteristic of many systems that process quantum information; all possibilities are present in the states already at the beginning. Only a final action by some observer determines how this will manifest it in actual observational outcomes.

Note: The teleportation process may also be used locally as a means to transfer a quantum state from one system to another. Nothing demands that systems 1 and 3 be of the same physical character. The process can thus be used to write quantum information from one medium to another.

Application: Quantum Dense Coding   The two parties A and B have prepared an entangled state

$$|\Psi_0\rangle = \frac{1}{\sqrt{2}}\left(|+\rangle_A|+\rangle_B + |-\rangle_A|-\rangle_B\right) \tag{2.121}$$

and distributed its two components so that each has access to one of the systems.

To write information onto this state, A applies one of the four operations $\{1, \sigma_1, i\sigma_2, \sigma_3\}$ to her system; she has now encoded two qubits into the system. Now A sends her system over to B, which transfers only one qubit across the quantum communication channel. When both systems are accessible to B, he can perform a Bell measurement to decide which state A had prepared. This gives B access to two bits of knowledge, even if only one qubit was transmitted. This process is termed *dense coding of information*. Of course, we must remember that the initial entanglement could only be prepared locally, so the particle at B's site had to be physically transferred there earlier. But at that time the information had not yet been imprinted on the quantum states.

General Teleportation   Let us consider the teleportation in the following way: Choose the initial state on three systems to be

$$|\Psi\rangle_{123} = \sum_i c_i |i\rangle_1 \sum_j \frac{|j\rangle_2 |j\rangle_3}{\sqrt{N}}. \tag{2.122}$$

This can now be probed in various ways; we choose to interrogate it in terms of a state in systems 1 and 2 written in the form

$$|\varphi_p\rangle_{12} = \sum_{a,b} d_{ab}^* |a\rangle_1 |b\rangle_2. \tag{2.123}$$

Conditional on observing this state, we find system 3 in the state

$$|\Psi_{ab}\rangle_3 = {}_{12}\langle\varphi_p|\Psi\rangle_{123} = \frac{1}{\sqrt{N}} \sum_k \left(\sum_i d_{ik} c_i\right) |k\rangle_3. \tag{2.124}$$

The coefficient in system 3 is thus given by the product

$$A_k = \sum_i c_i d_{ik}. \tag{2.125}$$

If these coefficients are any permutation of the original ones $\{c_i\}$, the quantum information has been transferred from system 1 to system 3. The only additional action needed is to transfer the classical information about the basis where the receiver should look for the quantum information. If needed, the basis system can then be transformed such that the quantum information is in a preselected basis. This implies that the matrix d_{ik} must be a linear representation of the permutation group on the initial states. However, by choosing another matrix we can transfer any linear combination of the initial state coefficients to the receiver. The teleportation process may thus be combined with a transformation on the original state. The sender receives the state $\sum_i c_i |i\rangle_1$ from somewhere and selects the transformation d_{ik} she wants to transmit to the receiver.

As the state received is conditional on the probe state the sender chooses, the information to be received is already coded in the initial state; only by performing the measurement on the probe state can the sender make this information actual for the receiver.

2.2.4 Bell Inequalities

We made it eminently clear above that the world described by quantum theory displays highly nonlocal correlations; what we do here and now will, in principle, require adjustments of our probability predictions for all places and all times. Sometimes this is trivial; a photon absorbed here and now will never be observed anywhere else. However, the nonlocality of quantum mechanical predictions has far stranger consequences.

One may speculate that a theory of variables not accessible to us may take care of the problem: Each quantum system carries some information stating where and when it can or will be absorbed. The fact that we have to be satisfied with probability statements only mirrors our lack of detailed information. Such *hidden variable theories* have acquired considerable attention, because it is still far from clear how to modify the concept of classical variable distributions to fit the probabilities obtained from quantum theory.

John Bell was the first to show that such hopes were in vain; quantum probabilities display effects conflicting with reasonable requirements imposed on any possible classical description in terms of internal hidden variables. The existence of such effects is easy to see in retrospect. Quantum interference may extinguish the probability to find a particle at a certain location where it should be according to classical predictions (cf. the famous double-slit interference fringes). Experimentalists, however, always find it difficult to verify the occurrence of a zero as noise tends to obscure the effect. On the other hand, the quantum interference must also give probabilities greater than those supplied by classical theory; interference cuts both ways.

Presently we have a number of inequalities referred to by the name of Bell. The literature concerning their validity and experimental verification is abundantly huge. Here we only want to present the general idea by taking the simplest case which illustrates the point.

Take a particle which can occur in either of two states $|+\rangle$ or $|-\rangle$, with the accompanying operators $\{a, b, c, d\}$ which take the corresponding eigenvalues ± 1. To be concrete we may think of the polarization states of a photon, which clearly can have only two values. These may be chosen as the rotation directions, or orthogonal linear polarizations in an arbitrarily chosen direction. We assume that two such systems are prepared in the state

$$|\Psi\rangle_{12} = \frac{1}{\sqrt{2}} \left(|+\rangle_1|-\rangle_2 - |-\rangle_1|+\rangle_2\right)$$

$$= \frac{1}{\sqrt{2}} \left(\begin{bmatrix} 1 \\ 0 \end{bmatrix}_1 \begin{bmatrix} 0 \\ 1 \end{bmatrix}_2 - \begin{bmatrix} 0 \\ 1 \end{bmatrix}_1 \begin{bmatrix} 1 \\ 0 \end{bmatrix}_2 \right). \tag{2.126}$$

As we showed in Sec. 2.1, this state is invariant under rotations of the axis chosen for the quantization. In the laboratory, such states can be prepared by a photon emission cascade where the two states are certain to have anticorrelated polarization directions.

We next assume that particle 1 is transferred to observer A and particle 2 to observer B without any adverse effects on their quantum state. This state is supposed to be prepared in a reproducible manner so that a series of measurements can be used to determine all desired correlations between observations chosen at will by A and B.

However, let us first see what a classical description may entail. Each particle can be found in either of two possible states, and the value is determined by some unobserved parameter fixed at the moment of state preparation. As any classical theory only allows the particle's internal state to be carried with it locally, the information from the preparation travels with the systems to each observer, and what happens there can no longer affect the outcome of what happens at the position of the other observer. The measurement values observed may, however, be correlated even in the classical case, but such correlations must then have been imposed locally by the process that prepared the initial state. We now assume that A chooses to observe the variables $\{a, c\}$ and B chooses to measure the variables $\{b, d\}$. If we assume these to be the classical variables carried by the individual particles, for any choice of observations, the values to be obtained are predetermined by information carried with the particles. In our case the variables can take only the values ± 1, and consequently,

$$(a + c)b + (a - c)d = \pm 2, \tag{2.127}$$

because either $|a + c| = 2$ or $|a - c| = 2$. If the variables are prepared at the source with some probability distributions, an ensemble of measurements will show any correlation between the variables imposed at their initiation. As any variable will have an average value lying between its possible extreme values, we conclude from (2.127) that

$$|\langle ab \rangle + \langle cb \rangle + \langle ad \rangle - \langle cd \rangle| \leq 2. \tag{2.128}$$

This is an inequality that we assume to be unavoidable, if we assume that the experimental outcomes are determined by local properties imprinted causally on the particles at the preparation of their initial state.

The inequality derived clearly also has a well-defined meaning in quantum theory. Let us calculate the expectation value of a simple operator representing the observation of the value of the two-valued observable in a direction chosen to be characterized by the angle φ. We define

$$\sigma(\varphi) = \cos \varphi \, \sigma_1 + \sin \varphi \, \sigma_2 = \begin{bmatrix} 0 & e^{-i\varphi} \\ e^{i\varphi} & 0 \end{bmatrix}. \tag{2.129}$$

When both A and B perform measurements, the corresponding observable is

$$\sigma_A(\varphi_a)\sigma_B(\varphi_b) = \left[\begin{array}{cc} 0 & \exp(-i\varphi_a) \\ \exp(i\varphi_a) & 0 \end{array} \right]_A$$
$$\times \left[\begin{array}{cc} 0 & \exp(-i\varphi_b) \\ \exp(i\varphi_b) & 0 \end{array} \right]_B. \qquad (2.130)$$

We now calculate the expectation value of this observable in the entangled quantum state (2.126). Because

$$\left[\begin{array}{cc} 1 & 0 \end{array} \right] \left[\begin{array}{cc} 0 & e^{-i\varphi} \\ e^{i\varphi} & 0 \end{array} \right] \left[\begin{array}{c} 1 \\ 0 \end{array} \right] = \left[\begin{array}{cc} 0 & 1 \end{array} \right] \left[\begin{array}{cc} 0 & e^{-i\varphi} \\ e^{i\varphi} & 0 \end{array} \right] \left[\begin{array}{c} 0 \\ 1 \end{array} \right] = 0, \qquad (2.131)$$

we obtain

$$_{12}\langle \Psi | \sigma_A(\varphi_a)\sigma_B(\varphi_b) | \Psi \rangle_{12}$$
$$= -\frac{1}{2} \left[\begin{array}{cc} 1 & 0 \end{array} \right]_A \left[\begin{array}{cc} 0 & \exp(-i\varphi_a) \\ \exp(i\varphi_a) & 0 \end{array} \right]_A \left[\begin{array}{c} 0 \\ 1 \end{array} \right]_A$$
$$\times \left[\begin{array}{cc} 0 & 1 \end{array} \right]_B \left[\begin{array}{cc} 0 & \exp(-i\varphi_b) \\ \exp(i\varphi_b) & 0 \end{array} \right]_b \left[\begin{array}{c} 1 \\ 0 \end{array} \right]_B + \text{c.c.} \qquad (2.132)$$

Evaluating this, we find that

$$\langle ab \rangle = {}_{12}\langle \Psi | \sigma_A(\varphi_a)\sigma_B(\varphi_b) | \Psi \rangle_{12} = -\cos(\varphi_a - \varphi_b). \qquad (2.133)$$

This result can now be used to check the validity of the inequality (2.128). We may, for instance, choose

$$\varphi_a = \frac{\pi}{2}; \qquad \varphi_b = \frac{3\pi}{4};$$
$$\varphi_c = \pi; \qquad \varphi_d = \frac{\pi}{4}. \qquad (2.134)$$

We find that

$$|\langle ab \rangle + \langle cb \rangle + \langle ad \rangle - \langle cd \rangle|$$
$$= \cos(\varphi_a - \varphi_b) + \cos(\varphi_c - \varphi_b) + \cos(\varphi_a - \varphi_d) - \cos(\varphi_c - \varphi_d)$$
$$= 4 \times \frac{1}{\sqrt{2}} = 2\sqrt{2} > 2. \qquad (2.135)$$

Thus, a simple quantum mechanical calculation shows that the inequality (2.128) is violated. There are more sophisticated derivations of similar inequalities, and many possible loopholes due to the detection process and contrived correlations have been eliminated. The bottom line is, however, that no theory assuming realistic values attached to local observables can emulate the results of quantum theory. The Bell inequalities are exceptional in that they eliminate such large classes of potential theories without really making very strong assumptions about their detailed formulations. The characteristic behavior of quantum correlations cannot be achieved by local realistic theories. These properties derive ultimately from the possibility to observe noncommuting variables utilizing entangled states, where the entanglement-imposed correlations are observable even over arbitrarily long distances, thanks to the probabilistic character of the quantum predictions.

Example   The Bell inequality states that

$$F \equiv |\cos(\varphi_a - \varphi_b) + \cos(\varphi_c - \varphi_b) + \cos(\varphi_a - \varphi_d) - \cos(\varphi_c - \varphi_d)| \leq 2. \tag{2.136}$$

This can be written as

$$F = |\cos\varphi_a\,(\cos\varphi_b + \cos\varphi_d) + \sin\varphi_a\,(\sin\varphi_b + \sin\varphi_d)$$
$$+ \cos\varphi_c\,(\cos\varphi_b - \cos\varphi_d) + \sin\varphi_c\,(\sin\varphi_b + \sin\varphi_d)\,|. \tag{2.137}$$

Choosing

$$\varphi_a = \frac{\pi}{2}; \quad \varphi_c = \pi, \tag{2.138}$$

we find that

$$F = |\sin\varphi_b - \cos\varphi_b + \sin\varphi_d - \cos\varphi_d|$$
$$= \sqrt{2}\left|\sin\left(\varphi_b - \frac{\pi}{4}\right) + \sin\left(\varphi_d + \frac{\pi}{4}\right)\right|. \tag{2.139}$$

From this we can see immediately that we may make $F = 2\sqrt{2}$, violating the Bell inequality.

The real significance of the Bell inequalities is that they can be subjected to experimental tests. Deviations from predictions by classical models that are on the order of 40% are not at the edge of what is feasible; now, clear experimental verifications of the quantum predictions exist, and they unequivocally show that quantum theory is not only the best theory we have, but it is the only theory we know that can describe the statistics observed for realistic experiments.

2.2.5   GHZ States and Reality

The great success achieved by the Bell inequalities is based on the fact that they can be subjected to experimental tests. Thus, the physicist can ask nature directly about the validity of the quantum description of reality. The conclusion is that the properties described by quantum variables cannot be assigned numerical values in a realistic way, which is taken to exclude all possible interpretation of quantum results in terms of variables well defined locally. As we will see, the mere acceptance of the rules of quantum calculations excludes the possibility of any such approach. If quantum theory is postulated, no experiment is needed to show that it is incompatible with realistic interpretations.

This point was brought out by Greenberger, Horne, and Zeilinger, who introduced the three-particle entangled state

$$|\Psi_0\rangle_{123} = \frac{1}{\sqrt{2}} \left(|+\rangle_1|+\rangle_2|+\rangle_3 + |-\rangle_1|-\rangle_2|-\rangle_3 \right), \qquad (2.140)$$

which is consequently called a *GHZ state*. To investigate the properties of this state, we introduce two alternative bases for our assumed observations.

The first one is a horizontal–vertical basis (X-basis):

$$|h\rangle = \frac{1}{\sqrt{2}} \left(|+\rangle + |-\rangle \right) = \frac{1}{\sqrt{2}} \begin{bmatrix} 1 \\ 1 \end{bmatrix},$$
$$|v\rangle = \frac{1}{\sqrt{2}} \left(|+\rangle - |-\rangle \right) = \frac{1}{\sqrt{2}} \begin{bmatrix} 1 \\ -1 \end{bmatrix}, \qquad (2.141)$$

and the second one is a right–left basis (Y-basis):

$$|r\rangle = \frac{1}{\sqrt{2}} \left(|+\rangle + i|-\rangle \right) = \frac{1}{\sqrt{2}} \begin{bmatrix} 1 \\ i \end{bmatrix},$$
$$|l\rangle = \frac{1}{\sqrt{2}} \left(|+\rangle - i|-\rangle \right) = \frac{1}{\sqrt{2}} \begin{bmatrix} 1 \\ -i \end{bmatrix}. \qquad (2.142)$$

In each case the second state corresponds to the eigenvalue -1.

We now have three particles, and we can choose to measure each one on an arbitrary basis. We designate a chosen set of observations on these particles by a sequence of symbols X and Y. Thus, we may choose to measure particles 1 and 2 in basis Y and particle 3 in basis X; this measurement is denoted by YYX. The state (2.140) expressed in the corresponding basis sets becomes, with (2.141) and (2.142),

$$|\Psi_0\rangle_{123}^{YYX} = \frac{1}{2} \left(|r\rangle_1|l\rangle_2|h\rangle_3 + |l\rangle_1|r\rangle_2|h\rangle_3 + |r\rangle_1|r\rangle_2|v\rangle_3 + |l\rangle_1|l\rangle_2|v\rangle_3 \right). \quad (2.143)$$

We next choose to interpret this state in a realistic fashion (i.e., we assert that each variable must really take the value indicated by the corresponding state). This gives rise to several observations:

1. Each single-particle state occurs with equal probability; the state is maximally random from the point of view of each particle.

2. As the states $|l\rangle$ and $|v\rangle$ correspond to the eigenvalue -1 of the observable σ_3 in the basis chosen, the product of measuring this variable on all three systems gives the product -1 for each term. Thus, fixing any two of the states by observing the variable σ_3, we unambiguously know the value of the third state.

3. The same conclusions can be drawn from imagining the measurements YXY and XYY, giving the states

$$|\Psi_0\rangle_{123}^{YXY} = \frac{1}{2} \left(|l\rangle_1|h\rangle_2|r\rangle_3 + |r\rangle_1|h\rangle_2|l\rangle_3 + |r\rangle_1|v\rangle_2|r\rangle_3 + |l\rangle_1|v\rangle_2|l\rangle_3 \right),$$
(2.144)

$$|\Psi_0\rangle_{123}^{XYY} = \frac{1}{2} \left(|h\rangle_1|r\rangle_2|l\rangle_3 + |h\rangle_1|l\rangle_2|r\rangle_3 + |v\rangle_1|r\rangle_2|r\rangle_3 + |v\rangle_1|l\rangle_2|l\rangle_3 \right);$$
(2.145)

these are obtained most easily by permutation of the states in (2.143).

4. According to the requirements by a local realistic interpretation of the state of the three-particle system, we have to assert that whichever measurement set we consider, the individual particles must be in states compatible with all the various representations of the quantum state. To eliminate all interactions between the measurements, we assume that these are to be performed at different locations without any communications. No causal influence between the observations can thus occur, and no information is transmitted. Let us look at the consequences of this realism assumption:

- Assume that we want to assign a definite value to the states of the three particles on the horizontal–vertical basis. Quantum mechanically, this corresponds to a measurement of type XXX. We assume that we observe the value -1 for both systems 2 and 3 (i.e., their states are $|v\rangle$).

- Consider the value -1 in system 3 (i.e., $|v\rangle_3$). Then Eq. (2.143) states that the first two particles must be in either of the states $|r\rangle_1|r\rangle_2$ or $|l\rangle_1|l\rangle_2$.

- However, if system 2 is also in state $|v\rangle_2$, then Eq. (2.144) similarly implies that systems 1 and 3 are in the state $|r\rangle_1|r\rangle_3$ or $|l\rangle_1|l\rangle_3$.

- In this case these states represent reality, and the conclusions above combine to state that systems 2 and 3 are in state $|r\rangle_2|r\rangle_3$ or $|l\rangle_2|l\rangle_3$.

- From (2.145), this implies that system 1 must be in the state $|v\rangle_1$.

- Consequently, we conclude that having the state $|v\rangle_2|v\rangle_3$, we must also have the state $|v\rangle_1$.

- Going through analogous arguments four times shows that the states allowed are

$$\{|v\rangle_1|v\rangle_2|v\rangle_3, |h\rangle_1|h\rangle_2|v\rangle_3, |h\rangle_1|v\rangle_2|h\rangle_3, |v\rangle_1|h\rangle_2|h\rangle_3\}.$$
(2.146)

- Another way to reach the same conclusion is to utilize fact 2 above: that the products of the eigenvalues of the terms allowed have to multiply to -1. Thus, we may construct Table 2.1. This is seen to single out the same states as (2.146).

TABLE 2.1   Eigenvalues and Products

State	Eigenvalues			Product	Allowed by Realism
$\lvert h\rangle_1\lvert h\rangle_2\lvert h\rangle_3$	1	1	1	1	No
$\lvert h\rangle_1\lvert h\rangle_2\lvert v\rangle_3$	1	1	-1	-1	Yes
$\lvert h\rangle_1\lvert v\rangle_2\lvert h\rangle_3$	1	-1	1	-1	Yes
$\lvert v\rangle_1\lvert h\rangle_2\lvert h\rangle_3$	-1	1	1	-1	Yes
$\lvert v\rangle_1\lvert v\rangle_2\lvert h\rangle_3$	-1	-1	1	1	No
$\lvert v\rangle_1\lvert h\rangle_2\lvert v\rangle_3$	1	1	-1	1	No
$\lvert h\rangle_1\lvert v\rangle_2\lvert v\rangle_3$	1	-1	-1	1	No
$\lvert v\rangle_1\lvert v\rangle_2\lvert v\rangle_3$	-1	-1	-1	-1	Yes

- It is, however, easy to derive the state predicting the outcomes of the measurement of type XXX. We find that

$$\lvert\Psi_0\rangle_{123}^{\text{XXX}} = \frac{1}{2}(\lvert h\rangle_1\lvert h\rangle_2\lvert h\rangle_3 + \lvert h\rangle_1\lvert v\rangle_2\lvert v\rangle_3$$
$$+ \lvert v\rangle_1\lvert h\rangle_2\lvert v\rangle_3 + \lvert v\rangle_1\lvert v\rangle_2\lvert h\rangle_3). \qquad (2.147)$$

This result is highly remarkable. Of the eight possible combinations of states $\lvert h\rangle$ and $\lvert v\rangle$, the four that are possible according to quantum theory (2.147) are just those that are not possible according to the realistic interpretation (2.146). Thus, the very existence of the GHZ state brings in a drastic contradiction between quantum theory and the local realistic interpretation of physical variables having values when not observed.

In addition to providing an excellent logical argument, the conclusions above have been subject to experimental tests, and the quantum predictions have been excellently verified on real correlated three-particle systems (Fig. 2.1).

Three-Particle Entangled States and Local Operations   We start by looking at the GHZ state

$$\lvert\Psi\rangle_{\text{GHZ}} = \frac{1}{\sqrt{2}}\left(\lvert000\rangle + \lvert111\rangle\right). \qquad (2.148)$$

A party having access only to the first of the systems in this tripartite state can apply any local operation to his state. We choose, in particular, the unitary operation

$$\lvert0\rangle \Rightarrow \cos\theta\lvert0\rangle + \sin\theta\lvert1\rangle,$$
$$\lvert1\rangle \Rightarrow -\sin\theta\lvert0\rangle + \cos\theta\lvert1\rangle. \qquad (2.149)$$

This can be effected by a suitably chosen Hamiltonian.

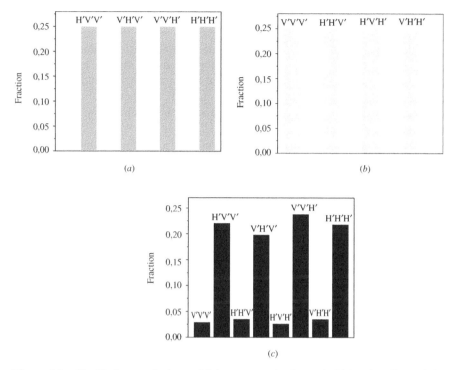

Figure 2.1 Conflicting predictions of *(a)* quantum physics and *(b)* local realism of the fractions of the various outcomes in an XXX experiment for perfect correlations. *(c)* The experimental results are in agreement with quantum physics within the experimental errors and in disagreement with local realism. (From [74]; reprinted here with the kind permission of Anton Zeilinger.)

The GHZ state is now transformed into

$$|\Psi\rangle_{GHZ} \Rightarrow \frac{1}{\sqrt{2}} (\cos\theta|000\rangle + \sin\theta|100\rangle - \sin\theta|011\rangle + \cos\theta|111\rangle). \quad (2.150)$$

It is easily seen that this contains either four states or possibly only two. Thus, there are tripartite states that cannot be reached by such local operations. One of them is the Werner state:

$$|\Psi\rangle_W = \frac{1}{\sqrt{3}} (|100\rangle + |010\rangle + |001\rangle). \quad (2.151)$$

Applying the local transformation (2.149) to this state, we find the state

$$|\Psi\rangle_W \Rightarrow \frac{1}{\sqrt{3}} (\cos\theta|100\rangle - \sin\theta|000\rangle + \sin\theta|110\rangle + \cos\theta|010\rangle$$
$$+ \cos\theta|001\rangle + \sin\theta|101\rangle). \quad (2.152)$$

This state contains six terms or possibly three only. Thus, despite the fact that all the three-system basis states occur in the two states, they cannot reach all entangled tripartite states. Using a more general local transformation, and allowing all parties to carry out their own transformations locally, we can show that all entangled states can be obtained from the two states $|\Psi\rangle_{GHZ}$ and $|\Psi\rangle_W$. They thus form the prototype tripartite entangled states. For higher numbers of parties, the situation becomes extremely complex and has not been totally systematized at the present moment.

Also, the concept of a physically relevant local operation is not transparent. Those effected by Hamiltonians are, obviously, allowed. On the other hand, irreversible spontaneous transitions between the levels may introduce unwanted features into the argument.

2.3   THE PROCESS OF MEASUREMENT

2.3.1   Introducing the Meter

In Sec. 2.1.1 we discussed the influence on the system of interest under the action of an observation as described by Rule 2 of Sec. 2.1. Here we proceed to formulate this approach to quantum theory by making a simple model of the measurement. This is a most trivial formulation, which is much less sophisticated than the many formal discussions available in the literature. However, following our general view that only the minimal assumptions are to be introduced, we present a formalism that is adequate to produce the results needed in practice.

The very act of observation must have an influence on the object observed. If this were not so, we could determine the properties of the system without affecting its state after the observation, and we could then determine the values of all its relevant observables by successive observations. Thus, a single copy of the system would suffice to fix the quantum state uniquely, which is in conflict with the unavoidable quantum uncertainty imposed by the existence of noncommuting variables. Any formal description of the measurement process must embrace this fact.

The general feature of a measurement process is to transfer the value of some physical parameter characterizing a quantum state to a device which we term a *meter*. If the system to be observed is denoted by S and the meter is called Σ, the measurement is a mapping $S \rightarrow \Sigma$. We do not know the exact requirement we need to impose on a quantum system for it to qualify as a meter. An essential feature of the Copenhagen interpretation is that such devices exist and that we are able to read the value their quantum state indicates. These states are defined by the complete set of states $\{|\varphi_n\rangle\}$; for the reading to be unambiguous, these states have to be orthogonal, and we assume them to be normalized.

System S is in the initial state $|\psi\rangle$, and the meter is in its reset initial state $|\varphi_0\rangle$. The measurement map is now assumed to be such that we obtain

$$|\Psi_i\rangle \equiv |\psi\rangle|\varphi_0\rangle \Rightarrow \sum_n |\psi_n\rangle|\varphi_n\rangle. \tag{2.153}$$

We write all equations for the case of a discrete spectrum, and in addition, when needed, we assume that the linear state space is of finite dimensions D. Except for mathematical simplifications, these assumptions impose no restrictions on the argument.

After we have observed the meter in the state $|\varphi_n\rangle$, we find the system in the state $|\psi_n\rangle$. Its quantum nature must depend entirely on the measurement device and not on the state observed. This is accomplished if the dependence on the initial state resides in a constant of proportionality a_n only. Thus, we write

$$|\psi_n\rangle = a_n|u_n\rangle. \tag{2.154}$$

The linearity of any quantum mechanical process implies that a_n is a linear functional of the state $|\psi\rangle$, which guarantees the existence of a quantum state $|v_n\rangle$ such that

$$a_n = \langle v_n|\psi\rangle. \tag{2.155}$$

According to the rules of quantum theory, the quantity $|\langle v_n|\psi\rangle|^2$ indicates the probability that the system S is found in the state $|v_n\rangle$. If the measurement is complete, such that we always obtain an outcome, these probabilities must sum to unity, and hence

$$\sum_n |\langle v_n|\psi\rangle|^2 = \langle\psi|\sum_n |v_n\rangle\langle v_n|\psi\rangle = 1. \tag{2.156}$$

This holds for all states $|\psi\rangle$ only if

$$\sum_n |v_n\rangle\langle v_n| = 1. \tag{2.157}$$

This requires the states $\{|v_n\rangle\}$ to form a complete set, but they need not necessarily be orthogonal. If they are not, they are termed *overcomplete*. If they are orthogonal, they form a basis in terms of which the measurement is carried out (see Rule 4); we will see below that the more general case is useful, too.

The state after the measurement mapping is written as

$$|\Psi_f\rangle \equiv \sum_n a_n|u_n\rangle|\varphi_n\rangle. \tag{2.158}$$

Consequently, reading the meter to be in the state $|\varphi_n\rangle$, we find the system to be in the state $|u_n\rangle$, but we have tested for the probability of finding it in the state $|v_n\rangle$ as seen above. There are no conditions on the states $|u_n\rangle$ except that they are defined uniquely by the device. Thus, the repetition of the measurement does not usually reproduce the result obtained in the first observation. This is the case only if $|u_n\rangle = |v_n\rangle$ ($\forall n$). In this case the measurement is called a *von Neumann measurement* or a *measurement of the first kind*; if the measurement is not repeatable it is called a *measurement of the second kind*.

2.3.2   Measurement Transformation

Using the results above, we find that we can write down a quantum operator effecting the measurement transformation (2.153). To achieve this, we need to label the meter in a cyclic manner so that we identify

$$|\varphi_{n+D}\rangle \equiv |\varphi_n\rangle. \tag{2.159}$$

It is then easy to see that the transformation can be written as

$$\hat{M} = \sum_{nm} |\varphi_{n+m}\rangle |u_n\rangle \langle v_n| \langle \varphi_m|. \tag{2.160}$$

This gives

$$\hat{M}|\Psi_i\rangle = |\Psi_f\rangle = \sum_n a_n |u_n\rangle |\varphi_n\rangle. \tag{2.161}$$

As the states $|\varphi_n\rangle$ are orthonormal, we find that the states $|\Psi_f\rangle$ are always normalized; hence the measurement transformation preserves the norm of the states. It is, however, not unitary because $\hat{M}\hat{M}^\dagger$ is not unity in the general case. If we calculate the reduced density matrix of the system after the measurement operation, the state (2.161) gives directly

$$\rho_f^S = \text{Tr}_\Sigma \left(|\Psi_f\rangle\langle\Psi_f|\right) = \sum_n |u_n\rangle |a_n|^2 \langle u_n|. \tag{2.162}$$

This describes an ensemble of quantum systems where the state $|u_n\rangle$ occurs with probability $|a_n|^2$. If we disregard the transfer of the information about the quantum state to the meter and the subsequent reading of this, we may think that the pure quantum state $|\psi\rangle$ has been replaced by the mixed state (2.162), which cannot be achieved by a unitary transformation. Much of the effort to explain quantum measurements has gone into explaining how this occurs. However, as we explained in Sec. 2.1.2, this may not be necessary. The mere assumption that we can read the meter state forces us to replace the state $|\psi\rangle$ by $|u_n\rangle$. Performing a sequence of such measurements, we have prepared an ensemble of postmeasurement systems where each is in one of the states $|u_n\rangle$, which occurs with probability $|a_n|^2$. Any subsequent predictions for future observations must be based on this ensemble, and this is just described by the result (2.162). Thus, the assumption about the existence of systems acting as meters implies the introduction of the reduced ensembles.

2.3.3   Observation on Nonorthogonal States

We noted above that the necessary condition for a measurement is given by the relation (2.157) even when the states are not orthogonal. If we want to describe the process of measurement entirely in system space S, we may introduce the information transfer operators

$$\hat{\Pi}_n \equiv |u_n\rangle\langle v_n|. \tag{2.163}$$

These satisfy the relation

$$\sum_n \hat{\Pi}_n^\dagger \hat{\Pi}_n = \sum_n |v_n\rangle\langle v_n| = 1. \tag{2.164}$$

The probability of finding the system in the state $|v_n\rangle$ is now given by

$$\langle\psi|\hat{\Pi}_n^\dagger\hat{\Pi}_n|\psi\rangle = |\langle v_n|\psi\rangle|^2 = |a_n|^2. \tag{2.165}$$

After the measurement the state is found to be

$$|u_n\rangle = \frac{\hat{\Pi}_n|\psi\rangle}{\langle v_n|\psi\rangle}. \tag{2.166}$$

The relations (2.164) to (2.166) are postulated in the general theory of measurements as the most general description of an observation compatible with the probability interpretation of quantum mechanics. Here we have been led to a similar situation from the simple assumption that there are meter devices whose state can be read.

A set of operators postulated to satisfy the definitions given by (2.164) to (2.166) are called POVM (positive operator-valued measures) or *effects*. The operators $\hat{\Pi}_n$ are then called *operations*.

Remark: The existence of overcomplete states can be shown easily in the case of the harmonic oscillator. As discussed in Sec. 1.2, we can use the ordinary creation and annihilation operators, which obey bosonic commutation relations $[\hat{a}, \hat{a}^\dagger] = 1$ and have a vacuum such that $\hat{a}|0\rangle = 0$. These may be assumed to describe, for example, the photons of a quantized electromagnetic field.

We now define the *coherent state* by introducing the operator

$$\hat{D}(\alpha) = \exp(\alpha\hat{a}^\dagger - \alpha^*\hat{a}) = \exp\left(-\frac{1}{2}|\alpha|^2\right)\exp(\alpha\hat{a}^\dagger)\exp(-\alpha^*\hat{a}), \tag{2.167}$$

where the Baker–Campbell–Hausdorff formula has been used.[1] The parameter α is any complex number and the operator $\hat{D}(\alpha)$ is easily seen to be unitary. The coherent state is labeled by the complex number α and defined as

$$|\alpha\rangle = \hat{D}(\alpha)|0\rangle$$

$$= \exp\left(-\frac{1}{2}|\alpha|^2\right)\sum_{n=0}^\infty \frac{\alpha^n}{\sqrt{n!}}|n\rangle, \tag{2.168}$$

---

[1]This states that for any operators A and B that commute with their commutator $[A, B]$, the relation $\exp(A + B) = \exp(-\frac{1}{2}[A, B])\exp(A)\exp(B)$ holds.

where $|n\rangle$ is the eigenstate of the occupation number operator $\hat{a}^\dagger \hat{a}$. These states are found to be right eigenstates of the annihilation operator

$$\hat{a}|\alpha\rangle = \alpha|\alpha\rangle, \tag{2.169}$$

and they have a Poissonian distribution of the excitation number

$$P(n) = \exp(-|\alpha|^2)\frac{|\alpha|^{2n}}{n!}. \tag{2.170}$$

These states have a phase attached to them, and they are the quantum states closest to a classical state of the harmonic oscillator.

The coherent states are not orthogonal because

$$|\langle\alpha|\beta\rangle|^2 = |\langle 0|\hat{D}^\dagger(\alpha)\hat{D}(\beta)|0\rangle|^2$$

$$= \exp(-|\alpha - \beta|^2). \tag{2.171}$$

The interpretation of this is that being in the state $|\beta\rangle$, the system has the probability (2.171) to be found in the state $|\alpha\rangle$ (or vice versa). The probability is appreciably different from zero in a unit circle around the complex number β, which is an indication of the quantum uncertainty of the photon number ensuing when one tries to pin down the phase of the quantum system. This is sometimes referred to as quantum noise, even if it is basically a consequence of quantum uncertainty.

The coherent states form a complete set; in fact, they are overcomplete and do not provide a unique resolution of an arbitrary quantum state. We have, however, the completeness condition

$$\int |\alpha\rangle\frac{d^2\alpha}{\pi}\langle\alpha| = \frac{1}{\pi}\sum_{n,m}\frac{|n\rangle\langle m|}{\sqrt{n!m!}}\int_0^\infty dr\, r^{m+n+1}e^{-r^2}\int_0^{2\pi}d\theta\, e^{i(m-n)\theta}$$

$$= 2\sum_n \frac{|n\rangle\langle n|}{n!}\int_0^\infty dr\, r^{2n+1}e^{-r^2}$$

$$= \sum_n |n\rangle\langle n| = 1. \tag{2.172}$$

The operators $|\alpha\rangle\langle\alpha|$ thus satisfy a generalization of the result (2.164), which shows that they offer an example of a set of POVM operators. Their range of values is continuous; it is possible to select a denumerable subset of these states which still retains the completeness property, but this construction is far from trivial. As they stand, the coherent states form a simple and useful way of presenting the information contained in a quantum state of a harmonic oscillator.

The amplitudes of the coherent states add almost like classical amplitudes. It is straightforward to show that

$$D(\alpha)D(\beta)|0\rangle = \exp\left[\frac{1}{2}\left(\alpha\beta^* - \alpha^*\beta\right)\right]D(\alpha + \beta)|0\rangle, \tag{2.173}$$

where the exponent is an inessential phase factor only.

2.3.4   Special Cases

Measurements of the First Kind   In this case

$$|u_n\rangle = |v_n\rangle; \quad (\forall n). \tag{2.174}$$

In addition, we assume these states to be orthonormal (i.e., they form a basis). Then the measurement operators (2.163) are projection operators

$$\hat{\Pi}_n^2 = \hat{\Pi}_n, \tag{2.175}$$

and $\hat{\Pi}_n = \hat{\Pi}_n^\dagger$. The probability to find the system in the state $|v_n\rangle$ is then given by

$$|\langle v_n|\psi\rangle|^2 = \langle\psi|\hat{\Pi}_n|\psi\rangle. \tag{2.176}$$

Consequently, we reproduce the conventional result introduced in (2.29). After the measurement, the system is found in the state

$$|v_n\rangle = \frac{\hat{\Pi}_n|\psi\rangle}{|\langle v_n|\psi\rangle|}, \tag{2.177}$$

and a repeated observation will give the same value as the first one. This is the situation usually described in quantum mechanics textbooks; as in Sec. 2.3.1, we call it a von Neumann measurement or a projective measurement. As we have seen above, this situation is not necessarily prevailing. In fact, it is quite difficult to envisage a physical situation corresponding exactly to this ideal case.

Absorptive Measurement   In many cases it is clear that the measurement operation erases all information about the incoming state in the process. A case in point is the observation of the polarization state of a single photon. Any device recording this will necessarily involve absorption of the photon, which leaves the system in the vacuum state after the event. Then we call the measurement *absorptive* and find that

$$|u_n\rangle = |u_0\rangle; \quad (\forall n). \tag{2.178}$$

In this case the state after the measurement is

$$|\Psi_f\rangle \equiv |u_0\rangle \sum_n a_n|\varphi_n\rangle, \tag{2.179}$$

and the reduced density matrix of the system (2.162) is

$$\rho_f^S = |u_0\rangle\langle u_0|, \tag{2.180}$$

which describes a pure state and carries no information; its entropy S_S (2.78) is clearly zero.

   Remark: The concept of a von Neumann measurement can be utilized to define the concept of a POVM. We assume that we can perform an ideal measurement in the joint space $S \otimes \Sigma$, which we describe by the projection operators

$$\hat{P}^{\nu}_{S\Sigma} \hat{P}^{\mu}_{S\Sigma} = \delta_{\nu\mu} \, \hat{P}^{\nu}_{S\Sigma}, \tag{2.181}$$

and these are supposed to be complete:

$$\sum_{\nu} \hat{P}^{\nu}_{S\Sigma} = 1. \tag{2.182}$$

Choosing an orthonormal basis $\{|v_{\nu}\rangle\}$, we write the initial state as

$$|\Psi_i\rangle \equiv |\psi\rangle|\varphi_0\rangle = \sum_{\nu} a_{\nu} |v_{\nu}\rangle|\varphi_0\rangle. \tag{2.183}$$

Calculating the probability of obtaining the value ν, we find that

$$P_{\nu} = \langle\Psi_i|\hat{P}^{\nu}_{S\Sigma}|\Psi_i\rangle \equiv \langle\psi|\hat{\Pi}^{\dagger}_{\nu}\hat{\Pi}_{\nu}|\psi\rangle, \tag{2.184}$$

where

$$\hat{\Pi}^{\dagger}_{\nu}\hat{\Pi}_{\nu} \equiv \langle\varphi_0|\hat{P}^{\nu}_{S\Sigma}|\varphi_0\rangle \geq 0 \tag{2.185}$$

with the property

$$\sum_{\nu} \hat{\Pi}^{\dagger}_{\nu}\hat{\Pi}_{\nu} = \langle\varphi_0| \sum_{\nu} \hat{P}^{\nu}_{S\Sigma}|\varphi_0\rangle = \langle\varphi_0|\varphi_0\rangle = 1. \tag{2.186}$$

As the operator $\langle\varphi_0|\hat{P}^{\nu}_{S\Sigma}|\varphi_0\rangle$ in the space S is positive, the operators $\hat{\Pi}_{\nu}$ exist. They are not necessarily projectors and hence they form a set of POVMs. This is the conventional way to introduce them, but as we have seen, they emerge in a natural way also from a simple approach to measurements.

Application: State Truncation   In Fig. 2.2 we show a configuration of beamsplitters and detectors, where an arbitrary state is given in terms of a photon expansion as

$$|\psi_{\text{in}}\rangle = \sum_{n=0}^{\infty} c_n |n\rangle; \tag{2.187}$$

$|0\rangle$ and $|1\rangle$ are the vacuum and one-photon states, respectively. Labeling the arms of the device by the numbers $\{1, 2, 3, 4, 5, 6\}$, we want to determine the state $|\psi_{\text{out}}\rangle$ conditioned on one count in D_6 and no count in D_5; we assume perfect counters of incoming photons. Using the beamsplitter transformations (1.28), we find, that

$$\begin{bmatrix} a^{\dagger}_1 \\ a^{\dagger}_2 \\ a^{\dagger}_3 \end{bmatrix} = \frac{1}{2} \begin{bmatrix} 0 & \sqrt{2} & i\sqrt{2} \\ \sqrt{2} & -1 & i \\ i\sqrt{2} & i & 1 \end{bmatrix} \begin{bmatrix} a^{\dagger}_4 \\ a^{\dagger}_5 \\ a^{\dagger}_6 \end{bmatrix}. \tag{2.188}$$

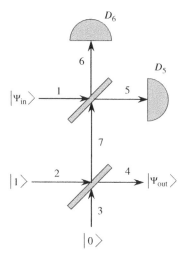

Figure 2.2   Beamsplitter configuration for state truncation.

The total incoming state is now written as

$$|\Psi_{\text{inc}}\rangle = a_2^\dagger \left(c_0 + c_1 a_1^\dagger + \cdots \right) |0\rangle$$

$$= \frac{1}{2} \left(\sqrt{2} a_4^\dagger - a_5^\dagger + i a_6^\dagger \right) \left[c_0 + \frac{c_1}{\sqrt{2}} \left(a_5^\dagger + i a_6^\dagger \right) + \cdots \right] |0\rangle. \qquad (2.189)$$

Projecting this on the state $\left(a_5^\dagger \right)^0 \left(a_6^\dagger \right) |0\rangle$, we find the conditional state in the output to be

$$|\psi_{\text{out}}\rangle = \frac{i}{2} \left(c_0 + c_1 a_4^\dagger \right) |0\rangle \propto (c_0 |0\rangle_4 + c_1 |1\rangle_4) . \qquad (2.190)$$

Thus, we have truncated out the first two components of the incoming state.

2.4   INTRODUCTION OF IRREVERSIBILITY

2.4.1   Master Equation

When a quantum system is isolated from perturbations by any environment, its time evolution is determined by a Hamiltonian, and the quantum ensemble described by a density matrix evolves according to (2.60). In most cases, however, the evolution is perturbed by random interventions from an uncontrolled environment. This may be the thermal radiation field, the collisional encounters with perturbers or random vibrations in a solid background. All these make the time evolution irreversible and carry away information about the state represented. They tend to decrease quantum coherence and cause many observational results to deteriorate. In some situations, however, the description of irreversibility can be based on simple considerations. There exists a great deal of literature about quantum dissipation, but here we can only present a most elementary treatment and the most important consequences.

We assume that the environment is huge in some sense, so that we can represent it by a reservoir only little influenced by its effect on the system of interest. Its degrees of freedom are assumed to decohere very rapidly, so that it has no memory of its earlier encounters with the system. This is the *Markov limit*, where we may describe the influence of the environment by short uncorrelated interactions, which last for very brief intervals Δt only. To achieve this, the reservoir must have access to a broad band of spectral frequencies; thus, it is most often taken to have a continuous spectrum. The quantum character of the environment induces uncertainties in the time evolution of the system of interest. These are usually described as reservoir fluctuations, even if their origin derives entirely from quantum mechanics and no stochastic variations are involved.

After the interaction, the system becomes entangled with the reservoir, and if we have access to the state of the reservoir, we can draw conclusions about the properties of the system of interest. In that case all future predictions have to be conditioned on the information gained. Then the intervention can be considered as a measurement. In most cases, however, the environment is not monitored, and the information it carries becomes lost. As the next uncorrelated encounter takes place, the memory of the preceding one is irrevocably forgotten. The effect on the system of interest is like a series of measurements without recording.

In general, the derivation of irreversible time evolution equations is done by a perturbative elimination of the dynamics of the unobserved environment. This is a cumbersome procedure, which offers both challenging and controversial features that have given rise to much discussion. Here we choose to approach the situation in a different manner. We utilize the fact that the perturbative encounters can be considered as a series of brief interactions between system and environment, which last for a time Δt. This is taken to be short with respect to the ordinary dynamics determined by the Hamiltonian, but long from the point of view of the evolution of the interaction with the reservoir. Thus, we may assume that the effect of the interaction is given by a scattering matrix $\mathbf{S}(\Delta t)$, effecting the change

$$\rho(t + \Delta t) = \mathbf{S}(\Delta t)\rho(t)\mathbf{S}^{\dagger}(\Delta t) \tag{2.191}$$

on the density matrix; during this time, the Hamiltonian time evolution can be neglected. If no interaction with the environment occurs in Δt, the evolution is governed by the Hamiltonian.

To proceed, we express the scattering matrix in terms of the reaction matrix $\mathbf{T}$:

$$\mathbf{S} = \mathbf{1} + i\mathbf{T}. \tag{2.192}$$

The scattering matrix has to preserve the normalization of the density matrix in (2.191) and hence we must have

$$\mathbf{S}^{\dagger}\mathbf{S} = \left(\mathbf{1} - i\mathbf{T}^{\dagger}\right)\left(\mathbf{1} + i\mathbf{T}\right) = \mathbf{1}, \tag{2.193}$$

which gives

$$-i\left(\mathbf{T} - \mathbf{T}^{\dagger}\right) = 2\mathbf{T}_{\text{imag}} = \mathbf{T}^{\dagger}\mathbf{T}. \tag{2.194}$$

It is easy to see that with these relations, $\text{Tr}\rho$ is conserved, as is necessary if the probability interpretation is to remain valid. We assume next that the system may experience a series of encounters distinguished by different reactions $\mathbf{T}_j$, each occurring with the rate r_j. The number of such encounters then becomes $r_j \Delta t$ in the given time interval. Calculating the change in the density matrix over the ensemble of encounters, we obtain

$$\begin{aligned}
\Delta\rho &= \rho(t + \Delta t) - \rho(t) \\
&= \sum_j r_j \left[i \left(\mathbf{T}_j \rho - \rho \mathbf{T}_j^{\dagger}\right) + \mathbf{T}_j \rho \mathbf{T}_j^{\dagger} \right] \Delta t.
\end{aligned} \tag{2.195}$$

Denoting this average by an overbar and combining the two possible time evolutions in Δt, we can derive the equation of motion with the irreversible encounters to be of the form

$$\frac{d\rho}{dt} = -\frac{i}{\hbar}[H, \rho] + i\left(\overline{\mathbf{T}}\rho - \rho\overline{\mathbf{T}^{\dagger}}\right) + \overline{\mathbf{T}\rho\mathbf{T}^{\dagger}}. \tag{2.196}$$

If we now separate the reaction matrix into real and imaginary parts,

$$\mathbf{T} = \mathbf{T}_{\text{real}} + i\mathbf{T}_{\text{imag}}, \tag{2.197}$$

we find, from Eq. (2.195),

$$\begin{aligned}
\frac{d\rho}{dt} &= -\frac{i}{\hbar}\left[\left(H - \hbar\overline{\mathbf{T}}_{\text{real}}\right), \rho\right] - \left(\overline{\mathbf{T}}_{\text{imag}}\rho + \rho\overline{\mathbf{T}_{\text{imag}}^{\dagger}}\right) + \overline{\mathbf{T}\rho\mathbf{T}^{\dagger}} \\
&= -\frac{i}{\hbar}\left[\left(H - \hbar\overline{\mathbf{T}}_{\text{real}}\right), \rho\right] - \frac{1}{2}\left(\overline{\mathbf{T}^{\dagger}\mathbf{T}}\rho + \rho\overline{\mathbf{T}^{\dagger}\mathbf{T}}\right) + \overline{\mathbf{T}\rho\mathbf{T}^{\dagger}},
\end{aligned} \tag{2.198}$$

where we have used the relation (2.194). We see that the real part of the reaction matrix contributes a modification of the system Hamiltonian. This is often called a *renormalization*, and it is a universal feature of reservoir interactions. However, in many problems it may become divergent, and then the combination $(H - \hbar\mathbf{T}_{\text{real}})$ is regarded as the observed Hamiltonian, whose energy eigenstates correspond to the observationally determined energy levels. Here we neglect its influence in the following, as it does not affect our arguments. Equation (2.198) is our final result, and an equation of this type is usually called a *master equation*.

To obtain a useful equation we have to reexpress the master equation in a more tractable form. Hence we assume the system-reservoir encounters to consist of well-defined state changes such that each system state $|\psi_k\rangle$ entering the encounter is taken to an outgoing state $|\chi_k\rangle$. We then find that the reaction matrix can be written in the form

$$\mathbf{T} = \sum_k \lambda_k t_k, \tag{2.199}$$

where

$$t_k = |\chi_k\rangle\langle\psi_k|. \tag{2.200}$$

If we assume that these various possible reaction channels lack coherence, we can take the average to mean

$$\overline{\lambda_k \lambda_n} = \lambda_k^2 \delta_{kn}, \tag{2.201}$$

which gives in Eq. (2.198),

$$\frac{d\rho}{dt} = -\frac{i}{\hbar}[H, \rho] - \frac{1}{2}\sum_k \lambda_k^2 \left(t_k^\dagger t_k \rho + \rho t_k^\dagger t_k - 2t_k \rho t_k^\dagger\right). \tag{2.202}$$

In Sec. 2.4.4 we argue that this form of the dissipative master equation is the most general memoryless evolution equation, which preserves the essential properties of the density matrix. An evolution equation of this type is called a *Lindblad equation*.

Damped Harmonic Oscillator The quantum mechanical harmonic oscillator is described by the Hamiltonian

$$H = \hbar\omega a^\dagger a. \tag{2.203}$$

If we add dissipative terms to the equation of motion for the density matrix, we may write

$$\frac{d}{dt}\rho = -i\omega\left[a^\dagger a, \rho\right] - \frac{C}{2}\left(a^\dagger a\rho - 2a\rho a^\dagger + \rho a^\dagger a\right)$$
$$- \frac{A}{2}\left(aa^\dagger\rho - 2a^\dagger\rho a + \rho aa^\dagger\right). \tag{2.204}$$

This is easily seen to be of the Lindblad form (2.202), and the probability is conserved, $d(\mathrm{Tr}\rho)/dt = 0$.

We can directly calculate the equation of motion for the operators. Using the relation $\mathrm{Tr}(A[B, C]) = \mathrm{Tr}([A, B]C)$, we derive

$$\frac{d}{dt}\langle a\rangle = \mathrm{Tr}\left(a\frac{d}{dt}\rho\right)$$
$$= -i\omega\mathrm{Tr}\left([a, a^\dagger a]\rho\right) - \frac{C}{2}\mathrm{Tr}\left([a, a^\dagger a]\rho\right) - \frac{A}{2}\mathrm{Tr}\left([aa^\dagger, a]\rho\right)$$
$$= \left(-i\omega - \frac{C - A}{2}\right)\langle a\rangle. \tag{2.205}$$

Taking real and imaginary parts of this expression, we obtain the classical equations of the damped oscillator. The solution is given by

$$\langle a(t) \rangle = \exp\left[-\left(i\omega + \frac{C - A}{2}\right)t\right]\langle a(0)\rangle. \tag{2.206}$$

This shows that as long as $C > A$, the amplitude is damped in the way expected from a classical solution. We want to emphasize that this behavior relates to the expectation value only. The operator cannot be damped, as this would violate the commutation rules. The correct behavior of the operator is restored by the quantum fluctuations of the reservoir effecting the damping.

If $C < A$, the equations describe a quantum amplifier. This description is, however, incomplete, because the exponential growth can continue for a limited period only. After that, nonlinear saturation effects must set in and limit growth.

As in the derivation (2.205), we derive

$$\frac{d}{dt}\langle a^{\dagger}a \rangle = \text{Tr}\left(a^{\dagger}a\frac{d}{dt}\rho\right)$$

$$= A(\langle a^{\dagger}a \rangle + 1) - C\langle a^{\dagger}a \rangle. \tag{2.207}$$

The population of the oscillator $\bar{n} = \langle a^{\dagger}a \rangle$ thus obeys the equation

$$\frac{d}{dt}\bar{n} = -(C - A)\bar{n} + A. \tag{2.208}$$

For $C > A$ this agrees with the damping of the amplitude (2.206), but the inhomogeneous term displays the effects of the fluctuations deriving from the reservoir providing the damping. In steady state, we have

$$\bar{n} = \frac{A}{C - A}. \tag{2.209}$$

We thus see that for a reservoir providing no amplification, $A = 0$, the oscillator relaxes to its ground state. With a thermal reservoir, however, we expect the steady state to be of thermal character

$$\bar{n} = n_B = \frac{1}{\exp(\hbar\omega/k_BT) - 1}. \tag{2.210}$$

This implies the detailed balance condition

$$\frac{C}{A} = \exp\left(\frac{\hbar\omega}{k_BT}\right), \tag{2.211}$$

which is satisfied by writing

$$A = \Gamma n_B,$$
$$C = \Gamma(n_B + 1),$$
(2.212)

which allows us to take Γ independent of temperature as $\lim_{T \to 0} C$.

Exercise   The Lindblad equation for a damped two-level system can be written in the form

$$\frac{d}{dt}\rho = -i\frac{\omega}{2}[\sigma_3, \rho] - \frac{\gamma}{2}(\rho - \sigma_3\rho\sigma_3) - \frac{C}{2}(\sigma^+\sigma^-\rho - 2\sigma^-\rho\sigma^+ + \rho\sigma^+\sigma^-)$$
$$- \frac{A}{2}(\sigma^-\sigma^+\rho - 2\sigma^+\rho\sigma^- + \rho\sigma^-\sigma^+),$$
(2.213)

where

$$\sigma^\pm = \frac{1}{2}(\sigma_1 \pm i\sigma_2)$$
(2.214)

and $[\sigma^+, \sigma^-] = \sigma_3$. Show that the trace of the density operator is a conserved quantity. Show using the results of Sec. 1.3.1 that the Bloch vector $\vec{R} = \{\langle\sigma_1\rangle, \langle\sigma_2\rangle, \langle\sigma_3\rangle\} \equiv \{u, v, w\}$, satisfies the equation

$$\frac{d}{dt}\vec{R} = \vec{\Omega} \times \vec{R} - \frac{1}{T_1}(w - w_0)\hat{e}_3 - \frac{1}{T_2}(u\hat{e}_1 + v\hat{e}_2),$$
(2.215)

where we have

$$\frac{1}{T_1} = A + C,$$
$$\frac{1}{T_2} = \gamma + \frac{A + C}{2},$$
$$w_0 = \frac{A - C}{A + C}.$$
(2.216)

Here T_1 is called the *longitudinal* or *energy relaxation time*. T_2 is called the *transverse* or *phase relaxation time*; in addition to the dependence on the parameters contributing to the energy relaxation, this may contain a phase relaxation contribution γ which does not affect the population difference.

In the thermal situation (2.211) the equilibrium population is given by

$$w_0 = -\tanh\frac{\hbar\omega}{2k_BT}.$$
(2.217)

At zero temperature, only the lower level is populated; $w_0 = -1$, as we expect.

2.4.2   Unraveling the Master Equation

Equations of Lindblad type (2.202) have an interesting interpretation. Usually, we cannot unravel a quantum ensemble in terms of individual histories making up the ensemble, but for an evolution of the Lindblad type we can achieve this in a certain sense.

We start by combining the first three terms on the right-hand side of (2.202) as derived from an effective Hamiltonian:

$$H_{\text{eff}} = H - \frac{i\hbar}{2} \sum_k \lambda_k^2 t_k^\dagger t_k; \tag{2.218}$$

acting on the right of the density matrix, this is replaced by $H_{\text{eff}}^\dagger$. Evolving a quantum state with this Hamiltonian over a brief time interval gives

$$|\Phi(t + \Delta t)\rangle = \exp(-i H_{\text{eff}} \Delta t / \hbar)|\Psi(t)\rangle$$

$$= \left(1 - \frac{i}{\hbar} H \Delta t - \frac{1}{2} \sum_k \lambda_k^2 t_k^\dagger t_k \Delta t\right)|\Psi(t)\rangle. \tag{2.219}$$

Because the Hamiltonian is now nonhermitian, the norm of the state decreases, which we interpret as a decreasing probability of finding the system in the original state,

$$\langle\Phi(t + \Delta t)|\Phi(t + \Delta t)\rangle = \langle\Psi(t)|\exp\left(-\sum_k \lambda_k^2 t_k^\dagger t_k \Delta t\right)|\Psi(t)\rangle$$

$$= 1 - \sum_k \Delta p_k = 1 - \Delta p, \tag{2.220}$$

where Δp_k is the probability lost through process k and Δp is the total loss of probability. We have, from (2.219),

$$\Delta p_k = \lambda_k^2 \, ||t_k|\Psi(t)\rangle||^2 \Delta t. \tag{2.221}$$

This we interpret as a probability to jump out of the initial state through the channel described by t_k.

We now introduce a simulation technique in the following manner: Select a random number $r \in [0, 1]$. Then:

- If $r > \Delta p$, we conclude that no transition has taken place in the time Δt, and we normalize the state (2.219) to give unit probability; that is,

$$|\Psi(t + \Delta t)\rangle^{(1)} = \frac{\exp(-i H_{\text{eff}} \Delta t / \hbar)|\Psi(t)\rangle}{\sqrt{1 - \Delta p}}. \tag{2.222}$$

- If $r < \Delta p$, we conclude that a transition has taken place in the time Δt, and we replace the state at time $t + \Delta t$ by the normalized state

$$|\Psi_k(t + \Delta t)\rangle^{(2)} = \frac{\lambda_k t_k|\Psi(t)\rangle}{\sqrt{||\lambda_k t_k|\Psi(t)\rangle||^2}}. \tag{2.223}$$

These states are chosen at random by a second process designed in such a way that their relative probabilities become distributed according to the various Δp_k.

- After this we have determined the state $|\Psi(t + \Delta t)\rangle$ and may proceed to the next time interval. In this way we are building up an ensemble of state vectors undergoing a history of jump processes or evolution with decreasing probability. If the jumps correspond to recorded measurements, we are simultaneously building up a sequence of possible actual observations.

It is easy to show that the ensemble describes the evolution of the density matrix in the manner determined by the master equation. We write down the matrix at time $t + \Delta t$ as an average over the various histories possible at this single jump. We write

$$\rho(t + \Delta t) = (1 - \Delta p)\,|\Psi(t + \Delta t)\rangle^{(1)(1)}\langle\Psi(t + \Delta t)|$$
$$+ \sum_k \Delta p_k |\Psi_k(t + \Delta t)\rangle^{(2)(2)}\langle\Psi_k(t + \Delta t)|. \qquad (2.224)$$

Using the relations (2.219), (2.222), and (2.223), we write

$$\rho(t + \Delta t) = \rho(t) - \frac{i}{\hbar}\left(H|\Psi(t)\rangle\langle\Psi(t)| - |\Psi(t)\rangle\langle\Psi(t)|H\right)\Delta t$$
$$- \frac{1}{2}\sum_k \lambda_k^2 \left(t_k^\dagger t_k|\Psi(t)\rangle\langle\Psi(t)| + |\Psi(t)\rangle\langle\Psi(t)|t_k^\dagger t_k\right)\Delta t$$
$$+ \sum_k \lambda_k^2 t_k|\Psi(t)\rangle\langle\Psi(t)|t_k^\dagger \Delta t + O(\Delta t^2). \qquad (2.225)$$

Letting Δt go to zero and identifying the appropriate averages, we obtain the correct master equation (2.202).

The procedure described above does indeed generate an ensemble which is equivalent with that described by the master equation. The procedure is, however, not unique; the choice of relaxation operators can be modified at our will. We can perform transformations on the operators $\{t_k\}$ in (2.199) and retain the same ensemble but unraveled differently. In some cases the variable chosen for the observation can be used to select which dissipative processes are most propitious. The condition (2.201) also imposes some conditions on possible choices.

2.4.3 Continuous Measurements

So far we have considered primarily the effect of the environment as a purely destructive influence on the system of interest. However, as pointed out above, the measurement process can also be seen as a disruptive intervention by an environment. The gathering of information from a system will also introduce irreversibility and loss of coherence during the time evolution. If the device of observation is coupled to the system continuously, we obtain a formulation termed *continuous measurements*.

To evolve this point of view, we introduce a set of measurement operators $\{\hat{\Pi}_\nu\}$ analogous to those introduced in Sec. 2.3.3, but now they are taken to describe continuous measurements. These have to be normalized so that the probability of the observation of the value ν in a time interval Δt is given by

$$\Delta p_\nu = ||\hat{\Pi}_\nu|\psi\rangle||^2 \Delta t, \qquad (2.226)$$

when the system is in the state $|\psi\rangle$. This is analogous to the relation (2.221), and according to relation (2.177), observation of the value ν leaves the system in the state

$$|\psi_f\rangle = \frac{\hat{\Pi}_\nu|\psi\rangle}{\sqrt{||\hat{\Pi}_\nu|\psi\rangle||^2}} = \sqrt{\frac{\Delta t}{\Delta p_\nu}}\,\hat{\Pi}_\nu|\psi\rangle, \qquad (2.227)$$

which should be compared with the relation (2.223). The setup is thus very similar to the simulation sequence described above. The continuously observed system is perturbed through the randomly occurring extraction of information by the measuring setup. The effect on the system is thus described by an evolution equation analogous with (2.202):

$$\frac{d\rho}{dt} = -\frac{i}{\hbar}[H,\rho] - \frac{1}{2}\sum_\nu \left(\hat{\Pi}_\nu^\dagger\hat{\Pi}_\nu\rho + \rho\hat{\Pi}_\nu^\dagger\hat{\Pi}_\nu - 2\hat{\Pi}_\nu\rho\hat{\Pi}_\nu^\dagger\right). \qquad (2.228)$$

For a single run, the simulation process described above will generate a random sequence of pairs $\{(t_i, \nu_i)\}$, where t_i indicates the time of a random observation and ν_i is the corresponding recorded outcome of the measurement. Each individual sequence here gives a possible series of events in the laboratory and a record of possible observations. If we generate an ensemble of such sequences, the ensemble-averaged expectation values are identical with those obtained by solving the density matrix equation of motion. In this case, however, all information stored in the observed values ν_i will be lost. If the ensemble is large enough, the probability will become large that an experimentally observed sequence can be found as a member of the ensemble. In the limit of an infinite ensemble, we may surmise that the probability of this happening will approach unity.

2.4.4 Completely Positive Maps

The probabilistic interpretation of the density matrix assumes that its eigenvalues are nonnegative and sum to unity. The physical interpretation imposes, however, one less self-evident condition: Let a general linear transformation act on a state where the system of interest is entangled with an arbitrary additional system not directly affected by the transformation. If we then require that the ensuing map, acting on the state of the combined system, still produces a nonnegative state operator, this retains its probability interpretation. This is imposed by the physics; the entanglement with a distant system without direct interaction with the system of interest should not make the transformed state operator unphysical. A map fulfilling this condition is called *completely positive* (CP), which thus is more restrictive than the ordinary positivity.

The discussion of CP is usually carried through within the mathematical framework of C^* algebras and dynamical semigroups. It goes beyond the frame of the present text to enter these highly mathematical issues. The final result is, however, that a transformation of the general form

$$\Gamma\rho = \sum_i A_i^\dagger \rho A_i \qquad (2.229)$$

is the necessary and sufficient condition to make the transformation Γ completely positive. An operation of the form $A_i^\dagger \rho A_i$ is called a *Kraus operator*. If, in addition, we have

$$\sum_i A_i A_i^\dagger = 1, \qquad (2.230)$$

the mapping is trace preserving. Thus, density matrices are mapped onto density matrices even when possible entanglements are included. This result is not going to be proved in its generality here, but we will elucidate the situation by some simple considerations.

We start by noting that any linear map must obey the condition

$$\Gamma\rho = \sum_\alpha p_\alpha \Gamma \left(|\varphi_\alpha\rangle\langle\varphi_\alpha| \right), \qquad (2.231)$$

where we have chosen the customary representation of an arbitrary density matrix.

First we present a simple example showing the special role of complete positivity. Let us take a 2×2 density matrix

$$\rho = \begin{bmatrix} \rho_{00} & \rho_{01} \\ \rho_{10} & \rho_{11} \end{bmatrix}. \qquad (2.232)$$

A linear transformation on this state can be defined as

$$\Gamma\rho = \frac{1}{2}\mathrm{Tr}\rho + \gamma \begin{bmatrix} 0 & \rho_{01} \\ \rho_{10} & 0 \end{bmatrix}, \qquad (2.233)$$

where γ is a real number. Because the density matrix is normalized, the eigenvalues of the transformed state are nonnegative if

$$2\gamma\sqrt{\rho_{01}\rho_{10}} \leq 1. \qquad (2.234)$$

On the other hand, we have

$$\rho_{01}\rho_{10} \leq \rho_{00}\rho_{11} \leq \frac{1}{4}. \qquad (2.235)$$

Thus, the necessary condition for a positive map is

$$\gamma \leq 1. \qquad (2.236)$$

We now proceed to look at a state where the two-level system is entangled with an independent two-level system. Take the state

$$|\Psi\rangle_{12} = \frac{1}{\sqrt{2}} \left(|00\rangle + |11\rangle \right), \qquad (2.237)$$

which gives the matrix

$$\rho^{(12)} = \frac{1}{2} \left(|00\rangle\langle 00| + |00\rangle\langle 11| + |11\rangle\langle 00| + |11\rangle\langle 11| \right). \qquad (2.238)$$

The transformation Γ acting on these terms gives with $x \in \{0, 1\}$, the mapping

$$\Gamma : |0x\rangle\langle 0x| \Rightarrow \frac{|0x\rangle\langle 0x| + |1x\rangle\langle 1x|}{2};$$

$$\Gamma : |1x\rangle\langle 1x| \Rightarrow \frac{|0x\rangle\langle 0x| + |1x\rangle\langle 1x|}{2}; \qquad (2.239)$$

$$\Gamma : |00\rangle\langle 11| \Rightarrow \gamma |00\rangle\langle 11|;$$

$$\Gamma : |11\rangle\langle 00| \Rightarrow \gamma |11\rangle\langle 00|.$$

In the basis

$$\mathcal{B} = \{|00\rangle, |01\rangle, |10\rangle, |11\rangle\}, \qquad (2.240)$$

the result of the mapping (2.239) is given by

$$\Gamma\rho^{(12)} = \frac{1}{4} \begin{bmatrix} 1 & 0 & 0 & 2\gamma \\ 0 & 1 & 0 & 0 \\ 0 & 0 & 1 & 0 \\ 2\gamma & 0 & 0 & 1 \end{bmatrix}. \qquad (2.241)$$

This is easily seen to have positive eigenvalues only if

$$\gamma \leq \frac{1}{2}, \qquad (2.242)$$

which shows that the condition of CP is more restrictive than simple positivity as given by (2.236).

In the case when (2.242) is satisfied, we may define an angle θ by setting

$$\gamma = \frac{1}{2} \sin 2\theta. \qquad (2.243)$$

Now we introduce the matrix transformations

$$A_1 = \frac{1}{\sqrt{2}}\begin{bmatrix} \cos\theta & 0 \\ 0 & \sin\theta \end{bmatrix}; \qquad A_2 = \frac{1}{\sqrt{2}}\begin{bmatrix} \sin\theta & 0 \\ 0 & \cos\theta \end{bmatrix};$$

$$A_3 = \frac{1}{\sqrt{2}}\begin{bmatrix} 0 & 0 \\ 1 & 0 \end{bmatrix}; \qquad A_4 = \frac{1}{\sqrt{2}}\begin{bmatrix} 0 & 1 \\ 0 & 0 \end{bmatrix}. \tag{2.244}$$

Combining these, we find the result

$$\sum_{\nu=1}^{4} A_\nu^\dagger \rho A_\nu = \frac{1}{2}\begin{bmatrix} \rho_{00} + \rho_{11} & \sin 2\theta \rho_{01} \\ \sin 2\theta \rho_{10} & \rho_{00} + \rho_{11} \end{bmatrix}; \tag{2.245}$$

with the definitions (2.243) this agrees with the definition (2.233) of the mapping Γ. Thus, we find that in this particular example, the requirement of CP agrees with the general form (2.229).

We should now look at a more general transformation

$$\Gamma \rho^{(12)} = A_{(1)}^\dagger \rho^{(12)} A_{(1)}, \tag{2.246}$$

where the subscript on $A_{(1)}$ indicates that it operates on system 1 only. For simplicity we consider only one term in the expansion (2.229). We note that if an operator is positive on the product space $S_1 \otimes S_2$, its restriction to S_1 turns out positive as required by CP.

We take an arbitrary quantum state $\rho^{(12)}$; if it is nonnegative, we may write it as a product

$$\rho^{(12)} = R^\dagger R. \tag{2.247}$$

If the mapping Γ is to give a positive result, the resulting state must necessarily have a positive trace if the probability interpretation is to be preserved. Consequently, we should conclude that

$$\mathrm{Tr}\, \Gamma \rho^{(12)} = \sum_\alpha \langle \alpha | A_{(1)}^\dagger R^\dagger R A_{(1)} | \alpha \rangle$$

$$= \sum_{\alpha,\beta} |\langle \beta | R A_{(1)} | \alpha \rangle|^2 \geq 0. \tag{2.248}$$

Because the state $\rho^{(12)}$ was chosen arbitrarily, this shows that Γ effects a nonnegative mapping. A straightforward extension of the argument works for a sum of terms of the form (2.246).

The proof that any CP map Γ is of the form (2.229) is slightly more convoluted. The mapping we consider is of the form

$$\Gamma = G_1 \otimes I_2, \tag{2.249}$$

where I_2 is the unit operator on space 2 and G_1 is a positive operator on space 1.

Let us first introduce the auxiliary density matrix

$$\rho^{(12)} = |\Psi\rangle\langle\Psi|, \tag{2.250}$$

where the pure state is taken to be the totally entangled one,

$$|\Psi\rangle = \frac{1}{\sqrt{N}} \sum_{\nu} |v_\nu\rangle_1 |u_\nu\rangle_2. \tag{2.251}$$

We next define a mapping on $S_1 \otimes S_2$, which is positive according to our assumptions

$$\widehat{\Sigma} = (G_1 \otimes I_2) |\Psi\rangle\langle\Psi| = \frac{1}{N} \sum_{\nu,\mu} G_1 \left(|v_\nu\rangle_1 \, _1\langle v_\mu|\right) |u_\nu\rangle_2 \, _2\langle u_\mu|. \tag{2.252}$$

This is chosen to be diagonalized in the state space of the combined systems,

$$\widehat{\Sigma} = \sum_{k} |\varphi_k\rangle_{12} \, \lambda_k^2 \, _{12}\langle\varphi_k|; \tag{2.253}$$

this is a spectral resolution of the operator.

We now want to apply the map to an arbitrary pure state in S_1 of the form

$$|\psi\rangle_1 = \sum_{\nu} c_\nu |v_\nu\rangle_1 \tag{2.254}$$

and we introduce its "shadow" state in S_2:

$$|\widetilde{\psi}\rangle_2 = \sum_{\nu} c_\nu^* |u_\nu\rangle_2. \tag{2.255}$$

We now define a linear operator on space 1 by setting

$$\Gamma_k |\psi\rangle_1 \equiv \, _2\langle\widetilde{\psi}|\varphi_k\rangle_{12}. \tag{2.256}$$

This is clearly seen to be a linear mapping on the coefficients $\{c_\nu\}$. It follows that

$$\sum_{k} \lambda_k^2 \Gamma_k |\psi\rangle_1 \, _1\langle\psi|\Gamma_k^\dagger = \sum_{k} \, _2\langle\widetilde{\psi}|\varphi_k\rangle_{12} \, \lambda_k^2 \, _{12}\langle\varphi_k|\widetilde{\psi}\rangle_2$$

$$= \, _2\langle\widetilde{\psi}|\widehat{\Sigma}|\widetilde{\psi}\rangle_2$$

$$= N^{-1} \sum_{\nu,\mu} G_1 \left(|v_\nu\rangle_1 \, _1\langle v_\mu|\right) \, _2\langle\widetilde{\psi}|u_\nu\rangle_2 \, _2\langle u_\mu|\widetilde{\psi}\rangle_2$$

$$= N^{-1} \sum_{\nu,\mu} G_1 \left(|v_\nu\rangle_1 \, _1\langle v_\mu|\right) c_\nu c_\mu^*$$

$$= N^{-1} G_1 \left(|\psi\rangle_1 \, _1\langle\psi|\right). \tag{2.257}$$

Now defining the operators

$$A_k = \sqrt{N} \, \lambda_k \Gamma_k^\dagger, \tag{2.258}$$

we find that the arbitrary CP operator G_1 can be expressed in the form (2.229) when acting on S_1. This proves that the operation (2.249) is of the form (2.229) when applied to a pure state. The corresponding result for mixed states follows from (2.231).

After having outlined the proof of the general form of a CP operator, we wish to apply the result to the time evolution operator acting on the state density matrix. If the generator of the evolution is CP, we expect the density matrix to retain its physical property. To this end we write the equation of motion

$$\frac{d}{dt}\rho = \sum_i A_i^\dagger \rho A_i - X\rho - \rho X, \tag{2.259}$$

where the operator X has to be determined such that the trace of ρ is conserved. We find that

$$\frac{d}{dt}\mathrm{Tr}\rho = \sum_i \mathrm{Tr}\left(A_i A_i^\dagger \rho\right) - 2\mathrm{Tr}\left(X\rho\right) = 0. \tag{2.260}$$

This gives the result

$$X = \frac{1}{2}\sum_i A_i A_i^\dagger. \tag{2.261}$$

Consequently, we find that the equation of motion is of the form (2.202). This result was introduced in Sec. 2.4.1 as an equation of the *Lindblad form*. It was first written down by Lindblad but also by Gorini, Kossakowski, and Sudarshan. For a detailed mathematical derivation, we refer to the references in Sec. 2.5.

2.5 REFERENCES

There are many textbooks on quantum theory, and the basic formalism can be learned from any of these. Of special value for the purpose of our description is a book by Peres [78]. The description of the density matrix is still very valuable in the old reviews by Fano [35] and ter Haar [44]. The uniqueness of the density matrix is discussed in [48]. The Schmidt decomposition is discussed by Peres [78], but it had already been used in the discussion of quantum states by von Neumann [71]. The proof of Eq. (2.70) is adapted from Schrödinger [86]. The concept of quantum entropy was also introduced by von Neumann in [71].

The noncloning property of quantum states was proved by Dieks [31] and Wootters and Zurek [107]. The quantum copier was first suggested by Bužek and Hillery [22]. The teleportation procedure was suggested by Bennett et al. [11]; for more recent developments, see Chapter 2 of [17]. The Bell inequalities were originally suggested by John Bell [9]; for the history, see [28]. The recent experimental progress is reviewed by Aspect in [7]. The quantum dense coding is discussed in [18]. The GHZ states were introduced by Greenberger et al. in [40] and first observed (with photons) in Zeilinger's group [16]. For recent progress, see Chapter 6.3 of [17] and references [73] and [74].

The quantum measurement process has been discussed a great deal over the years. Much of the relevant literature is collected by Wheeler and Zurek in [105]. A detailed discussion of several aspects is found in the book by Belinfante [8], and the selected papers of van Kampen [66] present the conventional view on the interpretation of quantum theory. The approach presented here is based on the original work of Landau and Peierls [58], which has been modified to fit the contemporary description of measurements. A more formal presentation of measurements by Busch et al. is given in [20]. A distinction between measurements of the first and second kind was introduced by Pauli [75]. See also discussions of measurements in books by Peres [78] and Nielsen and Chuang [72]. A formal but readable account of the abstract approach to quantum observations is given in [57]. The example of quantum state truncation has been taken from an article by Pegg and Barnett [76].

The master equation of Lindblad form was written down in [61]; equivalent results were obtained by Gorini et al. [38]; see also [98]. A detailed exposition of the theory of dissipative systems is given by Breuer and Petruccione in [19]. A more formal presentation by Alicki and Fannes may be found in [3]; see also the textbook by Alicki and Lendi on dynamical semigroups [4]. The derivation of the master equation presented here is taken from [94]. The mathematical concept of positive mappings was introduced by Stinespring [97] and Kraus [56]. Its application to time-evolution generators was performed by Lindblad [61]. For a modern mathematical treatment, see the texts [4], [19], and [30]. Our approach is adapted from [19].

The unraveling of the master equation was introduced by several persons almost simultaneously; here we follow the discussion by Mølmer et al. in [69]. An alternative approach is given in the monograph by Carmichael [23]. Applications of this technique to quantum optics are given in lecture notes by Knight [55]; see also the review by Plenio and Knight [81]. A review of the physical situation is given in an article by Stenholm and Wilkens [96]. The theory of continuous measurements is discussed in a book by Mensky [67]. The general relation between quantum uncertainties and the stochastic description is given by Carmichael [24].

CHAPTER 3

QUANTUM COMMUNICATION AND INFORMATION

3.1 CLASSICAL COMMUNICATION

3.1.1 Information Theory

Entropy A very common event does not carry much information. If we want to catch someone's attention, we have to produce an unexpected effect, something that occurs with very low probability. If we merely splash ink on paper, we produce random blobs which are not very informative. However, if we deposit the ink in the form of letters, it is extremely unlikely that the pattern has appeared spontaneously and thus is able to carry information.

Thus, the less probable an occurrence is, the more information it can convey. If a single event is expected to occur with probability p, its rarity or surprise value can be measured by p^{-1}. This may thus be used to signify the information-carrying capacity of an event occurring with probability p. Such a measure is, however, not very expedient, because if we use two such events, the other one occurring with probability q, the information-carrying capacity of the two events should be the sum of the individual capacities if they are taken to be independent. On the one hand, we have

$$\frac{1}{p} + \frac{1}{q} = \frac{p+q}{pq},$$ (3.1)

but regarded as a single combined event, the two consecutive events should give the information capacity $1/pq$. This is true only if $p + q = 1$, which is an

---

Quantum Approach to Informatics, by Stig Stenholm and Kalle-Antti Suominen
Copyright © 2005 John Wiley & Sons, Inc.

exceptional special case. This shortcoming was overcome in 1948 when Shannon introduced his entropy concept,

$$H(p) = \log \frac{1}{p} = -\log p. \tag{3.2}$$

As a function, the logarithm is monotonic: It grows with p^{-1} but it satisfies the additivity requirement of combined events:

$$H(pq) = H(p) + H(q). \tag{3.3}$$

By mutual agreement we select a set of symbols $\{a_i\}$ for our communication. If these symbols occur with probabilities $\{p_i | \sum_i p_i = 1\}$, the definition of the Shannon entropy reads

$$H(\{p_i\}) = -\sum_i p_i \log p_i, \tag{3.4}$$

which can be interpreted as the average over the probability distribution $\{p_i\}$ of the information-carrying capacities of the individual events, each contributing $\log(1/p_i)$. This definition has turned out to be extremely useful in the theoretical treatment of communication methods.

Example   We want to transmit a message consisting of zeros and ones, a binary signal. Zero occurs with probability p_0 and 1 with probability $1 - p_0$. The entropy is then given by the expression

$$H(p_0) = -p_0 \log p_0 - (1 - p_0) \log(1 - p_0). \tag{3.5}$$

If either symbol occurs with a vanishing probability, $p_0 = 0$ or 1, we find zero entropy; no information can be transmitted. The maximum capacity $H = \log 2$ occurs when the probabilities are equal $p_0 = \frac{1}{2}$, when both possible symbols are used with equal frequency. This unit of information transfer, called a *bit*, constitutes the basic unit for measuring information-carrying capacity. For this reason, the basis for the logarithm used is often chosen to be 2, in which case the entropy of a bit is just 1. The binary system carries one bit of information per symbol.

The motivation for introducing the Shannon entropy given above can be generalized into a mathematical theorem as follows: We assume that our message is coded in an alphabet consisting of M symbols occurring with the probabilities $\{p_i | i = 1, \ldots, M\}$. We then impose the rather natural requirements:

1. For an equal distribution, $p_i = M^{-1}$, the information must be increasing with M:

$$H\left(\left\{\frac{1}{M_1}\right\}\right) < H\left(\left\{\frac{1}{M_2}\right\}\right) \tag{3.6}$$

if $M_2 > M_1$.

2. We must have additivity of the information:

$$H\left(\left\{\frac{1}{MN}\right\}\right) = H\left(\left\{\frac{1}{M}\right\}\right) + H\left(\left\{\frac{1}{N}\right\}\right). \tag{3.7}$$

3. The probabilities should be grouped so that when we divide the events into r events separated from the remaining $M - r$ events, we have the property

$$H\left(\{p_1, p_2, \ldots, p_M\}\right)$$
$$= H\left[(p_1 + p_2 +, \ldots, p_r), (p_{r+1}, p_{r+2}, \ldots, p_M)\right]$$
$$+ (p_1 + p_2 +, \ldots, p_r)H\left(\left\{\frac{p_1}{N_I}, \frac{p_2}{N_I}, \ldots, \frac{p_r}{N_I}\right\}\right)$$
$$+ (p_{r+1} + p_{r+2} +, \ldots, p_M)H\left(\left\{\frac{p_{r+1}}{N_{II}}, \frac{p_{r+2}}{N_{II}}, \ldots, \frac{p_M}{N_{II}}\right\}\right), \tag{3.8}$$

where the normalization constants are given by

$$N_I = \sum_{i=1}^{r} p_i,$$
$$N_{II} = \sum_{i=r+1}^{M} p_i. \tag{3.9}$$

4. Finally, we assume the entropy to be an analytic function of the probabilities.

With requirements 1 to 4 it is possible to derive the unique expression (3.4) for the Shannon entropy. We give a brief indication of the proof of this fundamental result. To this end we define the function

$$f(M) = H\left(\left\{\frac{1}{M}\right\}\right), \tag{3.10}$$

which according to requirement 4 is assumed analytic in its variable. From requirement 2 we conclude that

$$f(M^2) = f(M) + f(M) = 2f(M),$$
$$f(M^3) = f(M^2) + f(M) = 3F(M), \tag{3.11}$$
$$\vdots$$
$$f(M^k) = f(M^{k-1}) + f(M) = k\,f(M).$$

Setting $k = 0$, we find that

$$f(1) = 0. \tag{3.12}$$

Because requirement 4 is valid, we can take the derivative of (3.11) with respect to M and find that

$$f'(M^k)kM^{k-1} = kf'(M),$$ (3.13)

from which we obtain

$$f'(M^k)M^k = Mf'(M).$$ (3.14)

This can hold for all k only if each side is independent of M. Thus integration gives

$$f(M) = c\log(M).$$ (3.15)

The remaining degree of freedom is a multiplicative constant, which is equivalent with the freedom to choose the basis of the logarithm in an arbitrary manner.

Next, we take a fixed M, which we partition into the two sets with probabilities

$$p = \frac{r}{M}, \qquad 1 - p = \frac{M-r}{M}.$$ (3.16)

Using requirement 3, we find that

$$\begin{aligned}
f(M) &= H\left(\left\{\frac{1}{M}\right\}_r, \left\{\frac{1}{M}\right\}_{M-r}\right) \\
&= H\left(\frac{r}{M}, \frac{M-r}{M}\right) + \frac{r}{M}f(r) + \frac{M-r}{M}f(M-r).
\end{aligned}$$ (3.17)

The result (3.15) allows this to be written as

$$c\log M = H\left(\frac{r}{M}, \frac{M-r}{M}\right) + \frac{r}{M}c\log r + \frac{M-r}{M}c\log(M-r).$$ (3.18)

Writing $r = Mp$ and $M - r = (1-p)M$, we find the result

$$H(p, 1-p) = -c\left[p\log p + (1-p)\log(1-p)\right].$$ (3.19)

Using requirement 3, we can generalize this by induction. The first step is going from two cases $\{p, (1-p)\}$ to three probabilities $\{p_1, p_2, p_3\}$. The step is as follows:

$$\begin{aligned}
H(p_1, p_2, p_3) &= H(p_1 + p_2, p_3) + (p_1 + p_2)H\left(\frac{p_1}{p_1 + p_2}, \frac{p_2}{p_1 + p_2}\right) + p_3 H(1) \\
&= -\left[c(p_1 + p_2)\log(p_1 + p_2) + p_3\log p_3 + (p_1 + p_2)\right. \\
&\qquad \left.\cdot\left(\frac{p_1}{p_1 + p_2}\log\frac{p_1}{p_1 + p_2} + \frac{p_2}{p_1 + p_2}\log\frac{p_2}{p_1 + p_2}\right)\right] \\
&= -c(p_1\log p_1 + p_2\log p_2 + p_3\log p_3).
\end{aligned}$$ (3.20)

This result is easily extended to the general formula (3.4). It is expressed in bits if we use the base 2 for the logarithm and set $c = 1$.

The entropy has an interesting property, which we may formulate as a theorem:

Theorem   Let $\{p_i\}$ and $\{q_i\}$ be two arbitrary normalized probability distributions. Then we have the inequality

$$\sum_i p_i \log p_i \geq \sum_i p_i \log q_i. \qquad (3.21)$$

Proof: We use the inequality $\log x \leq x - 1$ on the quantity

$$\sum_i p_i \log \frac{q_i}{p_i} \leq \sum_i p_i \left(\frac{q_i}{p_i} - 1\right) = \sum_i q_i - \sum_i p_i = 0, \qquad (3.22)$$

which proves the inequality.

If the entropy is regarded as the average of $\log(1/q_i)$, it takes its lowest value when $q_i = p_i$. This theorem is used in the following.

The entropy has an interesting behavior when we combine two probabilities. Let us assume that we have two binary probability distributions $\{p_1, 1 - p_1\}$ and $\{p_2, 1 - p_2\}$. We now assume that the first one occurs with probability q and the second with probability $(1 - q)$. The first occurrence then takes place with probability

$$P = qp_1 + (1 - q)p_2; \qquad (3.23)$$

the second occurrence takes place with probability $1 - P = q(1 - p_1) + (1 - q)(1 - p_2)$. If we now define the function of any variable ξ,

$$h(\xi) \equiv H(\xi, 1 - \xi) = -\left[\xi \log \xi + (1 - \xi) \log(1 - \xi)\right]. \qquad (3.24)$$

Expressing for any x and y ($\in [0, 1]$) a new function

$$f(q) \equiv h(qx + (1 - q)y) \qquad (3.25)$$

of the variable q, we can write in the interval $q \in [0, 1]$

$$f(q) = h(y) + (h(x) - h(y))q + O(q^2). \qquad (3.26)$$

The first two terms on the right-hand side give the line joining the points $\{q = 0, f(0) = h(y)\}$ and $\{q = 1, f(1) = h(x)\}$. We find in the interval $q \in [0, 1]$ that

$$f''(q) = h''(qx + (1 - q)y)(x - y)^2 < 0. \qquad (3.27)$$

From Fig. 3.1 it is then easy to see that

$$f(q) = h(qx + (1 - q)y) \geq h(y) + (h(x) - h(y))q = qh(x) + (1 - q)h(y). \qquad (3.28)$$

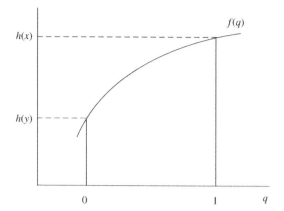

Figure 3.1 Concavity of the function $h(x)$.

Applied to the entropy function with $x = p_1$ and $y = p_2$, the inequality (3.28) says that

$$H(P, 1 - P) \geq qH(p_1, 1 - p_1) + (1 - q)H(p_2, 1 - p_2). \qquad (3.29)$$

This is the *concavity property* of the entropy function. It says, simply stated, that given the full probability distribution P, we have more information than just having the probabilities in the two subsystems with their appropriate weights.

Note: The quantum generalization of the Shannon entropy is the von Neumann entropy,

$$S(\rho) = -\text{Tr}(\rho \log \rho), \qquad (3.30)$$

where the density matrix takes the role of the probability distribution. Indeed, the density matrix can be seen as a probability distribution over vectors in the quantum state space, in the same manner as a classical probability distribution can be seen as giving probabilities over classical entities.

The inequality used in (3.22) can be written as

$$A(\log B - \log A) \leq B - A, \qquad (3.31)$$

which we may take to hold also for quantum operators. For operators this is called the *Klein inequality*. The proof is then less obvious, because A and B do not usually commute.

We next choose A to be a density matrix ρ and select an orthonormal basis $\{|\psi_i\rangle\}$. We define the operator B as the diagonal part of ρ in this basis,

$$\rho_D = \sum_i |\psi_i\rangle \rho_{ii} \langle \psi_i|. \qquad (3.32)$$

We take the trace of (3.31) and obtain

$$-\text{Tr}(\rho \log \rho_D) \geq -\text{Tr}(\rho \log \rho) = S(\rho). \qquad (3.33)$$

On the other hand, we find that

$$\text{Tr}\,(\rho \log \rho_D) = \sum_k \langle \psi_k | \rho \sum_i | \psi_i \rangle \log \rho_{ii} \langle \psi_i | \psi_k \rangle$$

$$= \sum_i \rho_{ii} \log \rho_{ii} = -H(\{\rho_{ii}\}). \tag{3.34}$$

Inequality (3.33) then states that

$$S(\rho) = -\text{Tr}\,(\rho \log \rho) \le -\sum_i \rho_{ii} \log(\rho_{ii}) = H\,(\{\rho_{ii}\}). \tag{3.35}$$

Consequently, when a quantum mechanical density matrix loses its off-diagonal elements (i.e., it decoheres), its entropy is increasing. This process does, however, depend on which basis we use. On the other hand, when decoherence is due to the effects of a thermal reservoir, the off-diagonal elements disappear in the energy representation, which makes the process correspond to the increase in thermodynamic entropy. In the general case, however, the decoherence processes have no relationship to thermodynamics, and the entropy defined in (3.35) is not identical with the thermodynamic entropy.

Also, a measurement implying projection of the density matrix onto some diagonal form will thus increase the entropy of the system. As pointed out in Sec. 2.4.3, there is a definite similarity between irreversible decoherence and observations; if the result observed is not recorded, the latter acts like an external reservoir on the system.

Entropy in Communication Systems   In communication theory, a channel is regarded as a statistically defined system, where a sender A emits a sequence of symbols $\{a_1, a_2, \ldots, a_r\}$ which in a long enough message occur with the probabilities $\{p_1, p_2, \ldots, p_r\}$. The receiver B similarly finds the symbols $\{b_1, b_2, \ldots, b_s\}$ with probabilities $\{q_1, q_2, \ldots, q_s\}$. Note that r and s need not in general be the same. For the most common binary channel, both A and B use the alphabet $\{0, 1\}$. The tacit assumption is that the sender and the receiver have agreed fully on the set of symbols and their meaning.

The channel is defined by its transmission function $Q(a_i|b_j)$, which states the conditional probability that a_i was transmitted assuming that b_j was received. This description obviously allows many complications; the channel may introduce errors or have losses. If we have

$$Q(a_i|b_j) = \delta_{ij} \tag{3.36}$$

the channel is lossless and faithful; it is said to be uniquely decodable. We may also introduce the opposite probability $P(b_i|a_j)$, which gives the probability that b_i reaches the receiver when a_j was sent. These are related by Bayes' theorem,

$$P(a_j, b_i) = P(b_i|a_j)p_j = Q(a_j|b_i)q_i. \tag{3.37}$$

These both give the joint probability $P(a_j, b_i)$ of the occurrence of a_j and b_i. As the joint probability must sum to the separate probabilities, we find the relations

$$\sum_j P(b_i|a_j)p_j = q_i,$$

$$\sum_i Q(a_j|b_i)q_i = p_j.$$

(3.38)

These relations agree with the fact that the conditional probabilities are normalized with respect to their first variable.

Example   In general, the representation of 2^N different symbols by a binary code would require N bits for faithful transmission. For various reasons, we sometimes want to introduce more symbols for the communication. Let us assume that to transmit three symbols, we choose the coding $\{0, 01, 11\}$. This is not a good choice because receiving the sequence $(01111\ldots)$, we cannot read the message this far; the reading is not instantaneous. The reason is that this could be part of either the message $(0, 11, 11, \ldots)$ or the message $(01, 11, 11, \ldots)$. Only after knowing the full message can we find the interpretation. If, instead, we choose the coding $\{0, 10, 11\}$, we have a code that can be interpreted on the run. Thus, the sequence received above has the unique beginning $(0, 11, 11, \ldots)$. The trick is to introduce the separator of the symbols at the end instead of the beginning. Thus, the code $\{0, 10, 110, 1110, 1111\}$ can be interpreted on the run. The final symbol, 1111, can always be interpreted because it contains the maximum number of 1's. Such a code is termed *instantaneous*.

The example above introduces the concept of a word length l_j. This indicates the binary length of the word used to denote the symbol number j. Thus, in the examples above, the word lengths are given by $\{1, 2, 2\}$ and $\{1, 2, 3, 4, 4\}$, respectively.

Here a warning may be needed. The information-carrying capacity of a message is defined only by its formal length. Thus, the two sequences

{UXQPREN QK SWATNUGN MYUQRTU}

and

{BEWARE OF NONSENSE MESSAGES}

formally carry the same amount of information. Meaning is not included in the definition.

Using the input and output probabilities of a channel, we can define the corresponding entropies

$$H(A) = -\sum_i p_i \log p_i,$$

$$H(B) = -\sum_i q_i \log q_i.$$

(3.39)

These represent the mean capacity of information input and output, respectively. The information interpretation of these is that $H(A)$ represents the leeway of system A when nothing is known about B. The coding of any message has to take place within this range of possibilities, and hence $H(A)$ is also a measure of the size of the message needed to utilize the channel input to encode an arbitrary message. We will make this aspect more precise below. A similar interpretation holds for $H(B)$.

We want, however, to continue. Which is the information conveyed when we have received a signal b_j? This is given by the conditional entropy

$$H(A|b_j) = -\sum_i Q(a_i|b_j) \log Q(a_i|b_j). \tag{3.40}$$

If we average over all possible outputs, we find the conditional entropy

$$H(A|B) = -\sum_{j,i} q_j Q(a_i|b_j) \log Q(a_i|b_j) = -\sum_{j,i} P(a_i, b_j) \log Q(a_i|b_j). \tag{3.41}$$

This quantity is a measure of how much information is still carried by A after we have had access to the information in B. It can also be interpreted as the uncertainty about A even after knowing B. A similar definition gives $H(B|A)$ with exactly the analogous interpretation

$$H(B|A) = -\sum_{j,i} p_j P(b_i|a_j) \log P(b_i|a_j). \tag{3.42}$$

There are relations between these various expressions: Thus, the ordinary entropy $H(A, B)$, denoting the magnitude of uncertainty if we know nothing about A and B, can be written as

$$
\begin{aligned}
H(A, B) &= -\sum_{i,j} P(a_i, b_j) \log P(a_i, b_j) \\
&= -\sum_{i,j} P(a_i, b_j) \log q_j Q(a_i|b_j) \\
&= -\sum_j \left[\sum_i P(a_i, b_j)\right] \log q_j - \sum_{i,j} P(a_i, b_j) \log Q(a_i|b_j) \\
&= -\sum_j q_j \log q_j - \sum_{i,j} q_j Q(a_i|b_j) \log Q(a_i|b_j) \\
&= H(B) + H(A|B). \tag{3.43}
\end{aligned}
$$

This says that the information in A and B consists of the information in B and the additional information residing in A once B is known. If the variables are uncorrelated, we have $H(A|B) = H(A)$ and the information capacities of the two systems add.

The quantity $H(A|B)$ tells us how uncertain A is even after we have learned about B. For communication purposes, it is, however, more interesting to know what we have learned about A by obtaining information about B. This is given by the *mutual information*, defined as

$$I(A : B) = H(A) - H(A|B). \tag{3.44}$$

This gives us a measure of the information about A that is conveyed by B. From $H(A)$ we remove the uncertainty that cannot be resolved by learning about B. This quantity is symmetric, because from (3.43) we can write

$$I(A : B) = H(A) + H(B) - H(A, B). \tag{3.45}$$

Thus, B tells us just as much about A as A can tell us about B.

The mutual information is always positive, $I(A : B) \geq 0$. This is shown from (3.45) as follows:

$$I(A : B) = -\sum_i p_i \log p_i - \sum_i q_i \log q_i + \sum_{i,j} P(a_i, b_j) \log P(a_i, b_j)$$

$$= -\sum_i \left(\sum_j P(a_i, b_j) \right) \log p_i - \sum_i \left(\sum_j P(a_j, b_i) \right) \log q_i$$

$$+ \sum_{i,j} P(a_i, b_j) \log P(a_i, b_j)$$

$$= \sum_{i,j} P(a_i, b_j) \left[\log P(a_i, b_j) - \log(p_i q_j) \right] \geq 0, \tag{3.46}$$

where we have applied the theorem (3.21) to the probability distributions $\{P(a_i, b_j)\}$ and $\{p_i q_j\}$. Equality ensues only if the probabilities factorize $P(a_i, b_j) = p_i q_j$.

From the various expressions for $I(A, B)$ and the relation (3.46), we obtain the relations

$$H(A) \geq H(A|B),$$

$$H(B) \geq H(B|A), \tag{3.47}$$

$$H(A, B) \leq H(A) + H(B).$$

These are easily interpreted like the relations above.

Because the mutual information $I(A : B)$ in (3.45) is symmetric, we may write

$$I(A : B) = H(A) + H(B) - H(A, B) = H(B) - H(B|A), \tag{3.48}$$

which indicates the amount of information in B that is resolved by A.

It is sometimes useful to interpret probabilities in terms of sets. Thus, the measure of the set P is assumed to be p, and the complementary set $(E - P)$

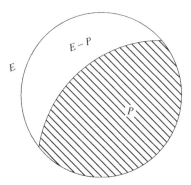

Figure 3.2 Relation between the sets E, $E - P$, and P.

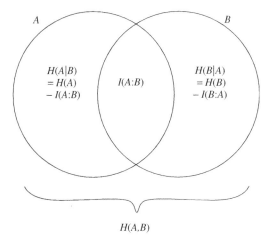

Figure 3.3 Relationships between the various entropies and the mutual information.

has the measure $(1 - p)$; here E is the set of measure unity. These relations are illustrated in Fig. 3.2. If we interpret the information measure given by the various entropy functions above as sets in the corresponding manner, we find the relationships given in Fig. 3.3. They are thus seen to correspond to the basic logical relationships between sets.

3.1.2 Coding Theory

Noiseless Coding A classical communication system with N bits available can send 2^N different symbols. If they all occur with equal probability, this is the most we can say. Only when there is a difference in the frequency of occurrence can we hope to utilize some trick to change the situation. This was the main result of the work by Shannon, who in 1948 pointed out the central role played by the concept of entropy in information transfer.

To see the general trend of the argument, we assume that for long enough messages with N binary symbols, we have

$$N_0 = \frac{N}{2} - m \tag{3.49}$$

occurrences of zero, and

$$N_1 = \frac{N}{2} + m \tag{3.50}$$

occurrences of 1. The probability of having a 1 is thus

$$p = \frac{1}{2} + \frac{m}{N}, \tag{3.51}$$

and the probability of zero is

$$1 - p = \frac{1}{2} - \frac{m}{N}. \tag{3.52}$$

These statements can, of course, be true only in a statistical sense, so they hold for asymptotically long messages.

The number of different messages we can send with such a string is

$$W = \frac{N!}{N_0! N_1!}. \tag{3.53}$$

Taking the logarithm and using Stirling's approximation, we find that

$$\log W = N \left[\log N - \left(\frac{1}{2} + \frac{m}{N} \right) \log N \left(\frac{1}{2} + \frac{m}{N} \right) - \left(\frac{1}{2} - \frac{m}{N} \right) \log N \left(\frac{1}{2} - \frac{m}{N} \right) \right]$$
$$= N \left[-p \log p - (1 - p) \log(1 - p) \right] = N H(p). \tag{3.54}$$

We thus find an estimate for the number of different messages that can be sent to be

$$W = \exp[N H(p)] = 2^{N H_2(p)}, \tag{3.55}$$

where we have replaced the logarithms in the entropy according to $\log_2 e \log p = \log_2 p$ (and $H \to H_2$). We thus see that we need $N H_2(p)$ bits to transmit the information strings characterized by the probability p. This amount of information-carrying capacity will be able to handle most *typical messages*. The risk that some messages do not fit into this scheme becomes negligible when the length of the message goes to infinity.

The result above can be formulated in a more general way by introducing the *noiseless coding theorem*:

Theorem   If a message of length N is coded in terms of r symbols $\{a_1, a_2, \ldots, a_r\}$ which occur with the probabilities $\{p_1, p_2, \ldots, p_r\}$, the number of bits needed to transmit the information is given by $N H_2(\{p_i\})$ bits.

This shows that the number of typical sequences is determined by the entropy. Atypical sequences are rare and can be neglected. This suggests that messages can be compressed, so that the longest strings are used to decode the rarest symbols. The efficient use of the method requires the introduction of rather long basic units (i.e., words) and asymptotically infinite messages.

Example   Let us look at the situation of binary symbols occurring with probability $p = 0.8$ for the symbol 1 and words of two symbols. The Shannon bound on the necessary capacity is then

$$2H(0.8) = -2\left(0.2\log_2 0.2 + 0.8\log_2 0.8\right) = 1.44. \qquad (3.56)$$

We now proceed to invent a coding utilizing intuition only. We select the word lengths $\{1, 2, 3, 3\}$ as follows:

Word	Probability	Code	
00	0.04	111	
01	0.16	110	(3.57)
10	0.16	10	
11	0.64	0	

The average word length is here given by

$$0.04 \times 3 + 0.16 \times 3 + 0.16 \times 2 + 0.64 \times 1 = 1.56. \qquad (3.58)$$

This is more than the entropy given in (3.56) but much less than the result 2, which would ensue if we used the original words directly. In addition, this is a code that can be interpreted on the run, as the separator zero is at the end of the code words.

This shows how we can simply compress the necessary magnitude of our messages by replacing the original words with different words. Unfortunately, detailed proof of the coding theorem is not constructive, so we cannot use it to find an optimal code. The next section is devoted to a discussion of this question. Then we also present a more detailed relationship between the entropy and the length of the code words.

Huffman Code   An important problem is to make a coding as economical as possible. The limit is set by the Shannon coding theorem, but there is no systematic way to reach this. We present this method in the case of binary coding with the elementary symbols $\{0, 1\}$.

The idea is to order the words to be decoded according to their increasing probability. We then take the two words with lowest probability and lump them together as a single entity, with its probability being the sum of the two combined symbols. The new entity is then moved to the proper place in the sequence of symbols, which is now one shorter than originally. This process is repeated until only two symbols remain. Their probabilities must add up to unity, and they are now assigned the code words "0" and "1." If either one then derives directly from the original sequence, its code word is retained. A combined symbol is then split up into its two previous components, and these are now coded by the original symbol but with the addition of a zero and a one after the symbol being split up. This procedure continues until no combined symbols remain. Every time a symbol found derives from the original sequence, it can no longer be split up and its code word is retained for the final choice of coding. The procedure is not entirely unique, but it always works to compress the information.

The procedure is best illustrated by an example. We have five original symbols, with the probability of occurrence being $\{0.1, 0.2, 0.2, 0.2, 0.3\}$. We note that this differs only marginally from an even distribution, and still considerable compression is possible. If we used straightforward binary numbers, we would need 3 bits to distinguish between all these, but using the Huffman method, we simplify the process. The reduction scheme is as follows: $\{0.1, 0.2, 0.2, 0.2, 0.3\} \Rightarrow \{0.2, 0.2, 0.3, 0.3\} \Rightarrow \{0.3, 0.3, 0.4\} \Rightarrow \{0.4, 0.6\}$. The assignment of code words is best presented as a matrix (Fig. 3.4). The upper half describes the reduction of probabilities; the lower half, the coding procedure of the method. The number used to perform the next step is the one enclosed by a frame. The final code is now found by attaching the code words on the bottom line to the symbols on the top line. We have thus found the code $\{010, 011, 10, 11, 00\}$, which is a code of the type $\{3, 3, 2, 2, 2\}$. It is also easy to see that this code can be interpreted on the run even if we have not given any formal criteria for such codes; such criteria do exist.

The average word length is now given by

$$0.1 \times 3 + 0.2 \times 3 + 0.2 \times 2 + 0.2 \times 2 + 0.3 \times 2 = 2.3, \qquad (3.59)$$

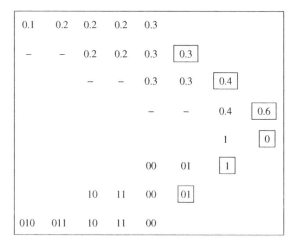

Figure 3.4 Assignment of code words.

which is considerably less than the 3 bits needed without the compression. To estimate how well we have done, we should calculate what the theoretical optimum is according to the Shannon theorem. We thus compute

$$- \left[0.1 \times \log_2(0.1) + 3 \times 0.2 \times \log_2(0.2) + 0.3 \times \log_2(0.3) \right] = 2.25. \quad (3.60)$$

This is less than the average word length (3.59), which cannot reach the theoretical channel capacity; this is the ultimate optimum. However, in view of the fact that the probabilities in the original case differ little from a uniform distribution, we find that the algorithm devised above works surprisingly well.

If the code constructed is uniquely decodable on the fly, we can prove that the average word length must always be bigger than or equal to the entropy. We carry out the proof for the case of a binary code only. We assume that our code consists of N words occurring with the probabilities $\{p_i | i = 1, \ldots, N\}$ and the corresponding word lengths $\{l_i | i = 1, \ldots, N\}$. The code is assumed to be uniquely decodable. We define the quantity

$$K = \sum_{l_i=m}^{M} \left(\frac{1}{2} \right)^{l_i}, \quad (3.61)$$

where $m = \min \{l_i\}$ and $M = \max \{l_i\}$. We consider the expression

$$K^n = \left[\sum_{l_i=m}^{M} \left(\frac{1}{2} \right)^{l_i} \right]^n \quad (3.62)$$

for an arbitrary integer n. In the expanded product, the terms are of the form $(\frac{1}{2})^j$, where $j = l_1 + l_2 + \cdots$. The values of j are bounded by $nm \leq j \leq nM$. Collecting the terms in (3.62) according to the values of j, we find that

$$K^n = \sum_{j=nm}^{nM} \frac{N(j, n)}{2^j}, \quad (3.63)$$

where $N(j, n)$ is the number of ways the sum j can be obtained for given n. It is thus the number of code words possible if the total length of the sequence of original words is given by j. As we assume that the code chosen is uniquely decodable, this can happen in only one way, and we conclude that this number is less than the total number of code words of length j [i.e., $N(j, n) \leq 2^j$], which states that the individual terms in (3.63) have to be smaller than unity. The total number of terms in the sum is $(nM + 1 - nm)$, and hence we obtain the inequality

$$K^n \leq n(M - m) + 1. \quad (3.64)$$

As this must hold for any number n, however, the left side grows exponentially with n and the right-hand side grows linearly. Hence, the inequality can hold only if

$$K \leq 1. \quad (3.65)$$

As an illustration, we choose the code discussed in (3.59)–(3.60):

$$K = 2 \times \frac{1}{2^3} + 3 \times \frac{1}{2^2} = 1,$$ (3.66)

which saturates the inequality.

We next introduce a normalized probability by setting

$$y_i = \frac{1}{K} \left(\frac{1}{2}\right)^{l_i}.$$ (3.67)

Using the theorem (3.21), we find the entropy to be

$$H_2(\{p_i\}) = -\sum_i p_i \log_2 p_i$$

$$\leq -\sum_i p_i \log_2 y_i$$

$$= \sum_i p_i \left(\log_2 K + l_i \log_2 2\right)$$

$$= \log_2 K + \sum_i p_i l_i$$

$$\leq \sum_i p_i l_i$$ (3.68)

because (3.65) guarantees that $\log K \leq 0$. This proves that the average word length $\sum_i p_i l_i$ must not be smaller than the entropy, giving the absolute bound on how far the compression can proceed. It is, however, as we can see, possible to reach the limit.

Example   Assume an alphabet consisting of three symbols $\{s_1, s_2, s_3\}$ with probabilities $\left\{\frac{1}{4}, \frac{1}{4}, \frac{1}{2}\right\}$. A Huffman code for this is obviously $\{00, 01, 1\}$, with average word length

$$\frac{1}{4}2 + \frac{1}{4}2 + \frac{1}{2} = \frac{3}{2}.$$ (3.69)

The entropy is

$$\frac{1}{4}\log_2 4 + \frac{1}{4}\log_2 4 + \frac{1}{2}\log_2 2 = \frac{3}{2},$$ (3.70)

which agrees with the word length. The reason here is that the probabilities are all powers of 2.

It is sometimes possible to improve the efficiency in transmitting information by extending the source symbols to contain several primary symbols in the basic alphabet. Let us illustrate this by the simple set of symbols $\{0, 1\}$ with the

$\frac{1}{9}$	$\frac{2}{9}$	$\frac{2}{9}$	$\frac{4}{9}$	
–	$\frac{2}{9}$	$\boxed{\frac{3}{9}}$	$\frac{4}{9}$	
		–	–	$\frac{4}{9}$	$\boxed{\frac{5}{9}}$
			0	$\boxed{1}$
	10	$\boxed{11}$	0	
111	10	110	0	

Figure 3.5 Matrix based on Huffman code.

probabilities $\{\frac{2}{3}, \frac{1}{3}\}$. The average word length is now unity, but we may improve this. The entropy is given by

$$-\left(\frac{2}{3}\log_2\frac{2}{3} + \frac{1}{3}\log_2\frac{1}{3}\right) = 0.92, \tag{3.71}$$

so it must be possible to improve on the result above.

We choose to use pairs of symbols as the basic alphabet $\{11, 01, 10, 00\}$ with the probabilities $\{\frac{1}{9}, \frac{2}{9}, \frac{2}{9}, \frac{4}{9}\}$. Constructing the Huffman code, we write the matrix shown in Fig. 3.5 and thus get the code $\{111, 110, 10, 0\}$ for the symbols $\{11, 10, 01, 00\}$. The average word length is now

$$\frac{1}{9} \times 3 + \frac{2}{9} \times 3 + \frac{2}{9} \times 2 + \frac{4}{9} \times 1 = \frac{17}{9}. \tag{3.72}$$

As each symbol now carries 2 bits, the word length per bit is

$$\left(\frac{17}{9}\right)\left(\frac{1}{2}\right) = 0.94 < 1. \tag{3.73}$$

We have thus decreased the average word length per bit at the expense of efficiency in decoding. We need to collect enough single bits to be able to interpret the code $\{111, 110, 10, 0\}$ instead of decoding each symbol in the set $\{0, 1\}$. However, we are still not reaching the limit set by the Shannon entropy (3.71).

The discussion above suggests that we have three different interpretations of the entropy $H(A) = -\sum_i p_i \log p_i$, which are useful in communication theory:

- $H(A)$ is the uncertainty we have about the value of A when no information has been received.
- $H(A)$ is the amount of information we can obtain if we get information about the value of A and no other information is available.
- $H(A)$ limits the average word length if we want to identify the value taken by A (i.e., the word length needed to encode the information carried by A).

Noisy Channel Coding Theorem   We now turn to the case of a communication channel which is less than perfect; we do not get out exactly what we put in. The message conveyed is afflicted with randomly occurring errors. The result is that the transmission of information is less efficient than in the case of a noiseless channel. It is, however, possible to estimate how much the errors decrease the channel performance.

We assume the information to be transmitted by a string of binary numbers carrying M_c bits. We want this string to carry M bits of essential information. In the limit of long messages, the error rate is characterized by the error probability q. Thus, the error (i.e., the number of incorrect bits) is given by

$$M_e = q M_c. \tag{3.74}$$

If we ask in how many ways these may occur, we have

$$P_{\text{error}} = \frac{M_c!}{M_e!(M_c - M_e)!}; \tag{3.75}$$

this measures the size of the incorrect information. As the errors in a binary system consist simply of flips $0 \Leftrightarrow 1$, we can correct the errors if we know where they occur. We assume that this information can be conveyed by m additional bits, which thus must carry more information than P_{error} measuring the errors. Then we conclude that the message can be transmitted faithfully if the total number of bits through the channel can carry both the essential information and that needed to correct the errors:

$$M_c \geq M + m. \tag{3.76}$$

This implies that

$$2^{M_c - M} \geq 2^m \geq \frac{M_c!}{M_e!(M_c - M_e)!}. \tag{3.77}$$

Introducing (3.74), taking the logarithm of both sides, and using the limit of large messages, we obtain

$$(M_c - M) \log 2 \geq M_c(\log M_c - 1) - q M_c(\log q M_c - 1)$$
$$- (M_c - q M_c)\left[\log(M_c - q M_c) - 1\right]$$
$$\Rightarrow \left(1 - \frac{M}{M_c}\right) \log 2 \geq -\left[q \log q + (1 - q) \log(1 - q)\right]. \tag{3.78}$$

Using base 2 for the logarithm, we find that the amount of information carried by the faulty channel is limited by

$$\frac{M}{M_c} \leq 1 + q \log_2 q + (1 - q) \log_2(1 - q) = 1 - H_2(q, 1 - q). \tag{3.79}$$

The interpretation is that we can use all the bits transmitted, decreased, however, by the disorder (i.e., loss of information) introduced by the error rate.

Result (3.79) is the *noisy channel coding theorem*. In mathematical formulations of information theory it is proved that this bound can be reached, but here we conclude only that such a result is intuitively reasonable. As before, the result holds only in the limit of long messages, and the mathematical proof is not constructive.

If we denote the channel efficiency by $R = M/M_c$, we write the result as

$$2^{RM_c} \leq 2^{M_c[1-H(q,1-q)]}. \tag{3.80}$$

The resulting efficiency can be seen from the following table:

q	0.001	0.01	0.1	0.25	0.333	0.5
R	0.99	0.92	0.53	0.19	0.08	0

Thus, after reaching 10% errors, the channel efficiency decreases rapidly; at a rate of 50% errors, no information can be conveyed. This is understandable; if half of the bits are wrong, the remaining bits cannot carry the information to correct the errors.

The communication channel theory introduced in Sec. 3.1.1 is also able to describe the case of imperfect transmission. We only have to have

$$Q(a_i|b_j) \neq \delta_{ij}, \tag{3.81}$$

which says that having received the symbol b_j, we only know a probability distribution for the symbol a_i sent. Similarly, if we send the symbol a_i, we only know the probability distribution $P(b_j|a_i)$ for the reception of b_j at the receiver. These are related by the equality (3.37). In Sec. 3.1.1, they are used to derive relations between various entropies.

In communication systems it is important to know the utmost ability that a channel has to convey information. If we have a transmitting system A and a receiving system B, the channel is used most efficiently when these two are maximally correlated (i.e., they contain a maximum amount of information about each other). We thus define the *channel capacity* as

$$C(A \Rightarrow B) = \max_A I(A : B), \tag{3.82}$$

where the optimization process is taken to be over all possible codings of the information contained in A. Sometimes a more efficient use of the channel can be obtained by maximizing the code used by both the sender and the receiver.

Binary Symmetric Channel   The simplest system we may consider is the binary-to-binary information transfer, but with errors included. Thus, A is described on the code $\{0, 1\}$ with probabilities $\{p, 1 - p \equiv \overline{p}\} \equiv [p_0, p_1]^T$, and B is described by the same $\{0, 1\}$ and probabilities $\{q, 1 - q \equiv \overline{q}\} \equiv [q_0, q_1]^T$. Here the subscripts refer to the value of the symbol, and $[\cdot]^T$ denotes transpose. The probability of faithful transfer is taken to be P, and the probability of an

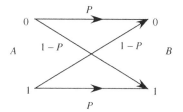

Figure 3.6   Binary symmetric channel.

error is $1 - P \equiv \overline{P}$. The situation is as shown in Fig. 3.6. Simple combination of the probabilities give for the transfer through the channel the matrix relation

$$\begin{bmatrix} q_0 \\ q_1 \end{bmatrix} = \begin{bmatrix} P & \overline{P} \\ \overline{P} & P \end{bmatrix} \begin{bmatrix} p_0 \\ p_1 \end{bmatrix}. \tag{3.83}$$

Referring to the discussion in Sec. 3.1.1, we identify

$$P(0|0) = P(1|1) = P, \tag{3.84}$$

which defines the probability of faithful transmission. The probability of erroneous transmission is given by

$$P(1|0) = P(0|1) = \overline{P}. \tag{3.85}$$

These relations define the *binary-symmetric channel* (BSC).

The quantities $P(b|a)$ give the probabilities of the output when the input is given. Using the Bayes' relations (3.37), we can derive the quantities $Q(a|b)$ which give the probabilities of the symbol a sent when the symbol b is received. We find that

$$\begin{aligned}
Q(0|0) &= \frac{p_0}{q_0} P(0|0) = \frac{pP}{pP + \overline{p}\,\overline{P}}, \\
Q(0|1) &= \frac{p_0}{q_1} P(1|0) = \frac{p\overline{P}}{p\overline{P} + \overline{p}P}, \\
Q(1|0) &= \frac{p_1}{q_0} P(0|1) = \frac{\overline{p}\,\overline{P}}{pP + \overline{p}\,\overline{P}}, \\
Q(1|1) &= \frac{p_1}{q_1} P(1|1) = \frac{\overline{p}P}{p\overline{P} + \overline{p}P}.
\end{aligned} \tag{3.86}$$

Example   Let us take $p = \overline{p} = \frac{1}{2}$. Then it follows that

$$q = \frac{1}{2}P + \frac{1}{2}\overline{P} = \frac{1}{2} = \overline{q}. \tag{3.87}$$

The probability of obtaining the right reading now becomes

$$Q(0|0) = Q(1|1) = \frac{\frac{1}{2}P}{\frac{1}{2}} = P. \tag{3.88}$$

The probability of incorrect reading becomes

$$Q(0|1) = Q(1|0) = \frac{\frac{1}{2}\overline{P}}{\frac{1}{2}} = \overline{P}. \tag{3.89}$$

This is what we expect, but let us look at another example:

Example   Assume an 80% faithful transmission, $P = 0.8$, and the symbol "0" occurring on the average nine times in every 10 symbols, $p_0 = p = 0.9$. The output probabilities are then given by

$$\begin{bmatrix} q_0 \\ q_1 \end{bmatrix} = \begin{bmatrix} 0.8 & 0.2 \\ 0.2 & 0.8 \end{bmatrix} \begin{bmatrix} 0.9 \\ 0.1 \end{bmatrix} = \begin{bmatrix} 0.74 \\ 0.26 \end{bmatrix}. \tag{3.90}$$

We can also calculate the coefficients $Q(a|b)$ as above, and we find that

$$Q(0|0) = 0.97; \; Q(1|0) = 0.03;$$
$$Q(1|1) = 0.31; \; Q(0|1) = 0.69. \tag{3.91}$$

Thus, if we receive a symbol "0," we can be almost certain that a "0" was sent. However, if we receive a symbol "1," in two cases out of three, a symbol "0" had been sent. Obviously, this is not a very favorable transmission situation.

We now want to calculate the conditional entropy

$$H_2(B|A) = -\sum_{i,j} p_i P(b_i|a_j) \log_2 P(b_i|a_j)$$

$$= -pP \log_2 P - p\overline{P} \log_2 \overline{P} - \overline{p}\overline{P} \log_2 \overline{P} - \overline{p}P \log_2 P$$

$$= -P \log_2 P - \overline{P} \log_2 \overline{P} = H_2(P, \overline{P}). \tag{3.92}$$

Thus, the uncertainty about B when we know A is determined by the faithfulness of the channel only. If $P = \frac{1}{2}$, it makes the channel useless.

We can also calculate the combined entropy

$$H(A, B) = H(A) + H(B|A)$$
$$= H(p, \overline{p}) + H(P, \overline{P})$$
$$= H(q, \overline{q}) + H(A|B). \tag{3.93}$$

This gives us

$$H(A|B) = H(p, \overline{p}) + H(P, \overline{P}) - H(q, \overline{q}). \qquad (3.94)$$

Because $q = pP + \overline{p}\overline{P}$, we have from the concavity (3.29),

$$H(q, \overline{q}) = H\left[pP + \overline{p}\overline{P}, 1 - (pP + \overline{p}\overline{P})\right]$$
$$\geq pH(P, \overline{P}) + (1 - p)H(\overline{P}, P) = H(P, \overline{P}). \qquad (3.95)$$

It then follows from (3.94) that

$$H(A|B) \leq H(p, \overline{p}) = H(A) \qquad (3.96)$$

and from (3.92) that

$$H(B|A) \leq H(B). \qquad (3.97)$$

These relations say that our leeway in assigning values to the system A (or B) decreases when we have learned the value of the other system, B (or A).

We can also calculate the mutual information

$$I(A : B) = H(B) - H(B|A) = H(q, \overline{q}) - H(P, \overline{P}). \qquad (3.98)$$

Because we know that this is positive, and using the logarithm in base 2, $H_2(q, \overline{q}) \leq 1$, we find the bounds

$$0 \leq I(A : B) \leq 1 - H_2(P, \overline{P}). \qquad (3.99)$$

As in Sec. 3.1.2, we can interpret the mutual information in three different ways:

- It is the amount of leeway in A determined by knowing B.
- It is the amount of information about A conveyed by B.
- It is the average number of individual symbols in a code for A which relate to B.

Finally, we can easily determine the channel capacity (3.82) of a BSC. As in (3.98), we write

$$I(A : B) = H_2(A) - H_2(B|A) = H_2(p, \overline{p}) - H_2(P, \overline{P}). \qquad (3.100)$$

It is, however, trivial to maximize this; the entropy $H_2(A)$ is maximized to one when $p = \overline{p} = \frac{1}{2}$. Thus, we have in this case

$$C(A \Rightarrow B) = 1 - H_2(P, \overline{P}). \qquad (3.101)$$

For $P = 1$, we have $H_2(P, \overline{P}) = 0$ and the channel does not deteriorate the message. On the other hand, when $P = \frac{1}{2}$, the channel is useless as $H_2(P, \overline{P}) = 1$.

In this section we have specified the various results for a binary-symmetric channel, where things are simple. The BSC is, however, also of more general interest, because in the case of quantum information, most discussions utilize the concept of a binary variable carrying the information, the qubit.

3.2 QUANTUM COMMUNICATION

3.2.1 Quantum Information

We have pointed out that the quantum counterpart of the Shannon entropy is the von Neumann entropy defined in terms of the density matrix:

$$S(\rho) = -\text{Tr}(\rho \log \rho). \tag{3.102}$$

This is manifestly representation invariant, and it is additive for independent systems with a density matrix $\rho = \rho_A \otimes \rho_B$. It is, however, zero for systems represented by a pure state, which thus carries no information in the sense of von Neumann. It may thus not be the most adequate measure of information in many physical situations. In communication theory, however, we will find that it in many ways plays the role of the Shannon entropy.

The quantum entropy has many physically interesting properties. First, assume that we select a subensemble by applying a set of filters based on the orthonormal projectors

$$\Pi_i = |\psi_i\rangle \langle \psi_i|. \tag{3.103}$$

This may also be regarded as the outcome of a perfect von Neumann measurement. The selected ensemble is now described by the density matrix

$$\rho_M = \sum_i \Pi_i \rho \Pi_i = \sum_i |\psi_i\rangle \rho_{ii} \langle \psi_i|. \tag{3.104}$$

From the relation (3.35) we find that

$$S(\rho) \leq S(\rho_M) = -\sum_i \rho_{ii} \log \rho_{ii}. \tag{3.105}$$

Thus, we conclude that filtering or projective measurements increase the entropy and thus the uncertainty about the system. This is a manifestation of the fact that from the point of view of the system, an unselective measurement is equivalent to a dissipative effect of an environment.

All the entropies introduced in Sec. 3.1.1 have their quantum mechanical counterparts. If we have two systems A and B described by the density matrix ρ_{AB}, we denote the reduced density matrices by ρ_A and ρ_B, respectively. We then define

$$\text{Relative entropy:} \quad S(\rho_1||\rho_2) = \text{Tr}\left[\rho_1\left(\log \rho_1 - \log \rho_2\right)\right],$$

$$\text{Conditional entropy:} \quad S(A|B) = S(\rho_{AB}) - S(\rho_B), \tag{3.106}$$

$$\text{Mutual information:} \quad S(A:B) = S(\rho_A) + S(\rho_B) - S(\rho_{AB}).$$

These definitions are standard, but notice that the first term in $S(\rho_1||\rho_2)$ is $-S(\rho_1)$. In quantum theory, these relations do not always have a self-evident interpretation, but the significance of the corresponding classical entities can be found in Sec. 3.1.1. There are many properties relating to these definitions, but we do not discuss all details here. Also, when the quantum entropies satisfy the same relations as their classical counterparts, the proofs are usually more intricate. Here a warning is necessary; all classically derivable results do not hold in the quantum case.

The Klein inequality (3.31) can be used to conclude that the relative entropy is always positive:

$$S(\rho_1||\rho_2) \geq 0. \tag{3.107}$$

The entropy of a combined system satisfies the inequalities

$$|S(\rho_A) - S(\rho_B)| \leq S(\rho_{AB}) \leq S(\rho_A) + S(\rho_B). \tag{3.108}$$

The first inequality is called the *triangle inequality* and the second, the *subadditivity* of entropy.

As demonstrations of the methods to prove results in quantum information theory, we briefly justify the results (3.108). To this end we set $\rho_1 = \rho_{AB}$ and $\rho_2 = \rho_A \otimes \rho_B$ in (3.107). We thus find that

$$S(\rho_{AB}||\rho_A \otimes \rho_B) = \text{Tr}_{AB}\left[\rho_{AB} \log\left(\rho_{AB}\right)\right]$$
$$- \text{Tr}_A\left[\rho_A \log\left(\rho_A\right)\right] - \text{Tr}_B\left[\rho_B \log\left(\rho_B\right)\right]$$
$$= -S(\rho_{AB}) + S(\rho_A) + S(\rho_B). \tag{3.109}$$

From (3.107) we now find that

$$S(\rho_{AB}) \leq S(\rho_A) + S(\rho_B), \tag{3.110}$$

and subadditivity follows.

To prove the triangle inequality, we use the trick of purification introduced in Sec. 2.1.2. We add to the systems A and B the fictitious Hilbert space $\mathcal{H}$, which makes the state pure in the combined space $AB\mathcal{H}$. We then use subadditivity and write

$$S(A\mathcal{H}) \leq S(A) + S(\mathcal{H}). \tag{3.111}$$

In the space $AB\mathcal{H}$ we have a pure state and thus $S(AB\mathcal{H}) = 0$. We partition the combined space into $A\mathcal{H} \otimes B$ and $AB \otimes \mathcal{H}$. As we start from a pure state, the entropy of each partitioning must be the same. We have

$$S(A\mathcal{H}) = S(B); \quad S(\mathcal{H}) = S(AB). \tag{3.112}$$

Inserting the relations (3.112) into (3.111), we find that

$$S(B) \le S(A) + S(AB). \tag{3.113}$$

Interchanging A and B in this inequality is seen to validate the triangle inequality of (3.108).

The result (3.105) can be generalized to the density matrix

$$\rho_A = \sum_k |\psi_k\rangle \rho_k \langle \psi_k|, \tag{3.114}$$

where the states $\{|\psi_k\rangle\}$ defining the ensemble need not be orthogonal. We introduce to this end a fictitious system B based on the orthonormal basis vectors $\{|k\rangle_B\}$ such that the combined state is purified to the state

$$|\Psi_{AB}\rangle = \sum_k \sqrt{\rho_k} |\psi_k\rangle |k\rangle_B. \tag{3.115}$$

The density matrix reduced to system A is then (3.114) and to system B it is

$$\rho_B = \sum_{k,n} \left(\langle \psi_n|\psi_k\rangle \sqrt{\rho_k \rho_n} \right) |k\rangle_{BB} \langle n|. \tag{3.116}$$

Because the combined system is in a pure state, the two subsystems must have the same entropy and hence

$$S(\rho_A) = S(\rho_B) \le S(\rho_B^{\text{diagon}}) = -\sum_k \rho_k \log \rho_k = H(\{\rho_k\}). \tag{3.117}$$

Here ρ_B^{diagon} is the diagonal part of (3.116). Because the states $\{|k\rangle_B\}$ are now orthonormal, the result (3.35) applies.

Density matrices may be thought of as representing ensembles of systems described by their members $\{\rho^{(i)}\}$ occurring with probabilities $\{p_i\}$; the states $\rho^{(i)}$ may here be pure or mixed. System A is thus described by the density matrix

$$\rho_A = \sum_i p_i \rho^{(i)}. \tag{3.118}$$

We introduce a fictitious auxiliary system B described by the orthonormal basis $\{|i\rangle\}$ and the corresponding density matrix

$$\rho_{AB} = \sum_i p_i \left(\rho^{(i)} \otimes |i\rangle\langle i| \right). \tag{3.119}$$

Note here the difference from the pure state (3.115). We find that the entropies of the reduced density matrices derived from (3.119) are given by

$$S(A) = S \left(\sum_i p_i \rho^{(i)} \right),$$

$$S(B) = S \left(\sum_i p_i |i\rangle\langle i| \right) = H(\{p_i\}). \tag{3.120}$$

We also have

$$
\begin{aligned}
S(AB) &= -\mathrm{Tr}_{AB} \left\{ \sum_i p_i \left(\rho^{(i)} \otimes |i\rangle\langle i| \right) \log \left[\sum_j p_j \left(\rho^{(i)} \otimes |j\rangle\langle j| \right) \right] \right\} \\
&= -\mathrm{Tr}_A \left\{ \sum_i p_i \rho^{(i)} \langle i| \log \left[\sum_j p_j \left(\rho^{(i)} \otimes |j\rangle\langle j| \right) \right] |i\rangle \right\} \\
&= -\mathrm{Tr}_A \left\{ \sum_i p_i \rho^{(i)} \left[\log \left(p_i \rho^{(i)} \right) \right] \right\} \\
&= \sum_i p_i S(\rho^{(i)}) + H(\{p_i\}). \tag{3.121}
\end{aligned}
$$

Applying the inequality $S(AB) \leq S(A) + S(B)$, we obtain

$$\sum_i p_i S\left(\rho^{(i)} \right) \leq S \left(\sum_i p_i \rho^{(i)} \right). \tag{3.122}$$

This is the *concavity* of the quantum entropy. It may be interpreted to say that the entropy in the mixture is larger than the weighted sum of the entropies in the individual subsystems. Alternatively, we may interpret this to say that the total ensemble can be used to carry more information than the sum of the individual subsystems. This interpretation seems rather natural, but we must always be careful not to overinterpret the quantum information relations; their exact meaning is not always divined from an interpretation of the corresponding classical relations.

An interesting quantum mechanical fact is that when the information carried by the separated subsystems is complemented by the classical entropy residing in the probabilities $\{p_i\}$, the resulting system can carry more information than the ensemble of the combined systems. To prove this, we assume that the individual density matrices $\rho^{(i)}$ in (3.118) are represented by their decomposition in terms of orthonormal states

$$\rho^{(i)} = \sum_k \pi_k^i |\eta_k^i\rangle\langle\eta_k^i|. \tag{3.123}$$

The states $\{|\eta_k^i\rangle\}$ form an orthonormal basis for each fixed i, but there is no simple relation between the states for different values of i. Hence, the total density matrix is written as

$$\rho_A = \sum_i p_i \rho^{(i)} = \sum_{i,k} p_i \pi_k^i |\eta_k^i\rangle\langle\eta_k^i|; \tag{3.124}$$

this is not a spectral decomposition of ρ_A. However, we can regard it as representing an ensemble where the state $|\eta_k^i\rangle$ occurs with probability $p_i \pi_k^i$.

Then the inequality (3.117) implies that

$$S(\rho_A) \leq - \sum_{i,k} p_i \pi_k^i \log \left(p_i \pi_k^i \right)$$

$$= - \sum_i p_i \log p_i \sum_k \pi_k^i - \sum_i p_i \sum_k \pi_k^i \log \pi_k^i$$

$$= H(\{p_i\}) + \sum_i p_i S(\rho^{(i)}). \tag{3.125}$$

Combining this with the concavity (3.122), we obtain the relations

$$\sum_i p_i S(\rho^{(i)}) \leq S\left(\sum_i p_i \rho^{(i)} \right) \leq \sum_i p_i S(\rho^{(i)}) + H(\{p_i\}). \tag{3.126}$$

This indicates the strange role that classical information plays in quantum theory; when added to the quantum information in the separated subsystems, it may carry more information than the combined systems. At least it gives the same amount of information as the combined systems.

We can use the relation (3.126) to show that a quantum system of dimensions D cannot carry more information than the corresponding classical system. We assume that the subsystems are in pure states $\rho^{(i)} = |\eta^i\rangle\langle\eta^i|$. Then the entropies $S(\rho^{(i)})$ are all zero, and we find that

$$S(\rho_A) \leq H(\{p_i\}). \tag{3.127}$$

This inequality says that because the states $|\eta^i\rangle$ are not necessarily orthogonal, they cannot be distinguished as well as classical signals; hence less information is conveyed. The optimal capacity to carry information is achieved when the states are orthogonal. Then they can be identified uniquely and the coding is essentially classical.

There is a stronger result referred to as the *Holevo bound*: If we choose any system B to observe the quantum system A, the classical information we can obtain is bounded by

$$I(A:B) \leq S(\rho_A) - \sum_i p_i S(\rho^{(i)}) \leq H(A). \tag{3.128}$$

This verifies our intuitive feeling: Whatever observational system B we choose, we cannot obtain the full information $H(A)$ about the system.

Exercise Discuss when equality holds in the inequalities introduced above.

3.2.2 Quantum Channel

Let us build up a communication system starting with sender A, who codes her alphabet by the symbols $\{a_i\}$. These are assigned to the quantum states $\{|a_i\rangle\}$. In a long enough message these occur with the probabilities $\{p_i\}$. The sender is thus characterized by the density matrix

$$\rho_A = \sum_i |a_i\rangle p_i \langle a_i|. \tag{3.129}$$

Receiver B detects the incoming signal by sorting the systems according to the states $\{|b_i\rangle\}$. These are received with the probabilities $\{q_i\}$ in a long message. The ensemble of received signals is thus described by the density matrix

$$\rho_B = \sum_i |b_i\rangle q_i \langle b_i|. \tag{3.130}$$

We thus have two systems characterized by the density matrices ρ_A and ρ_B, and all the quantum entropies introduced in the preceding section can be defined.

Of special interest is the mutual entropy $S(A:B)$, which tells how well correlated the input and output of the channel are. In general, if the sender sends $|a_i\rangle$ and the receiver observes $|b_i\rangle$, we get the matrix characterizing the channel given by

$$P_{ji} \equiv P(b_j|a_i) = |\langle b_j|a_i\rangle|^2 = Q(a_i|b_j) \equiv Q_{ij}, \tag{3.131}$$

where we have used the notation of Sec. 3.1.1. Unless the states transmitted are orthonormal and the receiver uses the same states, the channel is not faithful: $P_{ij} \neq \delta_{ij}$.

Following the example from the classical situation, we define the channel capacity in the quantum case as in (3.82):

$$C(A \Rightarrow B) = \max_A S(A:B), \tag{3.132}$$

where the optimization goes over varying the setup at the sender.

As in (3.37), we introduce the joint probabilities $p_{ij} = P(a_i, b_j)$ satisfying

$$p_{ij} = P_{ji} p_i = Q_{ij} q_j. \tag{3.133}$$

We can obtain the expression for the mutual entropy from (3.46) in the form

$$I(A : B) = \sum_{i,j} p_{ij} \log \frac{p_{ij}}{p_i q_j}$$

$$= \sum_{i,j} P_{ji} p_i \log \frac{P_{ji}}{q_j}, \tag{3.134}$$

where

$$q_j = \sum_i P_{ji} p_i. \tag{3.135}$$

This expresses the mutual information in terms of the channel parameters and the probabilities of the symbols sent. For a faithful channel we have $P_{ji} = \delta_{ij}$ (i.e., the symbol sent is the symbol received). The expression (3.134) then becomes

$$I(A : B) = \sum_i p_i \log \frac{1}{p_i} = H(\{p_i\}). \tag{3.136}$$

Thus, the mutual information coincides with the information in the sender's code. The channel capacity follows from the conditions

$$\frac{\partial I(A : B)}{\partial p_i} = 0, \tag{3.137}$$

which give exactly the correct number of equations to determine the probabilities $\{p_i\}$. This definition, however, is often difficult to use in practice. To illustrate the process, we look at the simpler binary channel next.

Binary Channel Examples   The two-dimensional state space for the qubit is assumed to be spanned by the states $\{|e_1\rangle, |e_2\rangle\}$. Assume that the receiver uses the states $|e_1\rangle$ and $|e_2\rangle$ to read "0" and "1," respectively, and the sender sends the state $|e_1\rangle$ as $|a_0\rangle$ but the state representing "1" is

$$|a_1\rangle = \cos\theta |e_1\rangle + \sin\theta |e_2\rangle. \tag{3.138}$$

Thus, the errors become in this case

$$P_{01} = \cos^2\theta; \quad P_{10} = 0. \tag{3.139}$$

In general, the properties of the channel are described by the transfer matrix

$$[P_{ij}] = \begin{bmatrix} P_{00} & P_{01} \\ P_{10} & P_{11} \end{bmatrix}. \tag{3.140}$$

As these are probabilities, the columns sum up to unity. The symbols "0" and "1" are transmitted with the probabilities p_0 and $p_1 = 1 - p_0$, respectively.

With these definitions, expression (3.134) becomes

$$
\begin{aligned}
I(A:B) = {} & \left(P_{00} \log_2 P_{00} + P_{10} \log_2 P_{10} \right) p_0 \\
& + \left(P_{01} \log_2 P_{01} + P_{11} \log_2 P_{11} \right) p_1 \\
& - (P_{00} p_0 + P_{01} p_1) \log_2 (P_{00} p_0 + P_{01} p_1) \\
& - (P_{10} p_0 + P_{11} p_1) \log_2 (P_{10} p_0 + P_{11} p_1),
\end{aligned}
\tag{3.141}
$$

where $p_1 = 1 - p_0$. Introducing the quantities

$$
\begin{aligned}
W_0 &= P_{00} p_0 + P_{01} p_1, \\
1 - W_0 &= P_{10} p_0 + P_{11} p_1,
\end{aligned}
\tag{3.142}
$$

we can write expression (3.141) as

$$
\begin{aligned}
I(A:B) = {} & \left[P_{00} \log_2 P_{00} + (1 - P_{00}) \log_2 (1 - P_{00}) \right] p_0 \\
& + \left[P_{11} \log_2 P_{11} + (1 - P_{11}) \log_2 (1 - P_{11}) \right] p_1 \\
& - W_0 \log_2 W_0 - (1 - W_0) \log_2 (1 - W_0).
\end{aligned}
\tag{3.143}
$$

In this form the first two terms give the weighted entropy of the transfer matrix of the channel. Because W_0 is the weighted probability of the output "0," the two second terms are the entropies of the channel transmission. Obtaining the channel capacity assumes that we take the derivative of this with respect to p_0. The ensuing expression is, however, still too unwieldy to be instructive. Thus, we look at a few simple examples.

Example 1: Symmetric Channel   We set $P_{00} = P_{11} = P$ and find that

$$
\begin{aligned}
I(A:B) = {} & P \log_2 P + (1 - P) \log_2 (1 - P) \\
& - W_0 \log_2 W_0 - (1 - W_0) \log_2 (1 - W_0),
\end{aligned}
\tag{3.144}
$$

with

$$
1 - W_0 = p_0 + P - 2P p_0.
\tag{3.145}
$$

Calculating the derivative, we now find that

$$
\frac{\partial I(A:B)}{\partial p_0} = \log_2 \left(\frac{1 - W_0}{W_0} \right) \frac{\partial W_0}{\partial p_0} = 0.
\tag{3.146}
$$

The condition gives

$$
W_0 = 1 - W_0 = p_0 (1 - 2P) + P = \frac{1}{2},
\tag{3.147}
$$

with the solution $p_0 = p_1 = \frac{1}{2}$. This result was derived differently in Sec. 3.1.2. Notice in particular that the value $P = \frac{1}{2}$ makes the procedure fail.

Example 2: Asymmetric Channel   We use the coding suggested in (3.138) (see Fig. 3.7). The transfer matrix becomes now

$$[P_{ij}] = \begin{bmatrix} 1 & \cos^2 \theta \\ 0 & \sin^2 \theta \end{bmatrix}. \tag{3.148}$$

The mutual information is

$$\begin{aligned} I(A:B) = {}& \left(\sin^2 \theta \log_2 \sin^2 \theta + \cos^2 \theta \log_2 \cos^2 \theta \right) p_1 \\ & - p_1 \sin^2 \theta \log_2 \left(p_1 \sin^2 \theta \right) \\ & - \left(1 - p_1 \sin^2 \theta \right) \log_2 \left(1 - p_1 \sin^2 \theta \right). \end{aligned} \tag{3.149}$$

We can easily optimize this by taking the derivative with respect to p_1. To get simple results, we choose $\theta = \pi/4$, giving $\cos^2 \theta = \sin^2 \theta = \frac{1}{2}$. We find that

$$I(A:B) = -p_1 - \frac{p_1}{2} \log_2 \frac{p_1}{2} - \left(1 - \frac{p_1}{2} \right) \log_2 \left(1 - \frac{p_1}{2} \right). \tag{3.150}$$

Now the derivative gives

$$2 = \log_2 \frac{1 - p_1/2}{p_1/2}. \tag{3.151}$$

Since the logarithm is taken in base 2, we find that

$$4 = \frac{2 - p_1}{p_1} \tag{3.152}$$

with the solution

$$p_1 = \frac{2}{5}; \quad p_0 = \frac{3}{5}. \tag{3.153}$$

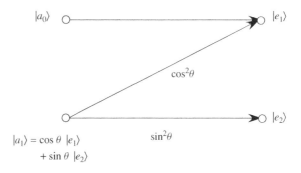

Figure 3.7   Asymmetric channel.

The corresponding mutual information then gives the capacity of this channel from (3.150) to be

$$C = \log_2 5 - 2 = 0.32. \qquad (3.154)$$

This is, of course, much less than the value $C = 1$ we had obtained using orthogonal states. But it is not the best possible result, as we see in Example 3.

Example 3: Symmetric Detector States   We assume that the coding now is chosen such that

$$|a_0\rangle = |e_1\rangle,$$
$$|a_1\rangle = \frac{1}{\sqrt{2}} (|e_1\rangle + |e_2\rangle). \qquad (3.155)$$

Using the states $\{|e_1\rangle, |e_2\rangle\}$ for the detection gives an intolerable 50% error [see Eq. (3.139)]. We choose the detection states orthogonal but in the form

$$|b_0\rangle = \cos\theta |e_1\rangle - \sin\theta |e_2\rangle,$$
$$|b_1\rangle = \sin\theta |e_1\rangle + \cos\theta |e_2\rangle. \qquad (3.156)$$

Choosing $\theta = \pi/8$, we find that $|b_0\rangle$ differs from $|a_0\rangle$ as much as $|b_1\rangle$ differs from $|a_1\rangle$ because then

$$2\theta + \frac{\pi}{4} = \frac{\pi}{2} \qquad (3.157)$$

(see Fig. 3.8). Because now $\cos^2\theta = 0.85$, the transfer matrix becomes

$$[P_{ij}] = \begin{bmatrix} 0.85 & 0.15 \\ 0.15 & 0.85 \end{bmatrix}. \qquad (3.158)$$

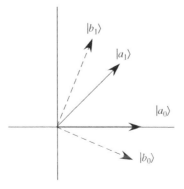

Figure 3.8   Symmetric detection states.

This is a symmetric channel, so $p = \frac{1}{2}$ is optimum, $W_0 = \frac{1}{2}$, and the result (3.144) gives

$$C = 1 + 0.15 \log_2 0.15 + 0.85 \log_2 0.85 = 0.39. \tag{3.159}$$

We thus see that by distributing the errors between the two components symmetrically, we can improve the capacity above (3.154), but we are still achieving only 39% of the capacity of the best transfer. In the next section we will see that there are strategies that allow us to do considerably better than in these examples.

3.2.3   Use of Generalized Measurements

In Sec. 2.3.3 we introduced the idea of a generalized measurement that was based on the concept of a positive operator-valued measure (POVM to be brief). This generalizes the concept of a projective measurement to introduce a set of positive operators, the POVMs, $\{M_i\}$, such that the expectation value of the outcome of an observation is given by the positive number

$$m_i = \langle M_i \rangle = \mathrm{Tr}(\rho M_i); \tag{3.160}$$

the operators have the property

$$\sum_i M_i = 1, \tag{3.161}$$

which guarantees normalization of the numbers m_i interpreted as probabilities. The results obtained do not exclude each other, the operators are not projectors and, consequently,

$$M_i (1 - M_i) = M_i \sum_{j \neq i} M_j \neq 0 \tag{3.162}$$

(i.e., the occurrence of the event i is not incompatible with the occurrence of some of the other events). The simplest example of such a system was the set of overcomplete basis vectors $\{|\varphi_i\rangle\}$, in which case $M_i = |\varphi_i\rangle\langle\varphi_i|$. In the following subsections we show how this concept can be utilized to improve communication in an imperfect quantum channel.

Binary Signaling   By a suitable choice of basis vectors, the general binary coding can be written in the form

$$\begin{aligned} |a_0\rangle &= \cos\theta |e_1\rangle + \sin\theta |e_2\rangle, \\ |a_1\rangle &= \cos\theta |e_1\rangle - \sin\theta |e_2\rangle. \end{aligned} \tag{3.163}$$

For $\theta \neq \pi/4$, the overlap between these vectors is

$$\langle a_1 | a_0 \rangle = \cos^2\theta - \sin^2\theta = \cos 2\theta \neq 0, \tag{3.164}$$

which allows misidentification of whichever detection basis the receiver chooses. We assume that the frequency of each state is the same in a long message, $p_0 = p_1 = \frac{1}{2}$.

We next address the question of how to find an optimal detection basis. If the receiver chooses

$$
\begin{aligned}
|b_0\rangle &= \sin\theta|e_1\rangle + \cos\theta|e_2\rangle, \\
|b_1\rangle &= \sin\theta|e_1\rangle - \cos\theta|e_2\rangle,
\end{aligned}
\tag{3.165}
$$

the probability of misidentification is zero, $\langle a_1|b_0\rangle = \langle a_0|b_1\rangle = 0$. These states do not, however, form an acceptable set of observational states which have to preserve probability. We find that the projector

$$
|b_0\rangle\langle b_0| + |b_1\rangle\langle b_1| = 2\sin^2\theta|e_1\rangle\langle e_1| + 2\cos^2\theta|e_2\rangle\langle e_2| \neq 1,
\tag{3.166}
$$

except when the original states are orthogonal, $\theta = \pi/4$.

The procedure we adopt here is to add to the states a third state which will make up an overcomplete set that can be used as the basis for POVMs. We try to define the modified detector states to be

$$
\begin{aligned}
|\tilde{b}_0\rangle &= N\left(\sin\theta|e_1\rangle + \cos\theta|e_2\rangle\right), \\
|\tilde{b}_1\rangle &= N\left(\sin\theta|e_1\rangle - \cos\theta|e_2\rangle\right), \\
|\tilde{b}_2\rangle &= C|e_1\rangle.
\end{aligned}
\tag{3.167}
$$

Now writing the sum of the projectors, we obtain

$$
\begin{aligned}
&|\tilde{b}_0\rangle\langle\tilde{b}_0| + |\tilde{b}_1\rangle\langle\tilde{b}_1| + |\tilde{b}_2\rangle\langle\tilde{b}_2| \\
&= 2N^2\left(\sin^2\theta|e_1\rangle\langle e_1| + \cos^2\theta|e_2\rangle\langle e_2|\right) + C^2|e_1\rangle\langle e_1|.
\end{aligned}
\tag{3.168}
$$

Setting this equal to the unit operator, we find that

$$
\begin{aligned}
2N^2\cos^2\theta &= 1, \\
2N^2\sin^2\theta + C^2 &= 1,
\end{aligned}
\tag{3.169}
$$

from which we get the states

$$
\begin{aligned}
|\tilde{b}_0\rangle &= \frac{1}{\sqrt{2}}\left(\tan\theta|e_1\rangle + |e_2\rangle\right), \\
|\tilde{b}_1\rangle &= \frac{1}{\sqrt{2}}\left(\tan\theta|e_1\rangle - |e_2\rangle\right), \\
|\tilde{b}_2\rangle &= \sqrt{\left(1 - \tan^2\theta\right)}|e_1\rangle.
\end{aligned}
\tag{3.170}
$$

Now we have two input states but three outputs. The channel transfer is given by the probabilities $P_{ji} = |\langle \tilde{b}_j | a_i \rangle|^2$, which form the matrix

$$[P_{ji}] = \begin{bmatrix} 2\sin^2\theta & 0 \\ 0 & 2\sin^2\theta \\ 1 - 2\sin^2\theta & 1 - 2\sin^2\theta \end{bmatrix}. \tag{3.171}$$

Thus, we have a case with no misidentification; if the result $|\tilde{b}_i\rangle$, $i = 0, 1$ is observed, we can exclude the possibility that the other state was sent. This, however, happens only with probability $2\sin^2\theta$; with probability $(1 - 2\sin^2\theta)$ we observe $|\tilde{b}_2\rangle$ and no conclusion can be reached. This is the price we pay for eliminating the possibility of misinterpretation. Note that these relations make sense only if $\theta \leq \pi/4$.

The POVM method used above can be modified to describe projective measurements in a bigger state space. We add to the basis $\{|e_1\rangle, |e_2\rangle\}$ one more vector $|e_3\rangle$ assumed to be orthogonal to the first two. We then choose the detection states such that the ones in (3.170) are projections on the space spanned by $\{|e_1\rangle, |e_2\rangle\}$: namely,

$$|\beta_0\rangle = \frac{1}{\sqrt{2}} \left(\tan\theta |e_1\rangle + |e_2\rangle - \sqrt{(1 - \tan^2\theta)}|e_3\rangle \right),$$

$$|\beta_1\rangle = \frac{1}{\sqrt{2}} \left(\tan\theta |e_1\rangle - |e_2\rangle - \sqrt{(1 - \tan^2\theta)}|e_3\rangle \right), \tag{3.172}$$

$$|\beta_2\rangle = \sqrt{(1 - \tan^2\theta)}|e_1\rangle + \tan\theta |e_3\rangle.$$

It is easy to see that these are orthonormal, and direct calculation shows that

$$|\beta_0\rangle\langle\beta_0| + |\beta_1\rangle\langle\beta_1| + |\beta_2\rangle\langle\beta_2| = 1. \tag{3.173}$$

In the extended space we can now form a projective measurement and obtain just the results given in (3.171). We introduce the projector $\Pi = (|e_1\rangle\langle e_1| + |e_2\rangle\langle e_2|)$ and find that

$$|\tilde{b}_i\rangle\langle\tilde{b}_i| = \Pi|\beta_i\rangle\langle\beta_i|\Pi. \tag{3.174}$$

The POVMs are thus the von Neumann projectors, which are projected down to the two-dimensional message space.

We still need to discuss the case when $\theta > \pi/4$. It then turns out that we should define the detection states such that they coincide with the signal states (3.163) in the two-dimensional space defined by the projection Π. Following the procedure to obtain the states (3.172), it now turns out that we should use the states

$$|\beta_0\rangle = \frac{1}{\sqrt{2}}\left(\cot\theta|e_1\rangle + |e_2\rangle - \sqrt{\left(1 - \cot^2\theta\right)}|e_3\rangle\right),$$

$$|\beta_1\rangle = \frac{1}{\sqrt{2}}\left(\cot\theta|e_1\rangle - |e_2\rangle - \sqrt{\left(1 - \cot^2\theta\right)}|e_3\rangle\right), \qquad (3.175)$$

$$|\beta_2\rangle = \sqrt{\left(1 - \cot^2\theta\right)}|e_1\rangle + \cot\theta|e_3\rangle.$$

These are easily shown to satisfy the relation (3.173) and the channel transfer matrix becomes

$$\left[P_{ji}\right] = \begin{bmatrix} \dfrac{1}{2\sin^2\theta} & \dfrac{\cos^2 2\theta}{2\sin^2\theta} \\[2ex] \dfrac{\cos^2 2\theta}{2\sin^2\theta} & \dfrac{1}{2\sin^2\theta} \\[2ex] -\cos 2\theta\cot^2\theta & -\cos 2\theta\cot^2\theta \end{bmatrix}. \qquad (3.176)$$

Because now $\sin^2\theta > \frac{1}{2}$ and $\cos 2\theta < 0$, these relations make sense. As an exercise, show that the columns add to unit probability. In this case no simplification is discernible, but the wrong identification is still down by a factor of $\cos^2 2\theta$ compared with the correct identification.

Ternary Coding   Assume that we have at our disposal a two-dimensional message space, a qubit, but we want to transmit three different symbols. Is it possible to do this, and how well can we do it?

As an example, let us choose the three code vectors to be given by

$$|a_0\rangle = |e_1\rangle,$$

$$|a_1\rangle = -\frac{1}{2}|e_1\rangle + \frac{\sqrt{3}}{2}|e_2\rangle, \qquad (3.177)$$

$$|a_2\rangle = -\left(\frac{1}{2}|e_1\rangle + \frac{\sqrt{3}}{2}|e_2\rangle\right).$$

These are symmetrically situated in the plane separated by an angle of $2\pi/3$.

From the treatment above we expect that a suitable approach is to augment the two-dimensional system with a third axis, choose a triad of orthogonal eigenvectors, and define the POVMs by taking their projections on the two-dimensional space. Here it seems advantageous to choose the projections to be the states (3.177) and add symmetrically the third component such that all three states are orthogonal. As these have the projections $-\frac{1}{2}$ on each other, we set the detection vectors to be

$$|\beta_i\rangle = \frac{1}{\sqrt{3}}\left(\sqrt{2}|a_i\rangle + |e_3\rangle\right). \tag{3.178}$$

These are seen to be properly orthonormalized. The corresponding POVM operators are then given by

$$M_i = \Pi|\beta_i\rangle\langle\beta_i|\Pi = \frac{2}{3}|a_i\rangle\langle a_i|. \tag{3.179}$$

The corresponding channel matrix $P_{ji} = |\langle\beta_j|a_i\rangle|^2$ now becomes

$$[P_{ji}] = \begin{bmatrix} \dfrac{2}{3} & \dfrac{1}{6} & \dfrac{1}{6} \\[2mm] \dfrac{1}{6} & \dfrac{2}{3} & \dfrac{1}{6} \\[2mm] \dfrac{1}{6} & \dfrac{1}{6} & \dfrac{2}{3} \end{bmatrix}. \tag{3.180}$$

Thus, the probability that the state received is the state sent is $\frac{2}{3} \approx 67\%$, and the probability that it was either one of the other two is $\frac{1}{3} \approx 33\%$. This is not bad if we remember that we are trying to transmit three states through a channel that can at its best transmit two faithfully.

Mutual Information The schemes introduced above have been considered from the point of view of optimizing the probability to obtain the correct result in a communication situation between sender A and receiver B. In fact, the optimal situation is when as much as possible of the information sent is conveyed to the receiver. This is measured by the mutual information (3.134), which tells how much correlation there is between the outgoing and the incoming message of a communication channel. The very definition of the channel capacity assumes that we optimize this over the coding distribution $\{p_i\}$, but for simplicity we assume, as we did above, that each coding symbol occurs with the same probability

$$p_i = p = D^{-1}, \tag{3.181}$$

where D is the number of symbols transmitted.

From (3.134) follows in this case

$$I(A:B) = p\sum_{i,j} P_{ji}\log_2 P_{ji} - p\sum_{i,j} P_{ji}\left(\log_2\sum_k P_{jk} + \log_2 p\right). \tag{3.182}$$

Because $\sum_j P_{ji} = 1$ and $p \sum_i = 1$, this becomes

$$I(A:B) = -\log_2 p + p \sum_{i,j} P_{ji} \log_2 P_{ji} - p \sum_j \Pi_j \log_2 \Pi_j, \qquad (3.183)$$

where

$$\Pi_j = \sum_k P_{jk}. \qquad (3.184)$$

In the case when $\Pi_j = 1$, the last term does not contribute; such a transfer channel is called *doubly stochastic*. Notice that the first term in (3.183) is the entropy $H(\{p\})$ of the original message. When the channel transfer matrix $[P_{ji}]$ is known, the channel modifications of the message can be obtained from expression (3.183).

We apply this to the scheme described by the matrix (3.180) and obtain

$$I(A:B) = -\log_2 \frac{1}{3} + \frac{1}{3}\left(3 \times \frac{2}{3}\log_2 \frac{2}{3} + 6 \times \frac{1}{6}\log_2 \frac{1}{6}\right)$$

$$= \frac{1}{3} = 0.33, \qquad (3.185)$$

where as usual we have evaluated the logarithm with the base 2. This result is not a very impressive transmission of a message containing the information $\log_2 3 = 1.59$.

It is, however, possible to improve on this by the following consideration. The probability of not observing the outcome corresponding to the POVM is

$$M_i^{\perp} = P_{ii} - M_i, \qquad (3.186)$$

as follows from (3.161). To make these to satisfy the normalization required by the POVM formalism, we define new observations derived from the POVMs:

$$\tilde{M}_i = \frac{2}{3}\left(1 - \frac{3}{2}M_i\right) = \frac{2}{3} - |\beta_i\rangle\langle\beta_i|, \qquad (3.187)$$

based on the states (3.178). From (3.180) we find that

$$[P_{ji}] = \begin{bmatrix} 0 & \dfrac{1}{2} & \dfrac{1}{2} \\[2mm] \dfrac{1}{2} & 0 & \dfrac{1}{2} \\[2mm] \dfrac{1}{2} & \dfrac{1}{2} & 0 \end{bmatrix}. \qquad (3.188)$$

For any outcome i, we know for sure that the message sent was not $|a_i\rangle$. The other two symbols have then to be assigned equal probability $= \frac{1}{2}$. This does not sound very useful, but which scheme we choose depends on whether it is more important to choose the right decision or to avoid making the wrong one. In fact, using (3.183) to calculate the mutual information in this case, we obtain

$$I(A : B) = \log_2 3 + \frac{1}{2} \times 6 \times \frac{1}{2} \log_2 \frac{1}{2} = \log_2 3 - 1 = 0.59, \qquad (3.189)$$

which is considerably more than the case (3.185). Thus, we learn that it may carry more information to be sure what is not the case than to be relatively certain what is. A similar conclusion can be obtained from the following example.

Example   Let us look at the case given in (3.176) with $\theta > \pi/4$. As an example, we choose $\theta = \pi/3$, to find that

$$\left[P_{ji} \right] = \begin{bmatrix} \dfrac{2}{3} & \dfrac{1}{6} \\[2mm] \dfrac{1}{6} & \dfrac{2}{3} \\[2mm] \dfrac{1}{6} & \dfrac{1}{6} \end{bmatrix}. \qquad (3.190)$$

If we calculate the mutual entropy here, we obtain

$$I(A : B) = \frac{13 - 5\log_2 5}{6} = 0.23. \qquad (3.191)$$

Thus, despite the fact that the probability of getting the right conclusion is $\frac{2}{3}$, the mutual information is rather small. The reason is partly due to the possibility of reaching no conclusion.

To illustrate the situation further, we choose the angle $\theta = \pi/8 < \pi/4$. Then we have to use scheme (3.171), which gives

$$\left[P_{ji} \right] = \begin{bmatrix} 0.3 & 0 \\ 0 & 0.3 \\ 0.7 & 0.7 \end{bmatrix}. \qquad (3.192)$$

In this situation we reach no conclusion in 70% of the cases. On the other hand, when we get an answer, it totally excludes the wrong conclusion. This is also mirrored in the mutual information

$$I(A : B) = 0.3, \qquad (3.193)$$

which clearly exceeds the value (3.191).

The latter case was discussed in Sec. 3.2.2, Example 3. There we found a scheme based on two detector states that gave $I(A : B) = 0.39$; that is better still. From this we should learn that extending the space of detector states to have larger dimensionality than the message space is not necessarily an advantage. The additional outcome signifying no conclusion introduces enough uncertainty to spoil the mutual information.

Example: Binary Coding   Instead of the ternary coding in Eq. (3.177), we choose the binary coding

$$|a_0\rangle = |e_1\rangle,$$
$$|a_1\rangle = -\frac{1}{2}|e_1\rangle + \frac{\sqrt{3}}{2}|e_2\rangle. \tag{3.194}$$

This is like the states in (3.177) except that we leave out the third state.
We choose the detector states as

$$|b_0\rangle = \cos\theta|e_1\rangle + \sin\theta|e_2\rangle,$$
$$|b_1\rangle = -\sin\theta|e_1\rangle + \cos\theta|e_2\rangle. \tag{3.195}$$

These are orthogonal, and the transfer matrix becomes

$$[P_{ji}] = \begin{bmatrix} \cos^2\theta & \left(\frac{1}{2}\cos\theta - \frac{\sqrt{3}}{2}\sin\theta\right)^2 \\ \sin^2\theta & \left(\frac{1}{2}\sin\theta + \frac{\sqrt{3}}{2}\cos\theta\right)^2 \end{bmatrix}. \tag{3.196}$$

Using the result of Sec. 3.2.2, Example 3, we expect good performance if the detector states are symmetric with respect to the signal states. The situation is shown in Fig. 3.9 giving

$$\theta = \frac{\pi}{12}. \tag{3.197}$$

With this we obtain

$$\cos^2\theta = \left(\frac{1}{2}\sin\theta + \frac{\sqrt{3}}{2}\cos\theta\right)^2 = 0.933 \tag{3.198}$$

and

$$\sin^2\theta = \left(\frac{1}{2}\cos\theta - \frac{\sqrt{3}}{2}\sin\theta\right)^2 = 0.067. \tag{3.199}$$

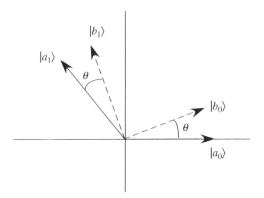

Figure 3.9   Binary coding states.

With equal incoming probabilities $p_i = \frac{1}{2}$ and a symmetric channel, we obtain $q_i = \frac{1}{2}$, too. The mutual information then becomes

$$
\begin{aligned}
I(A:B) &= \sum_{i,j} P_{ji}\, p_i \log_2 \frac{P_{ji}}{q_j} \\
&= \frac{1}{2} \left[\sum_{i,j} P_{ji} \left(\log_2 P_{ji} + \log_2 2 \right) \right] \\
&= \frac{1}{2} \sum_{i,j} P_{ji} \log_2 P_{ji} + 1 \\
&= 0.067 \log_2 0.067 + 0.933 \log_2 0.933 + 1 = 0.66. \qquad (3.200)
\end{aligned}
$$

This case is quite efficient because the maximum is unity. The ternary coding described above manages to obtain only $I = 0.3$, and in addition, three detector states had to be used. Ideally, this should transmit $\log_2 3 = 1.6$ qubits. Thus, it does not necessarily help to improve the detector system if the signal ambiguity resides in the states transmitted.

Two-Qubit Example   In the previous cases we have extended the two-dimensional qubit to have three dimensions; it is not obvious how to realize this in actual physical systems. If the coding is based on two-valued systems, the state space always has a dimensionality which is a power of 2. If we use two qubits to transmit the signal, we have a channel capacity of at most 2 bits.

Let us now ask the question: The sender transmits only one qubit to the receiver, but he wants to code 2 bits in this; how well can he do? Let us assume that the four message symbols are coded as

$$|a_0\rangle = \begin{bmatrix} s \\ c \end{bmatrix}; \qquad |a_1\rangle = \begin{bmatrix} s \\ -c \end{bmatrix};$$
$$|a_2\rangle = \begin{bmatrix} c \\ s \end{bmatrix}; \qquad |a_3\rangle = \begin{bmatrix} c \\ -s \end{bmatrix}. \tag{3.201}$$

We set

$$s = \sin\theta; \; c = \cos\theta, \tag{3.202}$$

which assures that

$$s^2 + c^2 = \sin^2\theta + \cos^2\theta = 1. \tag{3.203}$$

We assume that each symbol $\{a_0, a_1, a_2, a_3\}$ occurs with the same probability $p = \frac{1}{4}$.

We now extend the receiver's detection space to be four-dimensional by introducing the states

$$|\beta_0\rangle = \frac{1}{\sqrt{2}} \begin{bmatrix} s \\ c \\ s \\ c \end{bmatrix}; \qquad |\beta_1\rangle = \frac{1}{\sqrt{2}} \begin{bmatrix} s \\ -c \\ -s \\ c \end{bmatrix};$$
$$|\beta_2\rangle = \frac{1}{\sqrt{2}} \begin{bmatrix} c \\ s \\ -c \\ -s \end{bmatrix}; \qquad |\beta_3\rangle = \frac{1}{\sqrt{2}} \begin{bmatrix} c \\ -s \\ c \\ -s \end{bmatrix}. \tag{3.204}$$

These are clearly orthonormal and form a complete basis

$$\sum_i |\beta_i\rangle\langle\beta_i| = 1. \tag{3.205}$$

The sender now attempts to code 2 bits by sending one of the states (3.201), which requires the use of only one qubit. The receiver then uses the detection states (3.204) to construct the POVMs from the first two components:

$$M_0 = \frac{1}{2} \begin{bmatrix} s^2 & sc \\ sc & c^2 \end{bmatrix},$$
$$M_1 = \frac{1}{2} \begin{bmatrix} s^2 & -sc \\ -sc & c^2 \end{bmatrix},$$
$$M_2 = \frac{1}{2} \begin{bmatrix} c^2 & sc \\ sc & s^2 \end{bmatrix},$$
$$M_3 = \frac{1}{2} \begin{bmatrix} c^2 & -sc \\ -sc & s^2 \end{bmatrix}. \tag{3.206}$$

These clearly sum to unity:

$$\sum_{i=0}^{3} M_i = 1,$$

(3.207)

and thus form a set of proper POVMs.

Calculating the channel transmission probabilities $P_{ji} = \langle a_i | M_j | a_i \rangle$, we find that

$$[P_{ji}] = \begin{bmatrix} \frac{1}{2} & \frac{1}{2}\cos^2 2\theta & \frac{1}{2}\sin^2 2\theta & 0 \\ \frac{1}{2}\cos^2 2\theta & \frac{1}{2} & 0 & \frac{1}{2}\sin^2 2\theta \\ \frac{1}{2}\sin^2 2\theta & 0 & \frac{1}{2} & \frac{1}{2}\cos^2 2\theta \\ 0 & \frac{1}{2}\sin^2 2\theta & \frac{1}{2}\cos^2 2\theta & \frac{1}{2} \end{bmatrix}.$$

(3.208)

This scheme allows us to get the right assignment with 50% probability and definitely to exclude one possibility in each case. Remarkably, it has zeros in it. As we have seen above, this is likely to improve the mutual information between sender and receiver considerably. As the system is doubly stochastic, it is easy to calculate the mutual information, which gives

$$I(A : B) = 1 + \frac{1}{2}\left[\cos^2 2\theta \log_2\left(\cos^2 2\theta\right) + \sin^2 2\theta \log_2\left(\sin^2 2\theta\right)\right].$$

(3.209)

Looking for an extremum, we find $\cos 2\theta = \sin 2\theta$, giving $\theta = \pi/8$. This, however, is easily seen to be a minimum, which obviously is not a good choice. The maxima occur at the values $\theta = 0$ or $\theta = \pi/2$. In this case the mutual information is 1 bit. This derives from the fact that when $\theta = 0$, we can distinguish the two states

$$|a_2\rangle = |a_3\rangle = \begin{bmatrix} 1 \\ 0 \end{bmatrix}$$

(3.210)

from

$$|a_0\rangle = -|a_1\rangle = \begin{bmatrix} 0 \\ 1 \end{bmatrix}.$$

(3.211)

On the other hand, if $\theta = \pi/2$, then $\cos\theta = \sin\theta$, allowing us to distinguish the states

$$|a_0\rangle = |a_2\rangle = \frac{1}{\sqrt{2}}\begin{bmatrix} 1 \\ 1 \end{bmatrix}$$

(3.212)

from the states

$$|a_1\rangle = |a_3\rangle = \frac{1}{\sqrt{2}}\begin{bmatrix} 1 \\ -1 \end{bmatrix}.$$

(3.213)

These give exactly 1 bit of information, and as we have seen, the possibility to exclude some states with certainty leads to good mutual information.

To obtain four different possibilities, we choose the compromise $\theta = \pi/3$. Then the matrix in Eq. (3.208) becomes

$$
[P_{ji}] =
\begin{bmatrix}
\dfrac{1}{2} & \dfrac{1}{8} & \dfrac{3}{8} & 0 \\[2mm]
\dfrac{1}{8} & \dfrac{1}{2} & 0 & \dfrac{3}{8} \\[2mm]
\dfrac{3}{8} & 0 & \dfrac{1}{2} & \dfrac{1}{8} \\[2mm]
0 & \dfrac{3}{8} & \dfrac{1}{8} & \dfrac{1}{2}
\end{bmatrix}.
\tag{3.214}
$$

Calculating the mutual information, we obtain

$$
I(A:B) = \frac{3}{8} \log_2 3 = 0.59.
\tag{3.215}
$$

As this system is used to transmit 2 bits per qubit, we find that it seems to be rather advantageous compared with other schemes discussed.

3.2.4 Neumark Extension

Let us consider the case when we have a set of normalized states $\{|a_i\rangle; i = 1, \ldots, N\}$ that span a subspace S_1 of dimensionality $n < N$. The property of being overcomplete is given by the relation

$$
\sum_i |a_i\rangle\langle a_i| = C\, \mathbb{I}_n,
\tag{3.216}
$$

where $\mathbb{I}_n$ is the unit operator in the n-dimensional space S_1. The states $|a_i\rangle$ are not orthogonal, but taking the trace of both sides of (3.216), we obtain

$$
\mathrm{Tr}\left(\sum_i |a_i\rangle\langle a_i| \right) = \sum_i \langle a_i|a_i\rangle = N = Cn.
\tag{3.217}
$$

From this follows that the states

$$
|\tilde{a}_i\rangle = \sqrt{\frac{n}{N}}\, |a_i\rangle
\tag{3.218}
$$

form a set of POVMs

$$
\sum_i |\tilde{a}_i\rangle\langle \tilde{a}_i| = \mathbb{I}_n.
\tag{3.219}
$$

Following the procedure in Sec. 3.2.3, we add further components to the basis space to make the original vectors orthonormal. This space S_2 has to have $N - n$ dimensions in the present case, and we add vectors $|b_i\rangle \subset S_2$ in such a way that in the space $S_1 \oplus S_2$ the vectors are orthonormal. We write

$$|\beta_i\rangle = |\tilde{a}_i\rangle + |b_i\rangle, \qquad (3.220)$$

and we require that

$$\langle\beta_j|\beta_i\rangle = \frac{n}{N}\langle a_j|a_i\rangle + \langle b_j|b_i\rangle = \delta_{ij}. \qquad (3.221)$$

These relations can be used to find the auxiliary vectors $|b_i\rangle$ needed. In this extended space, the basis vectors are orthonormal and can be used as a convenient basis. In particular, they can be used to define projective measurements. If we define the projector Π restricting any vector to the space S_1 we have

$$|\tilde{a}_i\rangle\langle\tilde{a}_i| = \Pi|\beta_i\rangle\langle\beta_i|\Pi. \qquad (3.222)$$

Because $\Pi = \mathbb{I}_n$, this agrees with the relation (3.219).

The procedure described above is a special case of the mathematical procedure called the *Neumark extension* of the space. We have presented examples of its use in Sec. 3.2.3. A more general formulation can be obtained by interpreting the vectors $|\tilde{a}_i\rangle$ as N column vectors. Then we can form the operator

$$\mathbf{U} = \begin{bmatrix} |\tilde{a}_1\rangle & |\tilde{a}_2\rangle & \cdots & |\tilde{a}_{N-1}\rangle & |\tilde{a}_N\rangle \\ |b_1\rangle & |b_2\rangle & \cdots & |b_{N-1}\rangle & |b_N\rangle \end{bmatrix}. \qquad (3.223)$$

Using the relations (3.221), we see that this is a unitary operator on the space $S_1 \oplus S_2$. If we project this on the space S_1, we find an operator

$$\mathbf{U}_1 = \Pi\mathbf{U} = \begin{bmatrix} |\tilde{a}_1\rangle & |\tilde{a}_2\rangle & \cdots & |\tilde{a}_{N-1}\rangle & |\tilde{a}_N\rangle \\ 0 & 0 & \cdots & 0 & 0 \end{bmatrix}. \qquad (3.224)$$

For any state $|\Psi\rangle$ in $S_1 \oplus S_2$, this has the property

$$\langle\Psi|\mathbf{U}_1^\dagger\mathbf{U}_1|\Psi\rangle \leq \langle\Psi|\Psi\rangle = 1. \qquad (3.225)$$

The operator $\mathbf{U}_1$ is thus bounded by unity. This allows us to formulate *Neumark's theorem:*

Theorem Any operator $\mathbf{U}_1$ that is bounded by unity can be continued to be a unitary operator on an extended space.

The proof is, in principle, outlined above.

In particular, the considerations above have allowed us to show how to interpret the discussion at Sec. 2.4.4: Any trace-preserving map given by a set of POVMs can be extended to a unitary map on an extended space.

3.3 DISTANCE BETWEEN STATES

In the general situation of quantum communication, we may assume that sender A possesses a quantum state ρ_A which she wants to transmit to receiver B. If the latter obtains state ρ_B, we may ask how good a copy of ρ_A has come into B's possession. Using teleportation, we know that full identity may be achieved, but in practice even this transfer method may be afflicted with errors. If a cloning procedure is utilized, we know that full identity cannot be achieved. In the general case, the communication channel will introduce random distortions. It thus becomes an important issue how to compare states represented by density matrices. There is no unique procedure for this, and various methods prove to be advantageous in various connections. We proceed to look at the most common ones.

3.3.1 Trace Distance

In any set of operators we may introduce the bilinear functional

$$(A, B) = \mathrm{Tr}\left(A^\dagger B\right). \tag{3.226}$$

It is easily seen that this satisfies all the requirements defining a scalar product, and it is called the *Hilbert–Schmidt scalar product*. Applied to the set of density matrices, the hermitian conjugation has no influence, but it is formally necessary. This scalar product suggests the distance measure between quantum states:

$$||\rho_1, \rho_2||^2 = \mathrm{Tr}\left[(\rho_1 - \rho_2)^2\right] \le \mathrm{Tr}\left(|\rho_1 - \rho_2|\right). \tag{3.227}$$

A measure of distance has customarily been introduced in quantum information theory as

$$D(\rho_1, \rho_2) = \frac{1}{2}\mathrm{Tr}\left(|\rho_1 - \rho_2|\right). \tag{3.228}$$

This is clearly symmetric, and in the case when the two states are diagonal in the same representation,

$$\rho_1 = \sum_n |n\rangle r_n^{(1)} \langle n|,$$
$$\rho_2 = \sum_n |n\rangle r_n^{(2)} \langle n|, \tag{3.229}$$

the distance is simply

$$D(\rho_1, \rho_2) = \frac{1}{2}\sum_n |r_n^{(1)} - r_n^{(2)}|. \tag{3.230}$$

In case the quantum state spaces are two-dimensional, we can introduce the Bloch vectors $\vec{R}_i$ describing the states by writing

$$\rho_i = \frac{1}{2}\left(1 + \vec{R}_i \cdot \vec{\sigma}\right), \tag{3.231}$$

where $\vec{\sigma}$ is the Pauli spin vector. We then find that

$$\rho_1 - \rho_2 = \frac{1}{2} \left(\vec{R}_1 - \vec{R}_2 \right) \cdot \vec{\sigma}. \tag{3.232}$$

Choosing a suitable direction in the spin space, we find that the eigenvalues of $\left(\vec{R}_1 - \vec{R}_2 \right) \cdot \vec{\sigma}$ are $\pm \left| \vec{R}_1 - \vec{R}_2 \right|$, and hence we find that

$$D(\rho_1, \rho_2) = \frac{1}{2} \left| \vec{R}_1 - \vec{R}_2 \right|. \tag{3.233}$$

The trace distance between two states is consequently proportional to the distance between the corresponding Bloch vectors. From this it is obvious that the value is invariant under unitary transformations, because these correspond to rotations of the Bloch sphere. This is also manifest from the definition of the distance in (3.228).

The two-dimensional system is special: Calculating the Hilbert–Schmidt distance from (3.227), we obtain

$$\begin{aligned}
||\rho_1, \rho_2||^2 &= \mathrm{Tr} \left[(\rho_1 - \rho_2)^2 \right] \\
&= \frac{1}{4} \mathrm{Tr} \left[\left(\vec{R}_1 - \vec{R}_2 \right) \cdot \vec{\sigma} \right]^2 \\
&= \frac{\left(\vec{R}_1 - \vec{R}_2 \right) \cdot \left(\vec{R}_1 - \vec{R}_2 \right)}{4}.
\end{aligned} \tag{3.234}$$

From this it follows that

$$||\rho_1, \rho_2|| = D(\rho_1, \rho_2), \tag{3.235}$$

which holds for the two-dimensional case only.

The operator $\mathfrak{R} = \rho_1 - \rho_2$ is a hermitian operator with its spectrum confined to the interval $[-1, 1]$. We introduce the spectral resolution of this operator by setting

$$\mathfrak{R} = V^+ - V^- = \sum_{\nu} |v_\nu^+\rangle \lambda_\nu^+ \langle v_\nu^+| - \sum_{\mu} |v_\mu^-\rangle \lambda_\mu^- \langle v_\mu^-|, \tag{3.236}$$

where $\langle v_\nu^+ | v_\mu^- \rangle = 0$ for all ν and μ and also $\lambda_\nu^+, \lambda_\mu^- > 0$. There may also be zero eigenvalues, but they do not contribute to this expression. Because $\mathrm{Tr}\,\mathfrak{R} = 0$, we have

$$\sum_{\nu} \lambda_\nu^+ = \sum_{\mu} \lambda_\mu^-. \tag{3.237}$$

We also define the projector

$$\Pi = \sum_{\nu} |v_\nu^+\rangle \langle v_\nu^+|. \tag{3.238}$$

For any projector we have the property: If A is a nonnegative operator, we have

$$\mathrm{Tr}\,(\Pi A) \leq \mathrm{Tr}\,(A). \tag{3.239}$$

This works even when Π is an operator on the density matrix ρ (i.e., a superoperator).

The absolute value of an operator is obtained by changing the sign of all the negative eigenvalues. Thus, using the results (3.236) and (3.237), we may write

$$D(\rho_1, \rho_2) = \frac{1}{2}\mathrm{Tr}\,(|\rho_1 - \rho_2|) = \frac{1}{2}\mathrm{Tr}\,\left(V^+ + V^-\right)$$
$$= \mathrm{Tr}V^+ = \mathrm{Tr}\,[\Pi\,(\rho_1 - \rho_2)]. \tag{3.240}$$

As this is a linear relationship, we can write for any ρ_3,

$$D(\rho_1, \rho_2) = \mathrm{Tr}\,[\Pi\,(\rho_1 - \rho_3)] + \mathrm{Tr}\,[\Pi\,(\rho_3 - \rho_2)]. \tag{3.241}$$

As we have $\mathrm{Tr}\,(\Pi\rho) \leq \mathrm{Tr}\rho$, from (3.241) we conclude that

$$D(\rho_1, \rho_2) \leq D(\rho_1, \rho_3) + D(\rho_3, \rho_2). \tag{3.242}$$

In metric spaces this is called a *triangle inequality*, and it constitutes one of the defining properties of a measure of distance.

Let us introduce a trace-preserving operation $\mathcal{A}(\rho)$ such that $\mathrm{Tr}\,\left[\mathcal{A}(\rho)\right] = \mathrm{Tr}\rho$ for any ρ. Such operations were introduced in Secs. 2.3.3 and 2.4.4 in connection with quantum measurements and environmental perturbations. Using the result (3.240), we write

$$D\left[\mathcal{A}(\rho_1), \mathcal{A}(\rho_2)\right] = \mathrm{Tr}\,\left[\Pi\,(\mathcal{A}(\rho_1) - \mathcal{A}(\rho_2))\right] = \mathrm{Tr}\,\left[\Pi\,\left(\mathcal{A}(V^+) - \mathcal{A}(V^-)\right)\right]$$
$$\leq \mathrm{Tr}\,\left[\Pi(\mathcal{A}(V^+))\right]$$
$$\leq \mathrm{Tr}\,\left[\mathcal{A}(V^+)\right]$$
$$= \frac{1}{2}\mathrm{Tr}\,\left[\mathcal{A}(V^+) + \mathcal{A}(V^-)\right] = \frac{1}{2}\mathrm{Tr}\,\left(V^+ + V^-\right)$$
$$= \frac{1}{2}\mathrm{Tr}|V^+ - V^-| = D(\rho_1, \rho_2). \tag{3.243}$$

We have thus derived the result:

Theorem The applications of a trace-preserving map $\mathcal{A}(\rho)$ makes the distance between two quantum states shrink:

$$D\left[\mathcal{A}(\rho_1), \mathcal{A}(\rho_2)\right] \leq D(\rho_1, \rho_2). \tag{3.244}$$

This is in mathematics the definition of a *contractive mapping*. It is shown that such a mapping has a unique fixed point, which is not changed by the map; that is, there exists a state ρ_0 such that

$$\mathcal{A}(\rho_0) = \rho_0. \tag{3.245}$$

There also follows that if the space of the matrices σ is complete, any Cauchy sequence $\{\sigma_n\}$ with

$$\lim_{n,m \to \infty} D(\sigma_n, \sigma_m) = 0 \tag{3.246}$$

converges to a limit in the space. The proofs of these properties utilize the triangle inequality (3.242).

We see that the concept of a distance is of importance when proving exact relations in the space of quantum states. For a measure to be a proper distance, it has to satisfy the following criteria:

- It must be nonnegative ≥ 0.
- It must be nondegenerate (i.e., not give zero distance between different states).
- It must be symmetric.
- It must satisfy a triangle inequality.

We have shown that the trace distance may be used as a proper distance concept.

3.3.2 Fidelity

For two quantum states, a measure of their similarity may be $|\langle \varphi | \psi \rangle|$, which is unity only if they are identical. We can generalize this concept to two density matrix states by defining the fidelity

$$F(\rho_1, \rho_2) = \mathrm{Tr}\sqrt{\rho_1^{1/2} \rho_2 \rho_1^{1/2}}. \tag{3.247}$$

If the two states are diagonal in the same representation [see (3.229)], the fidelity is given by

$$F(\rho_1, \rho_2) = \sum_n r_n^{(1)} r_n^{(2)} \leq 1. \tag{3.248}$$

If one of the states is pure, $\rho_1 = |\psi\rangle\langle\psi|$ say, we find that

$$F(\rho_1, \rho_2) = \mathrm{Tr}\sqrt{|\psi\rangle\langle\psi|\rho_2|\psi\rangle\langle\psi|} = \sqrt{\langle\psi|\rho_2|\psi\rangle}. \tag{3.249}$$

This result is natural, and it was used in the connection with cloning in Sec. 2.2.2.

From the definition of fidelity, it is obvious that it is invariant with respect to unitary transformations. It is, however, far from obvious that it is symmetric in its arguments. To prove this we introduce the nonhermitian operator

$$A = \rho_2^{1/2}\rho_1^{1/2}. \tag{3.250}$$

The fidelity is then given by the expression $\mathrm{Tr}\left(\sqrt{A^\dagger A}\right)$. If we introduce the complete set of eigenfunctions of $A^\dagger A$ by setting

$$A^\dagger A|\varphi_n\rangle = \lambda_n|\varphi_n\rangle, \tag{3.251}$$

where $\lambda_n \geq 0$, we find that the fidelity is given by

$$F(\rho_1, \rho_2) = \sum_n \sqrt{\lambda_n}. \tag{3.252}$$

We also define the fidelity with the arguments exchanged:

$$F(\rho_2, \rho_1) = \mathrm{Tr}\sqrt{\rho_2^{1/2}\rho_1\rho_2^{1/2}} = \mathrm{Tr}\sqrt{AA^\dagger}. \tag{3.253}$$

Using the eigenfunctions defined by

$$AA^\dagger|\tilde{\varphi}_n\rangle = \tilde{\lambda}_n|\tilde{\varphi}_n\rangle, \tag{3.254}$$

we find that

$$F(\rho_2, \rho_1) = \sum_n \sqrt{\tilde{\lambda}_n}. \tag{3.255}$$

It is, however, easy to show that the operators $A^\dagger A$ and $AA^\dagger$ have the same nonvanishing eigenvalues. Namely, from (3.251) follow

$$AA^\dagger A|\varphi_n\rangle = \lambda_n A|\varphi_n\rangle,$$
$$AA^\dagger|\tilde{\varphi}_n\rangle = \lambda_n|\tilde{\varphi}_n\rangle, \tag{3.256}$$

where $|\tilde{\varphi}_n\rangle = A|\varphi_n\rangle$. Thus, the sums in (3.252) and (3.255) agree. This construction fails only if $\lambda_n = 0$ because then $\langle\varphi_n|A^\dagger A|\varphi_n\rangle = ||A|\varphi_n\rangle||^2 = 0$, and the corresponding state $|\tilde{\varphi}_n\rangle$ does not exist. These values do not, however, contribute to the sums. Thus, we have shown the symmetry of the fidelity:

$$F(\rho_2, \rho_1) = F(\rho_1, \rho_2). \tag{3.257}$$

The fidelity is, however, not a distance measure, as it does not satisfy a triangle inequality. It may be used to define such a measure, but we do not enter this aspect here.

Example   We specify the situation to one with two pure states in two dimensions, which without loss of generality, can be written

$$|\psi\rangle = |e_0\rangle,$$
$$|\varphi\rangle = \cos\theta|e_0\rangle + \sin\theta|e_1\rangle. \tag{3.258}$$

The fidelity is here given by

$$F(|\psi\rangle, |\varphi\rangle) = |\cos\theta|. \tag{3.259}$$

The density matrices give

$$|\psi\rangle\langle\psi| - |\varphi\rangle\langle\varphi| = \begin{bmatrix} 1 & 0 \\ 0 & 0 \end{bmatrix} - \begin{bmatrix} \cos^2\theta & \sin\theta\cos\theta \\ \sin\theta\cos\theta & \sin^2\theta \end{bmatrix}. \tag{3.260}$$

The eigenvalues are $\pm|\sin\theta|$, giving the trace distance

$$D(|\psi\rangle\langle\psi|, |\varphi\rangle\langle\varphi|) = \frac{1}{2}\text{Tr}\left(||\psi\rangle\langle\psi| - |\varphi\rangle\langle\varphi||\right) = |\sin\theta|. \tag{3.261}$$

Thus, we find the relation

$$D(|\psi\rangle\langle\psi|, |\varphi\rangle\langle\varphi|) = \sqrt{\left[1 - F(|\psi\rangle, |\varphi\rangle)^2\right]}. \tag{3.262}$$

For the general case it is possible to prove the relation

$$\left[1 - F(\rho_1, \rho_2)^2\right] \leq D(\rho_1, \rho_2) \leq \sqrt{\left[1 - F(\rho_1, \rho_2)^2\right]}. \tag{3.263}$$

This shows that the fidelity is equivalent with the trace distance as a measure of closeness between quantum states.

It is also possible to prove the relation equivalent with (3.244); namely, if $\mathcal{A}$ is a trace-preserving operation, we have

$$F\left[\mathcal{A}(\rho_1), \mathcal{A}(\rho_2)\right] \geq F(\rho_1, \rho_2). \tag{3.264}$$

This also says that applying trace-preserving mappings to different states makes them more alike. Without further discussions, we cannot apply the fixed-point theorem here, as the fidelity as such is not a proper distance measure.

3.3.3   Relative Entropy

One measure of the closeness of quantum states is the relative entropy, which was introduced in Sec. 3.2.1:

$$S(\rho_1||\rho_2) = \text{Tr}\left[\rho_1(\log\rho_1 - \log\rho_2)\right] \geq 0. \tag{3.265}$$

As this is zero only if $\rho_1 = \rho_2$, it does quantify the difference between the two distributions. It is, however, neither symmetric nor does it satisfy any triangular inequality. It is, hence, no natural distance measure.

It is obvious that the relative entropy is invariant under unitary transformations. If we take a system combined from the constituents A and B, we may define the reduced density matrix,

$$\rho_A = \text{Tr}_B \rho_{AB}. \tag{3.266}$$

This can be written as a mapping in the space of system AB,

$$D^{-1}\mathbb{I}_B \otimes \rho_A = D^{-1}\mathbb{I}_B \otimes \text{Tr}_B \rho_{AB} \equiv \Pi \rho_{AB}, \tag{3.267}$$

where $D = \text{Tr}_B \mathbb{I}_B$, and we identify the operator

$$\Pi \equiv D^{-1}\mathbb{I}_B \otimes \text{Tr}_B. \tag{3.268}$$

It is obvious that the operator introduced is a projector $\Pi^2 = \Pi$. Using the property (3.239), we find that

$$\begin{aligned}
S(\rho_A^{(1)} || \rho_A^{(2)}) &= \text{Tr}_{AB} \left[\Pi \rho_{AB}^{(1)} \left(\log \Pi \rho_{AB}^{(1)} - \log \Pi \rho_{AB}^{(2)} \right) \right] \\
&\leq \text{Tr}_{AB} \left[\rho_{AB}^{(1)} \left(\log \rho_{AB}^{(1)} - \log \rho_{AB}^{(2)} \right) \right] \\
&= S(\rho_{AB}^{(1)} || \rho_{AB}^{(2)}).
\end{aligned} \tag{3.269}$$

The two states can be related in more ways in the extended space AB.

The relative entropy also has the contractive property: If $\mathcal{A}$ is a trace-preserving operation, we have

$$S\left[\mathcal{A}\left(\rho^{(1)} \right) || \mathcal{A}\left(\rho^{(2)} \right) \right] \leq S(\rho^{(1)} || \rho^{(2)}). \tag{3.270}$$

This can be proved in the following way:

Take an arbitrary density matrix ρ in the space A. The most general trace-preserving map is given by

$$\mathcal{A}(\rho) = \sum_i A_i \rho A_i^\dagger, \tag{3.271}$$

with

$$\sum_i A_i^\dagger A_i = \mathbb{I}_A. \tag{3.272}$$

The unit operator on the right-hand side is of dimension equal to that of the original density matrix ρ. The operators thus constitute a set of POVMs. As shown in Sec. 3.2.4, we may introduce a complete orthonormal basis set $\{|\beta_i\rangle\}$ spanning an extended linear space AB such that

$$\sum_i |\beta_i\rangle\langle\beta_i| = \mathbb{I}_{AB}, \tag{3.273}$$

where $\mathbb{I}_{AB}$ is the unit operator in the extended space. Defining the projector Π on the space A, we may write

$$A_i = \Pi|\beta_i\rangle\langle\beta_i|\Pi. \tag{3.274}$$

We then have

$$
\begin{aligned}
S\left[A\left(\rho^{(1)}\right)||A\left(\rho^{(2)}\right)\right] &= S\left[\sum_i A_i\rho^{(1)}A_i^\dagger||\sum_j A_j\rho^{(2)}A_j^\dagger\right] \\
&= S\left[\sum_{i,k}\Pi|\beta_i\rangle\langle\beta_i|\rho^{(1)}|\beta_k\rangle\langle\beta_k|\Pi||\right. \\
&\quad \left.\times \sum_{j,n}\Pi|\beta_j\rangle\langle\beta_j|\rho^{(2)}|\beta_n\rangle\langle\beta_n|\Pi\right] \\
&= S\left[\Pi\rho^{(1)}\Pi||\Pi\rho^{(2)}\Pi\right] \leq S\left(\rho^{(1)}||\rho^{(2)}\right), \tag{3.275}
\end{aligned}
$$

which proves (3.270).

This does not, however, help to define convergence, but if we have $\rho^{(2)} = \rho_0$ such that $A(\rho_0) = \rho_0$, the quantity

$$S(A(\rho)||A(\rho_0)) = S(A(\rho)||\rho_0) \tag{3.276}$$

does indicate how far ρ is from the fixed point of the trace-preserving mapping A. Further applications of the relative entropy will be encountered later.

We can use the property (3.107) of the relative entropy to show that the entropy in thermal equilibrium is maximum. We write

$$0 \leq S(\rho||\rho_0) = \text{Tr}\,(\rho\log\rho) - \text{Tr}\,(\rho\log\rho_0). \tag{3.277}$$

We have the thermodynamic relation $\rho_0 = \exp\left[(F - H)/k_B T\right]$, where F is the free energy. We can now write

$$\frac{S(\rho)}{k_B} = -\text{Tr}\,(\rho\log\rho) \leq \frac{\text{Tr}\,(\rho H) - F}{k_B T}. \tag{3.278}$$

Now in thermal equilibrium we have $F = \langle H \rangle - T S_0$, where S_0 is now the equilibrium thermal entropy. Thus, if we consider density matrices with the energy $\mathrm{Tr}\,(\rho H)$ fixed, we find that all such states satisfy the relation

$$S(\rho) \le S_0, \tag{3.279}$$

which says that the relative entropy properly measures the distance to the equilibrium thermal state, which maximizes the entropy when the energy is fixed. But this is a generalization of the standard thermophysical statement.

3.4 REFERENCES

The classical theory of information has been discussed in many texts. The original work by Shannon [89] started the field, which also got pure formal mathematical presentations (see [53]). Of the many modern monographs covering the field, a typical one is that of Ash [6], where the most relevant aspects are discussed. A superficial but intuitively instructive presentation is given in the lectures by Feynman [36]. Many of the historically influential contributions to the field are reprinted in [59]. In a book by Jones and Jones [52], we find methods of classical communication theory, including a clear account of the Huffman code.

Quantum information theory is a comparatively recently developed field. The combination of quantum aspects and information theory is summarized in an article by Plenio and Vedral [82]. The main concepts and results are also reviewed by Werner [104]. It has turned out to be possible to generalize surprisingly many of the properties of classically defined entropy as a measure of information. These features are reviewed in recent textbooks by Gruska [43] and Nielsen and Chuang [72] together with the relations to classical information theory. Many mathematical aspects of quantum entropy are contained in an article by Wehrl [103]. A more global view of the various roles entropy may play in modern physics may be found in the proceedings [109] from a workshop at the Santa Fe Institute.

A discussion of communication with quantum states has been initiated by Helstrom [45]. In our presentation, we choose to illustrate the methods using simple examples. A modern review is given by Chefles [25]. The mathematical method of the Neumark extension is presented by Peres [78], but the mathematical proof behind it is given in a monograph by Akhieser and Glazman [1].

The various measures of distance in state space are presented and discussed in detail by Nielsen and Chuang [72]. For these formal aspects of quantum information, a book by Alicki and Fannes [3] is also a valuable source.

CHAPTER 4

QUANTUM COMPUTING

4.1 LOGIC OPERATIONS

4.1.1 Classical Logic Operations

Classical logic can be introduced in several ways. In philosophical discourse one usually introduces the truth value of a proposition by utilizing a variable taking the two values *false* and *true*. In algebraic terms, the former is usually denoted by 0 and the latter by 1; this is obviously highly useful in representing digital information in binary form. In this context the variable is, of course, the standard *bit* of information.

Functions defined on the set of values $\{0, 1\}$ are called *logical functions*, and the ensuing algebra is called a *Boolean algebra*. There are three basic logical functions, which have been given the names *NOT*, *OR*, and *AND*. The first one operates on a single input bit, whereas the other two operate on two input bits. They are denoted by

$$\text{NOT} : A \Rightarrow \overline{A},$$

$$\text{OR} : \{A, B\} \Rightarrow A \vee B,$$

$$\text{AND} : \{A, B\} \Rightarrow A \wedge B.$$

The functional dependence of the logical functions are represented in truth tables, which list the inputs to the left and the result of applying the function at

Quantum Approach to Informatics, by Stig Stenholm and Kalle-Antti Suominen
Copyright © 2005 John Wiley & Sons, Inc.

the right. Thus we obtain

$$
\begin{array}{c|c}
A & \overline{A} \\
\hline
0 & 1 \\
1 & 0
\end{array}
\tag{4.1}
$$

$$
\begin{array}{ccc}
A & B & A \vee B \\
\hline
0 & 0 & 0 \\
1 & 0 & 1 \\
0 & 1 & 1 \\
1 & 1 & 1
\end{array}
\tag{4.2}
$$

$$
\begin{array}{ccc}
A & B & A \wedge B \\
\hline
0 & 0 & 0 \\
1 & 0 & 0 \\
0 & 1 & 0 \\
1 & 1 & 1
\end{array}
\tag{4.3}
$$

The truth functions defined by these tables also have a set-theoretic representation (Fig. 4.1). Such pictures are called *Venn diagrams*.

The three logical functions defined above are sufficient to represent any logical operations, but they are not independent. They are connected by *deMorgan's rules*:

$$
\overline{A \vee B} = \overline{A} \wedge \overline{B},
$$
$$
\overline{A \wedge B} = \overline{A} \vee \overline{B}.
\tag{4.4}
$$

These are easily verified by a truth table or, even more simply, by looking at the set representation shown in Fig. 4.2.

All the basic logical functions can be represented by one single logical operation, (NOT A) AND (NOT B), defined by

$$
A|B \equiv \overline{A} \wedge \overline{B},
\tag{4.5}
$$

which is called the *Sheffer stroke*. That this is universal can be seen from

$$
\text{NOT}: \quad A|A = \overline{A} \wedge \overline{A} = \overline{A},
$$

$$
\text{OR}: \quad (A|B)|(A|B) = \overline{\left(\overline{A} \wedge \overline{B}\right)} \wedge \overline{\left(\overline{A} \wedge \overline{B}\right)} = \overline{\left(\overline{A} \wedge \overline{B}\right)} = A \vee B, \quad (4.6)
$$

$$
\text{AND}: \quad (A|A)|(B|B) = \overline{A}|\overline{B} = A \wedge B.
$$

From deMorgan's rules we see that $A|B \equiv \overline{A} \wedge \overline{B} = \overline{A \vee B}$. For this reason the function is also called *not or*, which is abbreviated as *NOR*.

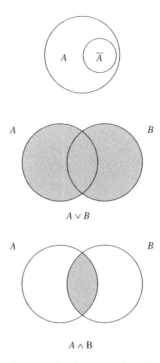

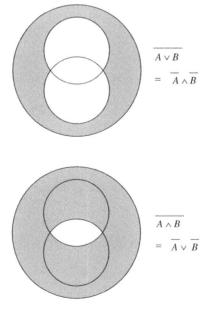

Figure 4.1   Venn diagrams for the operations NOT, OR, and AND.

$\overline{A \vee B}$

$= \ \overline{A} \wedge \overline{B}$

$\overline{A \wedge B}$

$= \ \overline{A} \vee \overline{B}$

Figure 4.2   DeMorgan's rules.

Exercise: Show that the logical operation (NOT A) OR (NOT B) is also universal.

In computations we need to introduce one more logical function because of the addition with carry; it is necessary to obtain in binary: $01 + 01 = 10$. Thus, we define the function *XOR*, called *exclusive or*. This is defined like OR in (4.2) with the exception that the input $\{1, 1\} \Rightarrow 0$. We denote this operation by $\oplus$, which is binary addition. The carry bit is seen to be given by $A \wedge B$, and hence binary addition can be represented as

$$\oplus : \{A, B\} \Rightarrow \{\text{XOR}(A, B), A \wedge B\}. \tag{4.7}$$

To be able to control a bit by the value of another bit, we introduce the function *controlled not* or *CNOT*. As a function of $\{A, B\}$ it gives out B if $A = 0$ and $\overline{B}$ if $A = 1$. These new functions can be represented by a truth table:

A	B	XOR	CNOT	A	
0	0	0	0	0	
1	0	1	1	1	(4.8)
0	1	1	1	0	
1	1	0	0	1	

As we see, CNOT, in fact, effects the same logical function as XOR.

It is easy to see that none of the standard logical functions is reversible; that is, the output does not determine the input uniquely. This is seen for *XOR* because both $\{0, 1\}$ and $\{1, 0\}$ give the output "1." In general, to obtain a reversible logical function, we need as many outputs as inputs. Thus, adding the column A to the output, we find the mapping

$$\{00, 10, 01, 11\} \Rightarrow \{00, 11, 10, 01\}, \tag{4.9}$$

which is obviously reversible. It is easily seen that for a logical function to be reversible, the outputs have to be a permutation of the inputs; the universal reversible logical function is thus a permutation P. The permutations form a group, and all its elements have an inverse. We also have for any permutation that there exists an integer N_P such that

$$P^{N_P} = 1. \tag{4.10}$$

Thus, the inverse is always $P^{-1} = P^{N_P - 1}$.

4.1.2 Quantum Logic Functions

To represent logical variables in quantum mechanics, we need to introduce an appropriate assembly of two-level systems. The carriers of these variables have to be regarded as classical entities, because we want to be able to assign the nth bit to a definite entity (i.e., we want to have a uniquely defined carrier of the first bit, the second bit, etc.). This may be realized, for example, by having large classical bodies or strictly localized systems as the carriers. For each bit we choose a uniquely defined orthonormal basis set $\{|0\rangle, |1\rangle\}$ which we call the *computational basis*. Note that the assignment of basis vectors to their respective symbols is arbitrary; in particular, there need be no simple relation between the assignments for the various bits.

In the computational basis, the general quantum state of the two-level system is written as

$$|\psi_1\rangle = \alpha|0\rangle + \beta|1\rangle; \tag{4.11}$$

this is the quantum equivalent of the classical bit; it is usually called a *qubit*.

The quantum mechanical representation of 2 bits is the state

$$|\psi_2\rangle = \alpha_{00}|00\rangle + \alpha_{01}|01\rangle + \alpha_{10}|10\rangle + \alpha_{11}|11\rangle, \tag{4.12}$$

where $|ab\rangle \equiv |a\rangle \otimes |b\rangle$. Thus, the quantum mechanical state can carry all possible combinations of 2 bits in a linear superposition. This is the origin of the power of quantum information processing over the classical one.

We now define a quantum computation by positing a device which acting on a quantum state effects the transformation

$$K : |AB\rangle \Rightarrow |f(A, B)\rangle, \tag{4.13}$$

where $f(A, B)$ is the Boolean function we want to implement in the calculation. Because the evolution of a quantum mechanical state is linear, it suffices to verify the validity of (4.13) for all classical inputs only; this guarantees that linear superpositions are transformed correctly. Thus, applying the transformation K to the state (4.12) we find the result

$$K|\psi_2\rangle = \alpha_{00}|f(0, 0)\rangle + \alpha_{01}|f(0, 1)\rangle + \alpha_{10}|f(1, 0)\rangle + \alpha_{11}|f(1, 1)\rangle. \tag{4.14}$$

Using the truth tables introduced in Sec. 4.1.1, we can see that this transformation can generalize all two-input logical functions to the quantum mechanical formulation.

The result (4.14) indicates that one application of a quantum operation performs the desired logical computation for all input variables. Here, however, a warning is in order; the process of quantum measurements implies that given one copy, we cannot access all the components of the ensuing state. There is usually no way of determining all the results of the computation from one computational cycle only. To find all the terms in (4.14), one would need to perform at least four experiments in the general case, and then quantum theory offers no advantage over the classical case. It is thus essential to find algorithms utilizing the large-scale parallelism offered by quantum states.

The general formulation of the quantum computing system is based on having two systems; system 1 is the input $|x\rangle_1$, where we assume that x is a 2^n binary number. We also introduce output system 2, which enters in a given state called the *fiducial state*; we choose $|0\rangle_2$ here. The input state is then taken to be

$$|\psi_{in}\rangle = \sum_x |x\rangle_1 |0\rangle_2. \tag{4.15}$$

The computing transformation is now required to effect the mapping

$$K \sum_x |x\rangle_1 |0\rangle_2 = \sum_x |x\rangle_1 |f(x)\rangle_2, \tag{4.16}$$

where $f(x)$ is the logical function we want to perform. We noted above that if we want a reversible computation, the values $\{f(x)\}$ have to be a permutation of the input values. Because the states $\{|x\rangle_1\}$ form a basis in the 2^n-dimensional state space of the input, the states $\{|f(x)\rangle_2\}$ also form a basis. Thus, we map a basis on another one, which guarantees that the mapping is unitary. Thus, the quantum operator K can be realized as a unitary transformation. If we define the quantum state labeling in a cyclic manner,

$$|y + 2^n\rangle = |y\rangle, \tag{4.17}$$

we can write the transformation as

$$K = \sum_{x,y} |y + f(x)\rangle_2 |x\rangle_1 \otimes {}_1\langle x|_2\langle y|. \tag{4.18}$$

In quantum information all state spaces are finite and the dimensions are usually powers of 2 because of the binary representation chosen. All sums are thus extended over the finite range $[0, 2^n - 1]$.

Because it is easily seen that

$${}_1\langle x|x'\rangle_1 \, {}_2\langle y + f(x)|y' + f(x')\rangle_2 = \delta_{xx'} \, {}_2\langle y + f(x)|y' + f(x)\rangle_2 = \delta_{xx'} \, \delta_{yy'}, \tag{4.19}$$

we find that

$$K^\dagger K = \sum_{x,y} |y\rangle_2 |x\rangle_1 \otimes {}_1\langle x|_2\langle y| = 1. \tag{4.20}$$

Similarly, we find that

$$KK^\dagger = \sum_{x,y} |y + f(x)\rangle_2 |x\rangle_1 \otimes {}_1\langle x|_2\langle y + f(x)| = 1, \tag{4.21}$$

because the set $\{|y + f(x)\rangle_2\}$ is a complete set for each value of x. We thus see that the transformation defined in (4.18) is unitary, and it can thus be realized by a Hamiltonian time evolution. It may not, however, be obvious how to achieve this in a given physical situation.

The transformation (4.18) is a special case of the measurement transformation introduced in Sec. 2.3.2. By relabeling the output states $\{|f(x)\rangle_2\}$, we can interpret them as pointer states, indicating the value carried by the input state. The relabeling defines the logical function we want to effect. If this is not reversible, the operator K is no longer unitary. As we assume that the input state $|x\rangle_1$ is to be preserved, the computation corresponds to a perfect von Neumann measurement. The process of computing could be generalized to the case when the input state is transformed, too: $|x\rangle_1 \rightarrow |g(x)\rangle_1$, where $g(x)$ is some well-defined function. In this generalization, much of the discussion of measurements can be carried over to the computational situation. In the following, however, we assume that the input state is conserved and the computation is reversible.

4.1.3 Simple Quantum Operations

It is easily realized that the most general operation on a single qubit is just a unitary transformation. This can be interpreted as changing the basis set from a computational basis to some other, in context propitious basis. Some simple examples are given below.

Hadamard Transformation   As usual, we choose to represent the quantum transformations in terms of the Pauli matrices:

$$\sigma_1 = \begin{bmatrix} 0 & 1 \\ 1 & 0 \end{bmatrix}; \quad \sigma_2 = \begin{bmatrix} 0 & -i \\ i & 0 \end{bmatrix}; \quad \sigma_3 = \begin{bmatrix} 1 & 0 \\ 0 & -1 \end{bmatrix}. \tag{4.22}$$

Now we define the Hadamard transformation by setting

$$U_2 = \frac{1}{\sqrt{2}} (\sigma_1 + \sigma_3) = \frac{1}{\sqrt{2}} \begin{bmatrix} 1 & 1 \\ 1 & -1 \end{bmatrix}. \tag{4.23}$$

This transforms the computational basis into a *complementary basis* according to

$$U_2 \begin{bmatrix} |0\rangle \\ |1\rangle \end{bmatrix} = \frac{1}{\sqrt{2}} \begin{bmatrix} |0\rangle + |1\rangle \\ |0\rangle - |1\rangle \end{bmatrix}. \tag{4.24}$$

In dimensions 2^n we can define the Hadamard transformation recursively by setting

$$U_{2^{n+1}} = \frac{1}{\sqrt{2}} \begin{bmatrix} U_{2^n} & U_{2^n} \\ U_{2^n} & -U_{2^n} \end{bmatrix}; \tag{4.25}$$

it is easy to see that this defines a sequence of unitary transformations. As an example we give

$$U_4 = \frac{1}{2} \begin{bmatrix} 1 & 1 & 1 & 1 \\ 1 & -1 & 1 & -1 \\ 1 & 1 & -1 & -1 \\ 1 & -1 & -1 & 1 \end{bmatrix}. \tag{4.26}$$

We notice that this distributes 2^{n-1} minus signs in all possible ways. From a given basis set in 2^n dimensions, it gives a transformation to new orthogonal basis vectors with equal projections on all the original states.

Physical Implementation   In optics the beamsplitter shown in Fig. 1.1 is represented by the transformation of the input signals $[a_1, a_2]$ to the output signals $[b_1, b_2]$ according to the rule

$$\begin{bmatrix} b_1 \\ b_2 \end{bmatrix} = \frac{1}{\sqrt{2}} \begin{bmatrix} 1 & i \\ i & 1 \end{bmatrix} \begin{bmatrix} a_1 \\ a_2 \end{bmatrix}. \tag{4.27}$$

It is easy to check that this transformation is unitary, and thus

$$|b_1|^2 + |b_2|^2 = |a_1|^2 + |a_2|^2. \tag{4.28}$$

In (4.27) the transformation is defined in a symmetric way, which is useful for systems of cascaded beamsplitters. Redefining the phases of the incoming and outgoing signals allows us to write the transformation as

$$\begin{bmatrix} b_1 \\ -ib_2 \end{bmatrix} = \frac{1}{\sqrt{2}} \begin{bmatrix} 1 & 1 \\ 1 & -1 \end{bmatrix} \begin{bmatrix} a_1 \\ ia_2 \end{bmatrix}, \tag{4.29}$$

which shows that the beamsplitter really performs a Hadamard transformation.

Square Root of NOT   Rewriting the beamsplitter transformation (4.27) in the form

$$\sqrt{-i} \begin{bmatrix} b_1 \\ b_2 \end{bmatrix} = \frac{1}{\sqrt{2}} \begin{bmatrix} \sqrt{-i} & \sqrt{i} \\ \sqrt{i} & \sqrt{-i} \end{bmatrix} \begin{bmatrix} a_1 \\ a_2 \end{bmatrix}, \tag{4.30}$$

we find a unitary transformation with the property

$$\left(\frac{1}{\sqrt{2}} \begin{bmatrix} \sqrt{-i} & \sqrt{i} \\ \sqrt{i} & \sqrt{-i} \end{bmatrix} \right)^2 = \frac{1}{2} \begin{bmatrix} -i+i & 2 \\ 2 & i-i \end{bmatrix} = \begin{bmatrix} 0 & 1 \\ 1 & 0 \end{bmatrix}. \tag{4.31}$$

Applied to the basis states in the computational basis, we find that

$$\begin{bmatrix} 0 & 1 \\ 1 & 0 \end{bmatrix} \begin{bmatrix} |0\rangle \\ |1\rangle \end{bmatrix} = \begin{bmatrix} |1\rangle \\ |0\rangle \end{bmatrix}; \tag{4.32}$$

this performs the NOT operation. The transformation (4.30) effects the *square root of NOT* (i.e., its square is the quantum version of the classical NOT function). Such an operation is not possible classically; the extra freedom offered by coherent superpositions allows quantum theory to introduce such a function. Physically, it is seen to be closely related to the simple beamsplitter.

Single-Qubit Phase Shift   We want to implement the phase shift transformation defined by

$$\Phi : \alpha|0\rangle + \beta|1\rangle \Rightarrow \alpha|0\rangle + \beta e^{i\varphi}|1\rangle, \tag{4.33}$$

which has basic significance in the processing of quantum information. This is easily seen to be generated by the Hamiltonian

$$H = \frac{\lambda}{2}(1 - \sigma_3) = \lambda \begin{bmatrix} 0 & 0 \\ 0 & 1 \end{bmatrix}. \tag{4.34}$$

We find trivially that

$$e^{-iHt}(\alpha|0\rangle + \beta|1\rangle) = \alpha|0\rangle + \beta e^{-i\lambda t}|1\rangle. \tag{4.35}$$

Choosing λ and t suitably gives any desired phase shift φ.

Controlled NOT (CNOT) Transformation   On the space of two qubits $\{|00\rangle, |01\rangle, |10\rangle, |11\rangle\}$ the CNOT transformation is given by

$$\begin{bmatrix} 1 & 0 & 0 & 0 \\ 0 & 1 & 0 & 0 \\ 0 & 0 & 0 & 1 \\ 0 & 0 & 1 & 0 \end{bmatrix} \begin{bmatrix} |00\rangle \\ |01\rangle \\ |10\rangle \\ |11\rangle \end{bmatrix} = \begin{bmatrix} |00\rangle \\ |01\rangle \\ |11\rangle \\ |10\rangle \end{bmatrix}. \tag{4.36}$$

Remark: It can be shown that the single-qubit transformations and CNOT can generate any general quantum transformation. They form a universal set of logical operations.

We use the two-dimensional Hadamard transformation (4.23) with the property

$$U_2^2 = \begin{bmatrix} 1 & 0 \\ 0 & 1 \end{bmatrix}, \tag{4.37}$$

to rewrite the CNOT transformation to give

$$\begin{bmatrix} |00\rangle \\ |01\rangle \\ |11\rangle \\ |10\rangle \end{bmatrix} = \begin{bmatrix} 1 & 0 \\ 0 & U_2 \end{bmatrix}^2 \begin{bmatrix} 1 & 0 & 0 & 0 \\ 0 & 1 & 0 & 0 \\ 0 & 0 & 0 & 1 \\ 0 & 0 & 1 & 0 \end{bmatrix} \begin{bmatrix} 1 & 0 \\ 0 & U_2 \end{bmatrix}$$

$$\times \begin{bmatrix} |00\rangle \\ |01\rangle \\ \frac{1}{\sqrt{2}}(|10\rangle + |11\rangle) \\ \frac{1}{\sqrt{2}}(|10\rangle - |11\rangle) \end{bmatrix}. \tag{4.38}$$

Because we have

$$U_2 \begin{bmatrix} 0 & 1 \\ 1 & 0 \end{bmatrix} U_2 = \begin{bmatrix} 1 & 0 \\ 0 & -1 \end{bmatrix}, \tag{4.39}$$

we find from (4.38) that

$$\begin{bmatrix} |00\rangle \\ |01\rangle \\ \frac{1}{\sqrt{2}}(|11\rangle + |10\rangle) \\ \frac{1}{\sqrt{2}}(|11\rangle - |10\rangle) \end{bmatrix} = \begin{bmatrix} 1 & 0 & 0 & 0 \\ 0 & 1 & 0 & 0 \\ 0 & 0 & 1 & 0 \\ 0 & 0 & 0 & -1 \end{bmatrix} \begin{bmatrix} |00\rangle \\ |01\rangle \\ \frac{1}{\sqrt{2}}(|10\rangle + |11\rangle) \\ \frac{1}{\sqrt{2}}(|10\rangle - |11\rangle) \end{bmatrix}, \tag{4.40}$$

which shows that if we can implement a controlled phase shift with $e^{i\varphi} = -1$, we can also implement the CNOT transformation. Note that the mapping between these transformations is acting only on the second bit of the two-qubit state.

4.1.4 The Deutsch Problem

We have already indicated that the utilization of the full state space allows us to perform a computation on all basis states in one operation, where the corresponding classical system would have to carry out the computation on each input separately. It is, however, not obvious that we can use this to facilitate any real calculational task because of the restrictions imposed by quantum observations. In this section we present a simple problem which can demonstrate that a quantum algorithm may be used to our advantage.

Let us assume that we have a device which maps states $\{0, 1\}$ on to themselves so that $f(x) = 0$ or 1. We do not know this function, but we assume that we can call it at will; such a device is called an *oracle* in quantum information contexts. There are then two possibilities:

$$\begin{aligned} f(0) = f(1) & \quad \text{constant function,} \\ f(0) \neq f(1) & \quad \text{balanced function.} \end{aligned} \tag{4.41}$$

To decide which is the case, classically we have to call the function twice and make the decision on the outcome. We will show that the procedure can be improved if a suitable quantum device is available.

We define the signature function of $f(x)$ giving the parity of the state by setting

$$V_f |x\rangle = (-1)^{f(x)} |x\rangle. \tag{4.42}$$

We introduce an auxiliary system, in this context called an *ancilla*, $|x\rangle_2$. We assume that we have available the transformation

$$U_f |x\rangle_1 |y\rangle_2 = |x\rangle_1 |y + f(x)\rangle_2, \tag{4.43}$$

where as usual, we assume a periodic arrangement of the states; $|1 + 1\rangle = |0\rangle$. We prepare the ancilla in the state $(1/\sqrt{2})\,(|0\rangle_2 - |1\rangle_2)$ and apply the transformation U_f:

$$|\psi_{\text{fin}}\rangle_{12} = U_f |x\rangle_1 \left(\frac{1}{\sqrt{2}}\,(|0\rangle_2 - |1\rangle_2) \right) = \frac{1}{\sqrt{2}}\,(|x\rangle_1 |f(x)\rangle_2 - |x\rangle_1 |1 + f(x)\rangle_2). \tag{4.44}$$

From this we conclude that

$$\begin{aligned}
|\psi_{\text{fin}}\rangle_{12} &= |x\rangle_1 \left(\frac{1}{\sqrt{2}}\,(|0\rangle_2 - |1\rangle_2) \right) && \text{if } f(x) = 0 \\
&= |x\rangle_1 \left(\frac{1}{\sqrt{2}}\,(|1\rangle_2 - |0\rangle_2) \right) && \text{if } f(x) = 1 \\
&= (-1)^{f(x)} |x\rangle_1 \left(\frac{1}{\sqrt{2}}\,(|0\rangle_2 - |1\rangle_2) \right).
\end{aligned} \tag{4.45}$$

The transformation U_f thus implements the signature function. The original decision problem can now be solved in the following manner:

- Using a Hadamard transform on the ancilla, we prepare the initial state

$$|\psi_{\text{in}}\rangle_{12} = \frac{1}{\sqrt{2}} \sum_x |x\rangle_1 \left(\frac{1}{\sqrt{2}}\,(|0\rangle_2 - |1\rangle_2) \right). \tag{4.46}$$

- We next apply the transformation U_f to obtain

$$|\psi_{\text{fin}}\rangle_{12} = \frac{1}{\sqrt{2}} \sum_x (-1)^{f(x)} |x\rangle_1 \left(\frac{1}{\sqrt{2}}\,(|0\rangle_2 - |1\rangle_2) \right). \tag{4.47}$$

- Now if $f(0) = f(1)$, we have

$$|\psi_{\text{fin}}\rangle_{12} = (-1)^{f(0)} \left(\frac{1}{\sqrt{2}}\,(|0\rangle_1 + |1\rangle_1) \right) \left(\frac{1}{\sqrt{2}}\,(|0\rangle_2 - |1\rangle_2) \right). \tag{4.48}$$

- If $f(0) \neq f(1)$, we find that

$$|\psi_{\text{fin}}\rangle_{12} = (-1)^{f(0)} \left(\frac{1}{\sqrt{2}}\,(|0\rangle_1 - |1\rangle_1) \right) \left(\frac{1}{\sqrt{2}}\,(|0\rangle_2 - |1\rangle_2) \right). \tag{4.49}$$

- Now because the states $(1/\sqrt{2})\,(|0\rangle_1 \pm |1\rangle_1)$ are orthogonal, a single measurement suffices to decide which one is present. This determines uniquely if the function $f(x)$ is balanced or constant without knowing its values.

The procedure discussed does not seem to give much improved efficiency: Instead of two classical measurements, we need to use only one quantum observation. The price is the availability of the function U_f, which we have not constructed. However, the example is designed to illustrate how quantum information processing can be utilized to facilitate a classical decision process.

4.2   THE COMPUTER

4.2.1   Classical Universal Computer

Alan Turing presented his conception of the most general computing device classically realizable, subsequently called a *Turing machine*. There are many different versions of it, but the simplest one possible is sufficient to make the case. It consists of the following items:

1. *Tape for data storage.* This is a simple sequence of squares, any one of which contains a symbol taken from a finite alphabet. The tape is of unlimited length in one direction.
2. *Processor.* This is the operative element of the computer and can be in a finite set of internal states.
3. *Finite instruction set.* This tells the processor what to do when in a given internal state it reads any symbol from the tape.
4. *Tape manipulation device.* This is a reading head, set to recognize the symbol just under it on the tape, to erase the symbol on the tape, and to write another one to the square if told to do so by the instruction set. Finally, the instruction tells the reading head to move right or left or, possibly, to stay where it is.

The general setup is illustrated in Fig. 4.3. The input data on the tape contain a START marker; the internal states contain an initial position and a STOP position, which indicates when the computation is finished. At each step in the process, the computer reads the current mark on the tape, recognizes its internal state, and looks up the corresponding action from the instruction set. The action consists of changing the internal state, rewriting the symbol on the tape, and possibly moving the read head to an adjacent location on the tape. This is one computing cycle. When the machine finds itself in the STOP state, it informs the operator in a suitable way.

There are several variations on the basic scheme of a Turing machine, but they are all equivalent in the end. If they are always restricted to move in one

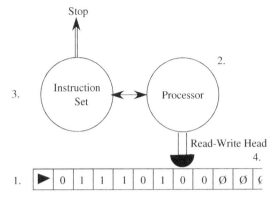

Figure 4.3 Scheme for a Turing machine.

direction only, they belong to a class of devices called *finite-state automatons*. These have attracted considerable interest in information-processing contexts. The concept can be extended to quantum systems, but this takes us out of the present discussion.

The central role played by the Turing machine derives from the following fact:

Theorem Any computation carried out on a classical computer can be emulated by a Turing machine.

This makes it the universal computer: If a process can be proved possible on a Turing machine, it can be carried out on a classical computer and conversely; impossible computations can be found by investigating what a Turing machine can do.

To illustrate the operation of such a device, we present the following simple example:

- The squares on the tape can contain any of the symbols $\{\triangleright, 0, 1, \emptyset\}$; the symbol $\triangleright$ indicates the starting position, the numbers $\{0, 1\}$ give the data on the tape in ordinary binary form, and finally, $\emptyset$ denotes a blank square (this is thus not the number zero).
- The internal state of the processor consists of four possible states $\{S, I, II, F\}$. S is the starting state and F is the STOP state, which indicates the end of the computation. At this point, the answer to the computation is written on the tape.

As an application, consider the instruction set below. We use the notation (internal state, symbol on square). We also assume that the reading head is moving one step along the tape for each cycle. We introduce the instructions

$$(S, \triangleright) \Rightarrow (I, \triangleright),$$
$$(I, 0) \Rightarrow (I, 0),$$
$$(I, 1) \Rightarrow (II, 0),$$
$$(II, 0) \Rightarrow (I, 1),$$
$$(II, 1) \Rightarrow (II, 1),$$
$$(II, \emptyset) \Rightarrow (I, 1),$$
$$(I, \emptyset) \Rightarrow (F, \emptyset).$$

(4.50)

Note that all instructions on the right are also assumed to comprise a move to the next square on the tape.

To demonstrate the action of this program, we give a few examples. Assume the initial tape to be given by

| $\triangleright$ | 0 | 0 | 1 | $\emptyset$ | $\emptyset$ | ... |

The program now proceeds according to the sequence

$(S, \triangleright) \Rightarrow (I, \triangleright);\ (I, 0) \Rightarrow (I, 0);\ (I, 0) \Rightarrow (I, 0);\ (I, 1) \Rightarrow (II, 0);$
$(II, \emptyset) \Rightarrow (I, 1);\ (I, \emptyset) \Rightarrow (F, \emptyset).$

The computation is now finished, and the tape contains

| $\triangleright$ | 0 | 0 | 0 | 1 | $\emptyset$ | ... |

As another example, the tape contains the input

| $\triangleright$ | 1 | 0 | 1 | $\emptyset$ | $\emptyset$ | ... |

The computational sequence now becomes

$(S, \triangleright) \Rightarrow (I, \triangleright);\ (I, 1) \Rightarrow (II, 0);\ (II, 0) \Rightarrow (I, 1);\ (I, 1) \Rightarrow (II, 0);$
$(II, \emptyset) \Rightarrow (I, 1);\ (I, \emptyset) \Rightarrow (F, \emptyset).$

The tape now contains

| $\triangleright$ | 0 | 1 | 0 | 1 | $\emptyset$ | ... |

The program we have devised thus performs the mapping

$$100 \Rightarrow 1000,$$
$$101 \Rightarrow 1010.$$

This is the simple shift operation, which in binary representation corresponds to multiplication by 2. It is easy to see that the instruction set provided will effect such a multiplication of any initial binary number on the tape. Because the process always moves right, it will always reach the STOP position and provide the answer on the tape. If the program is such that the machine can move in both directions or stop moving, there is no guarantee that the STOP position will be reached. This means that all possible instruction sets do not necessarily lead to a successful computation; the desired function is not computable.

Remark: By adding stochastic elements to the computing process, one may define a wider class of information-processing devices. They have a broader range of applications. Then it is also possible to define a probability that an answer is obtained. In this sense they are closer to quantum computers, but the role of probability in quantum physics is rather different from that in classical physics.

Historical remarks: The role of computability in the discussion about the foundations of mathematics is so central that presentation of some historical background may be justified. During a lecture in 1900, David Hilbert posed 23 problems for mathematics research in the coming century. These problems have turned out to be immensely influential on the development of mathematics during the past century. One of these problems gave rise to the following *entscheidungsproblem*:

> **Problem:** Given a mathematical statement, is there any algorithm to determine if this is true or false?

In 1936, Alan Turing turned this into a problem of computability; can we devise a function that states if any program will end successfully and has written the answer on the tape? Turing proved that this is not possible: It is not possible to construct an algorithm that can decide whether a computer reaches the STOP position in the case of an arbitrary program. This is called the *halting problem*. An equivalent result was reached independently by the logician Alonzo Church, and hence the result is called the *Church–Turing thesis*.

The proof by Turing is based on the fact that all parts of the machine consist of a finite number of elements. Thus, the set of all successful Turing machines can be ordered in a single sequence, and they can be assigned a unique Turing number. Because it can be shown that there are more possible functions than integers, all functions cannot be computed successfully. Thus, not all functions are computable, despite the fact that the proof does not explicitly display any such function. The procedure is similar to the one used by set theory to show that there are more rationals than integers.

4.2.2 Computational Complexity

Once we have at our disposal a model of a universal calculating device, the Turing machine, we may try to classify the various problems according to the number of operations needed to carry out a given computation. In conventional computing theory, this has led to a classification of computational problems. Note that this is not related to real time, which is determined by the duration of the basic computational cycle. The length required by a program is given in terms of the basic cycles only.

Let us assume that we want to add two binary numbers of magnitude 2^{n_1} and 2^{n_2}. If we define

$$n = \text{Max}(n_1 + 1, n_2 + 1), \tag{4.51}$$

we see that the addition can be accomplished in n operations. Each operation may, of course, imply the performance of several basic instructions, but this only leads to a finite scaling of n. Similarly, multiplication of the same numbers will imply a number of operations $\propto n_1 n_2$. Thus, the number of operations will in both cases grow as some power of the size of the problem to be solved.

We thus define the *polynomial class* of problems **P** as the set of all problems, the performance of which requires a number of operations that grows like n^p, where n is the size of the input and p is some integer.

A more general class of problems is called **NP**. They are usually defined to be such that once a solution is found, it can be verified by a procedure in the class **P**. It is easy to find a problem apparently not performable in a polynomial number of operations: Assume that we have an arbitrarily ordered list of 2^n elements. We want to know if a given element is to be found in the list. To decide this, we inspect the elements one by one. Because the element may be anywhere, this takes on the average 2^{n-1} operations. This grows exponentially with the length n of the list, and hence it is expected to belong to **NP** but not to **P**.

One problem is that there is no mathematical proof that there exist problems in **NP** that do not belong to **P**. We do not know if $\mathbf{P} \neq \mathbf{NP}$. Another problem that is believed not to be in **P** is the resolution of numbers into prime factors. If we have a number of order 2^n, a search for factors by trial and error implies a number of operations of the order $2^{n/2}$, which is again exponential. Of course, at first all even numbers can be excluded, at later stages various other numbers are obviously not factors, but the numbers remaining to be tried still grow exponentially. As stated above, however, we do not know if there exists an algorithm in **P** performing the task. The growth in popularity of the field of quantum computations was initiated by Shor's proof that a quantum computer can, in principle, factor a number in a polynomial number of operations.

4.2.3 Quantum Computer

The quantum computing transformation U_K is of the form (see Sec. 4.1.2)

$$U_K \left(\sum_x |x\rangle_1 |0\rangle_2 \right) = \sum_x |x\rangle_1 |f(x)\rangle_2, \tag{4.52}$$

where $f(x)$ is the function to be computed. From this representation, we draw the following conclusions:

- By using orthogonal states one by one, the quantum computer can always simulate the operation of a classical computer. This is in agreement with Holevo's bound and the discussion in Sec. 3.2.1.

- Quantum processes can be simulated on a classical computer, but the operation becomes more and more inefficient because the input number in (4.52) grows exponentially together with the number 2^n of states included.

- The large-scale parallelism implied by the ability to operate on the state (4.52) directly suggests the huge advantage offered potentially by quantum data processing.

- Quantum theoretical observations imply an essential limitation on the possibilities to read the desired result from the right-hand side of (4.52). This restricts the usefulness of quantum processing to cases where the parallelism can be utilized successfully. At present, we know only a few algorithms where this is possible.

- The performance of classical computers can be improved by the introduction of stochastic operations. The cost of this is often that the desired output may not be found in the first tries. In quantum systems the stochasticity derives from quantum uncertainties, and they are thus a necessary aspect of the entire approach.

It will be the task of the following sections to build up the formalism of general quantum computing and try to see when and how it may be useful. We want, however, to make one remark on the concept of quantum computation. In all examples presented so far, it is only the actual physical process of information handling that is quantum mechanical. The input data and the ultimate output are all defined in terms of a classically defined computational task. It is not obvious what a fully quantum mechanical process would involve. It may even be true that the classical input and output are necessary; then we would have an example of the quantum mechanical decree that state preparation and final observations have to be phrased in classical language. This view was always stressed by Niels Bohr.

4.2.4 Quantum Computing Circuits

As in classical information-processing systems, it has proved useful to introduce a pictorial representation of the basic devices building up a full-scale computer. Thus, we introduce symbols for the logical operations (i.e., quantum logical gates). Each one is, of course, representing a quantum mechanical transformation, and they can be interpreted as such. However, for those that want to work regularly with quantum computing systems, it is advantageous to be able to read off the logical operations directly from the symbols. Then the operation of an entire network can be inferred from its symbolic circuit in terms of gates.

Single-Qubit Operations The general operation on a single qubit can be written as

$$U\left(c_0|0\rangle + c_1|1\rangle\right) = a_0|0\rangle + a_1|1\rangle, \tag{4.53}$$

which is represented by Fig. 4.4.

Examples

1. The Hadamard transformation $H = U$ (Fig. 4.5):

$$H\left(c_0|0\rangle + c_1|1\rangle\right) = c_0 \frac{(|0\rangle + |1\rangle)}{\sqrt{2}} + c_1 \frac{(|0\rangle - |1\rangle)}{\sqrt{2}}$$

$$= \frac{1}{\sqrt{2}} \left[(c_0 + c_1)|0\rangle + (c_0 - c_1)|1\rangle\right]. \tag{4.54}$$

2. The NOT operator (Fig. 4.6):

$$\sigma_1\left(c_0|0\rangle + c_1|1\rangle\right) = c_0|1\rangle + c_1|0\rangle. \tag{4.55}$$

3. The phase shifter Φ (Fig. 4.7):

$$\Phi\left(c_0|0\rangle + c_1|1\rangle\right) = c_0\, e^{-i\varphi/2}|0\rangle + c_1\, e^{i\varphi/2}|1\rangle$$

$$= e^{-i\varphi/2}\left(c_0\,|0\rangle + c_1\, e^{i\varphi}|1\rangle\right). \tag{4.56}$$

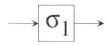

Figure 4.4 Gate symbol for a general single-qubit operation related to a unitary transformation U.

Figure 4.5 Symbol for a single-qubit Hadamard gate.

Figure 4.6 Symbol for a single-qubit NOT gate.

Figure 4.7   Symbol for a single-qubit phase gate.

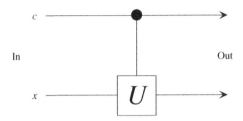

Figure 4.8   Symbol for a two-qubit conditional gate.

Two-Qubit Operations   The general two-qubit operation regards one bit as the control and the second as the target. The operation is to perform a unitary operation U_c on the second bit, where the transformation is chosen from a set $\{U_c\}$ according to the value of the control bit:

$$|c\rangle_1|x\rangle_2 \Rightarrow |c\rangle_1 U_c|x\rangle_2. \tag{4.57}$$

This is represented in Fig. 4.8.

Example: Controlled NOT   In the basis $\{|00\rangle, |01\rangle, |10\rangle, |11\rangle\}$, CNOT is given by

$$U_{\text{CNOT}} = \begin{bmatrix} 1 & 0 & 0 & 0 \\ 0 & 1 & 0 & 0 \\ 0 & 0 & 0 & 1 \\ 0 & 0 & 1 & 0 \end{bmatrix}, \tag{4.58}$$

and it is represented as shown in Fig. 4.9.

The CNOT can be used to perform selective state copying. We have found that we cannot copy an arbitrary state; quantum mechanics does not allow cloning. However, in information processing, we have a preselected basis, the computational basis. In this basis we can use the CNOT to duplicate quantum information. It is easily seen that the circuit in Fig. 4.9 effects the transformation

$$(\alpha|0\rangle_1 + \beta|1\rangle_1)\,|0\rangle_2 \Rightarrow \alpha|0\rangle_1|0\rangle_2 + \beta|1\rangle_1|1\rangle_2. \tag{4.59}$$

This deposits the quantum information $\{\alpha, \beta\}$ in both systems. This redundancy may be useful in securing quantum information against random losses.

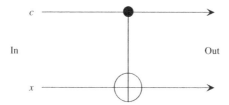

Figure 4.9   Symbol for a two-qubit controlled-NOT gate.

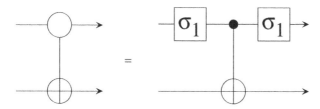

Figure 4.10   Symbol for an alternative two-qubit controlled-NOT gate.

Example: Alternative CNOT   The transformation

$$U_A = \begin{bmatrix} 0 & 1 & 0 & 0 \\ 1 & 0 & 0 & 0 \\ 0 & 0 & 1 & 0 \\ 0 & 0 & 0 & 1 \end{bmatrix} \tag{4.60}$$

can be realized as shown in Fig. 4.10. This is seen directly to give the desired result because σ_1 swaps the states $|0\rangle$ and $|1\rangle$.

Example: Multiple Control   Figure 4.11 shows a case where one control line performs the CNOT operation on two outgoing states. We can also implement multiple control so that one output is conditioned on the values of two control lines. In Fig. 4.12 we show a situation with three input qubits $\{a, b, c\}$. The output is defined to be $\{a, b, c \oplus (a \wedge b)\}$. From this we see that the output c is changed if and only if $\{a = 1, b = 1\}$. This is called a *Toffoli gate*, and it is easily seen to be reversible; the three outputs are permutations of the three inputs. The Toffoli gate is universal; any logical function can be constructed from such gates. A proof of this is shown in Fig. 4.13, where we construct the Sheffer stroke logical function $\overline{x} \wedge \overline{y}$ (see Sec. 4.1.1). From the figure we see that the circuit does, indeed, perform the desired operation. The Toffoli gate can be realized using CNOT and single-qubit gates. Such a circuit is shown in Fig. 4.14, where we have introduced the operator

$$V = \sqrt{\frac{-i}{2}} \begin{bmatrix} 1 & i \\ i & 1 \end{bmatrix}, \tag{4.61}$$

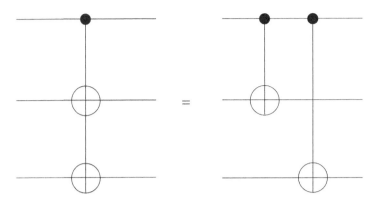

Figure 4.11   Symbol for a three-qubit controlled-NOT gate.

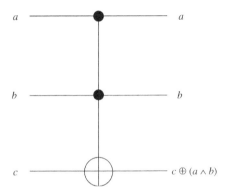

Figure 4.12   Symbol for a three-qubit Toffoli gate.

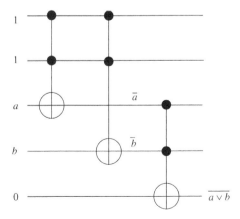

Figure 4.13   Sheffer stroke logical operation as a five-qubit circuit.

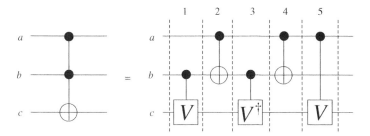

Figure 4.14 Breakdown of the Toffoli gate into two-qubit operations.

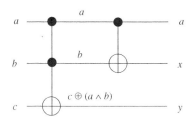

Figure 4.15 Binary addition circuit.

which is the square root of NOT and

$$V^2 = \sigma_1; \quad VV^\dagger = V^\dagger V = 1. \tag{4.62}$$

Cutting the circuit into consecutive steps denoted by the numbers $\{1, \ldots, 5\}$ in Fig. 4.14, we have the following transformations ($b = 0, 1$):

$$|0, 0, b\rangle \overset{1-5}{\to} |0, 0, b\rangle,$$

$$|0, 1, b\rangle \overset{1-2}{\to} |0, 1, Vb\rangle \overset{3-4}{\to} |0, 1, V^\dagger Vb\rangle \overset{5}{\to} |0, 1, b\rangle,$$

$$|1, 0, b\rangle \overset{1-2}{\to} |1, 1, b\rangle \overset{3-4}{\to} |1, 0, V^\dagger b\rangle \overset{5}{\to} |1, 0, VV^\dagger b\rangle = |1, 0, b\rangle,$$

$$|1, 1, b\rangle \overset{1-2}{\to} |1, 0, Vb\rangle \overset{3-4}{\to} |1, 1, Vb\rangle \overset{5}{\to} |1, 1, V^2 b\rangle = |1, 1, \sigma_3 b\rangle.$$

From this we can see that the circuit performs the operation of the Toffoli gate.

Application We denote addition modulo 2 by $\oplus$. The circuit in Fig. 4.15, with $c = 0$, is then seen to give the outputs

$$x = a \oplus b,$$
$$y = 0 \oplus (a \wedge b) = (a \wedge b). \tag{4.63}$$

It may thus be used in a computer to achieve binary addition, with y giving the carry bit.

Example: State Swapping We can represent the controlled NOT operation by the transformation

$$|a, b\rangle \Rightarrow |a, a \oplus b\rangle. \tag{4.64}$$

Using this formula, we can see that the gate given in Fig. 4.16 swaps the states

$$
\begin{aligned}
|a, b\rangle &\Rightarrow |a, a \oplus b\rangle \\
&\Rightarrow |a \oplus (a \oplus b), a \oplus b\rangle \\
&= |b, a \oplus b\rangle \\
&\Rightarrow |b, (a \oplus b) \oplus b\rangle \\
&= |b, a\rangle.
\end{aligned} \tag{4.65}
$$

This transformation performs the operation

$$
\begin{aligned}
&U_{SW} (c_0|0\rangle_1 + c_1|1\rangle_1)(a_0|0\rangle_2 + a_1|1\rangle_2) \\
&= (a_0|0\rangle_1 + a_1|1\rangle_1)(c_0|0\rangle_2 + c_1|1\rangle_2).
\end{aligned} \tag{4.66}
$$

An explicit representation of this operator is

$$
\begin{aligned}
U_{SW} = |0\rangle_1|0\rangle_2 \otimes {}_2\langle0|_1\langle0| + |1\rangle_1|1\rangle_2 \otimes {}_2\langle1|_1\langle1| \\
+ |0\rangle_1|1\rangle_2 \otimes {}_2\langle0|_1\langle1| + |1\rangle_1|0\rangle_2 \otimes {}_2\langle1|_1\langle0|.
\end{aligned} \tag{4.67}
$$

Exercise Show that the circuit in Fig. 4.17 transforms the input states in the computational basis into Bell states:

$$
\begin{aligned}
|00\rangle &\rightarrow \frac{1}{\sqrt{2}} (|00\rangle + |11\rangle), \\
|01\rangle &\rightarrow \frac{1}{\sqrt{2}} (|01\rangle + |10\rangle), \\
|10\rangle &\rightarrow \frac{1}{\sqrt{2}} (|10\rangle - |11\rangle), \\
|11\rangle &\rightarrow \frac{1}{\sqrt{2}} (|01\rangle - |10\rangle).
\end{aligned} \tag{4.68}
$$

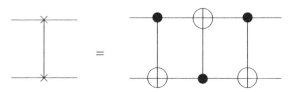

Figure 4.16 Bit-value swapping symbol and the circuit that performs swapping.

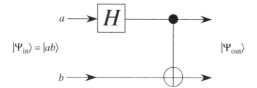

$$|\Psi_{\text{in}}\rangle = |ab\rangle \qquad\qquad |\Psi_{\text{out}}\rangle$$

Figure 4.17 Circuit for creating Bell states from computational basis states.

Figure 4.18 Two equivalent circuits.

Example We show that the two circuits in Fig. 4.18 effect the same transformation. This follows from showing that the first one transforms the state

$$|\psi_{\text{in}}\rangle = (a|0\rangle + b|1\rangle)\,(\alpha|0\rangle + \beta|1\rangle) \qquad (4.69)$$

into

$$|\psi_{\text{out}}\rangle = \left(\frac{(a+b)\,(|0\rangle + |1\rangle)}{2}\right)\left(\frac{(\alpha+\beta)\,|0\rangle + (\alpha-\beta)\,|1\rangle}{\sqrt{2}}\right)$$
$$+ \left(\frac{(a-b)\,(|0\rangle - |1\rangle)}{2}\right)\left(\frac{(\alpha+\beta)\,|1\rangle + (\alpha-\beta)\,|0\rangle}{\sqrt{2}}\right). \qquad (4.70)$$

The second circuit transforms the incoming state into

$$|\psi_{\text{out}}\rangle = \alpha\,(a|0\rangle + b|1\rangle)\left(\frac{(|0\rangle + |1\rangle)}{\sqrt{2}}\right)$$
$$+ \beta\,(a|1\rangle + b|0\rangle)\left(\frac{(|0\rangle - |1\rangle)}{\sqrt{2}}\right). \qquad (4.71)$$

It is easy to show that both these states are equal to

$$|\psi_{\text{out}}\rangle = \frac{1}{\sqrt{2}}\left[(\alpha a + \beta b)\,|00\rangle + (\alpha a - \beta b)\,|01\rangle\right.$$
$$\left. + (\alpha b + \beta a)\,|10\rangle + (\alpha b - \beta a)\,|11\rangle\right]. \qquad (4.72)$$

This shows the equivalence of the circuits.

4.2.5 Universal Quantum Gates

A set of quantum gates $\{U_i\}$ is said to be *universal* if any quantum logical operation can be written in the form

$$U_K = \prod_{U_k \subset \{U_i\}} U_k. \tag{4.73}$$

It is possible to show that this can always be achieved by the use of single-qubit operations. Thus, we can write the CNOT matrix (4.58) in the form

$$U_{\text{CNOT}} = \begin{bmatrix} \mathbf{1} & \mathbf{0} \\ \mathbf{0} & \sigma_1 \end{bmatrix}. \tag{4.74}$$

We note the similarity between this statement and the fact that an arbitrary rotation in dimensions d can be built up from a sequence of rotations around the basis axes.

In quantum computing we have the result:

Theorem   Single-qubit operations and CNOT gates form a universal set.

These can be used to construct a universal quantum logic network. Sometimes the exact construction of a complicated quantum operation may require excessively many components. Then an approximate system can be devised in which only a more limited number of parts are used.

4.2.6 Quantum Measurement Circuit

The special role played by measurements in quantum mechanics suggests the introduction of a special symbol to denote the presence of a measurement. This, however, implies the extraction of classical information from the system. The corresponding operation is no longer reversible; some quantum information is lost. The information acquired may, however, be used to control a later stage in information processing. Thus, care is needed in applying the operation of measurement in an information-processing network.

The symbol for a measurement circuit is shown in Fig. 4.19, illustrating both a quantum input and a classical measured value as output (double line). In Fig. 4.20 we indicate how the outcome of the measurement may be used to define which unitary transformation is applied to the data bit.

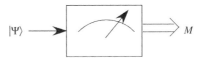

Figure 4.19 Symbol for a measurement gate.

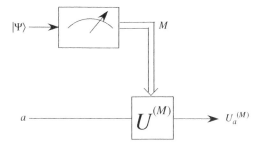

Figure 4.20   Measurement gate as part of a conditional logic circuit.

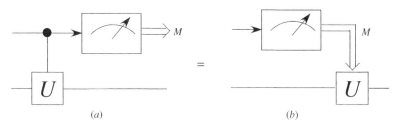

Figure 4.21   Two possible orders of performance for the measurement and unitary operation U.

Use of the measurement circuit is greatly facilitated by the following observation: As far as the data bit is concerned, it does not matter whether we measure the control state and select which unitary operator to apply, or alternatively, apply the unitary transformation as determined by the control state and measure this after the application.

The statement above can be shown by considering the circuit in Fig. 4.21a. The initial input state is taken to be

$$|\Psi_{in}\rangle = c_0|00\rangle + c_1|01\rangle + c_2|10\rangle + c_3|11\rangle, \tag{4.75}$$

which by the control is transformed into

$$|\Psi_{in}\rangle = c_0|00\rangle + c_1|01\rangle + c_2U|10\rangle + c_3U|11\rangle. \tag{4.76}$$

In the measurement of Fig. 4.21a, observing the value "0" on the first bit, we conclude that the data state is to be

$$|\psi_0\rangle = c_0|0\rangle + c_1|1\rangle. \tag{4.77}$$

If we observe the value "1," the state is

$$|\psi_1\rangle = c_0U|0\rangle + c_1U|1\rangle = U\left(c_0|0\rangle + c_1|1\rangle\right). \tag{4.78}$$

However, if we use the circuit in Fig. 4.21*b*, we decide in a classical way whether we apply the operator U or not, depending on the outcome. But the procedure will reproduce the states (4.77) and (4.78) exactly. Consequently, we find that measurement circuits can be moved to the end of the data information process. The ability to sustain linear superpositions offered by quantum theory makes it possible always to carry all potential outcomes of measurements to the end, where the ultimate choice of classical outputs can be recorded. The argumentation derives from the property of entangled states (see Sec. 2.3.2): When observations are made on one component of an entangled pair, the operation induces an incoherent mixture of the possible correlated outcomes in the other system. The corresponding reduced density matrix can be interpreted as describing an ensemble of recorded measurements or a prediction for outcomes obtained in possible future measurements. These interpretations closely correspond to the difference in Fig. 4.21*a* and *b*.

Application: Teleportation Circuit   We consider the teleportation process discussed in Sec. 2.2.3 as the information-processing circuit shown in Fig. 4.22*a*. The measurement circuit with two input lines denotes a Bell state measurement. The topmost input line contains the quantum data in the state

$$|\psi\rangle_1 = \alpha|0\rangle_1 + \beta|1\rangle_1, \qquad (4.79)$$

and the two lower inputs carry the entangled state

$$|\psi\rangle_{23} = \frac{1}{\sqrt{2}} \left(|00\rangle_{23} + |11\rangle_{23}\right); \qquad (4.80)$$

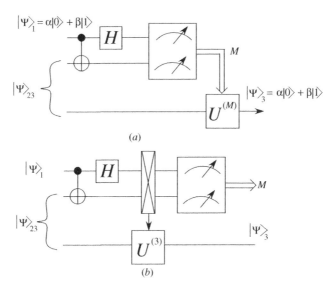

Figure 4.22   Two possible circuits for performing teleportation.

party A has access to the first two lines and party B, to the third line. Party A applies a CNOT gate to obtain the state

$$|\Psi\rangle_{123} = \frac{1}{\sqrt{2}} [\alpha|0\rangle_1 (|00\rangle_{23} + |11\rangle_{23}) + \beta|1\rangle_1 (|10\rangle_{23} + |01\rangle_{23})]. \qquad (4.81)$$

Party A then sends the first line through a Hadamard gate to obtain

$$|\Psi\rangle_{123} = \frac{1}{2} [\alpha (|0\rangle_1 + |1\rangle_1) (|00\rangle_{23} + |11\rangle_{23})$$
$$+ \beta (|0\rangle_1 - |1\rangle_1) (|10\rangle_{23} + |01\rangle_{23})]. \qquad (4.82)$$

Rearranging (4.82), we find that

$$|\Psi\rangle_{123} = \frac{1}{2} [|00\rangle_{12} (\alpha|0\rangle_3 + \beta|1\rangle_3) + |01\rangle_{12} (\alpha|1\rangle_3 + \beta|0\rangle_3)$$
$$+ |10\rangle_{12} (\alpha|0\rangle_3 - \beta|1\rangle_3) + |11\rangle_{12} (\alpha|1\rangle_3 - \beta|0\rangle_3)]. \qquad (4.83)$$

Next, party A performs a measurement in the basis $\{|ab\rangle_{12}\}$ and acquires 2 bits of classical information. Transmitting this information to party B, this person will then know in which basis the quantum information is to be found. If the person wishes, he or she can perform a rotation on the output state to restore the information to the computational basis $\{|0\rangle_3, |1\rangle_3\}$, which requires exactly the 2 bits of information available.

Using our earlier observation, we can rewrite the teleportation circuit of Fig. 4.22a in the form of Fig. 4.22b. The measurements have all been postponed to the end of the processing, but it is obvious that the same result will emerge upon application of the rotation $U_{ab}^{(3)}$ conditioned on the state in the basis $\{|ab\rangle_{12}\}$. The figure introduces the symbol signifying an application of a unitary transformation on state 3 conditioned on state $|\Psi\rangle_{12}$. It can be represented by the operator

$$S_c = \sum_{a,b} |ab\rangle_{12} \otimes {}_{12}\langle ab| U_{ab}^{(3)}. \qquad (4.84)$$

Subsequent final observation in this basis projects the state of system 3 on the correct quantum state $\alpha|0\rangle_3 + \beta|1\rangle_3$.

4.2.7 Quantum Fourier Transform

An operation of great utility in quantum information processing is the Fourier transform. The transform is applied to a finite space of N components defined by the dimensionality of the state space sustaining our quantum information. In most cases, this consists of qubits, so we have a dimensionality of the type $N = 2^n$.

The Fourier transformation is best expressed in terms of the Nth root of unity, defined by

$$(\omega_N)^N = 1. \qquad (4.85)$$

This equation has the N solutions

$$(\omega_N)^k = \left[\exp\left(i \frac{2\pi}{N} \right) \right]^k, \tag{4.86}$$

where $k \in \{0, 1, \ldots, N - 1\}$. We denote by ω_N the quantity $\exp[i(2\pi/N)]$. The Fourier transform is now defined on the basis $\{|0\rangle, |1\rangle, \ldots, |N - 1\rangle\}$ as follows:

$$|n\rangle_F = \frac{1}{\sqrt{N}} \sum_{k=0}^{N-1} (\omega_N)^{nk} |k\rangle, \tag{4.87}$$

where $n \in \{0, 1, \ldots, N - 1\}$. It is easily verified that this gives a complete orthonormal basis in the state space. Its inversion is easily obtained from the relation

$$\sum_{k=0}^{N-1} (\omega_N)^{k(n-m)} = N \delta_{nm}. \tag{4.88}$$

As a matrix, the transformation is given by

$$F_N = \frac{1}{\sqrt{N}} \begin{bmatrix} 1 & 1 & 1 & 1 & \cdots & 1 \\ 1 & \omega_N & \omega_N^2 & \omega_N^3 & \cdots & \omega_N^{N-1} \\ 1 & \omega_N^2 & \omega_N^4 & \omega_N^6 & \cdots & \omega_N^{2(N-1)} \\ 1 & \omega_N^3 & \omega_N^6 & \omega_N^9 & \cdots & \omega_N^{3(N-1)} \\ \cdots & \cdots & \cdots & \cdots & \cdots & \omega_N^{(N-2)(N-1)} \\ 1 & \omega_N^{N-1} & \omega_N^{2(N-1)} & \omega_N^{3(N-1)} & \cdots & \omega_N^{(N-1)(N-1)} \end{bmatrix}. \tag{4.89}$$

The general element is of the form $(\omega_N)^{kn}$, and if N is a prime, no product kn will ever be a multiple of N, and ones appear only at the top and the side of the matrix. Of course, when $nk = aN + b$, with integers a and b the term becomes $(\omega_N)^b$. If N has factors, some of the lines above will contain periods shorter than their full length. This is a property utilized later to find the factors of an integer.

The relation between the coefficients in the original basis and the Fourier basis follows from

$$\sum_{k=0}^{N-1} x_k |k\rangle = \sum_{n=0}^{N-1} y_n |n\rangle_F = \sum_{n=0}^{N-1} y_n \left(\frac{1}{\sqrt{N}} \sum_{k=0}^{N-1} (\omega_N)^{nk} \right) |k\rangle, \tag{4.90}$$

from which we see that

$$x_k = \frac{1}{\sqrt{N}} \sum_{n=0}^{N-1} (\omega_N)^{nk} y_n, \tag{4.91}$$

which is easily inverted using (4.88).

It is straightforward to show how to implement a Fourier transform on a quantum state. To be explicit, we carry out the construction in the case $N = 4$, when the transform is

$$
\begin{bmatrix} |0\rangle_F \\ |1\rangle_F \\ |2\rangle_F \\ |3\rangle_F \end{bmatrix} = \frac{1}{\sqrt{4}} \begin{bmatrix} 1 & 1 & 1 & 1 \\ 1 & \omega_4 & \omega_4^2 & \omega_4^3 \\ 1 & \omega_4^2 & 1 & \omega_4^2 \\ 1 & \omega_4^3 & \omega_4^2 & \omega_4 \end{bmatrix} \begin{bmatrix} |0\rangle \\ |1\rangle \\ |2\rangle \\ |3\rangle \end{bmatrix} .
\tag{4.92}
$$

We can rewrite this if we write the states in binary notation so that

$$
|k\rangle \equiv |2a + b\rangle \equiv |ab\rangle,
\tag{4.93}
$$

where a and b belong to $\{0, 1\}$. We now write

$$
\begin{aligned}
|k\rangle_F &= \frac{1}{2} \left(|0\rangle_1 + \omega_4^{2k}|1\rangle_1 \right) \left(|0\rangle_2 + \omega_4^{k}|1\rangle_2 \right) \\
&= \frac{1}{2} \left(|00\rangle_{12} + \omega_4^{k}|01\rangle_{12} + \omega_4^{2k}|10\rangle_{12} + \omega_4^{3k}|11\rangle_{12} \right) .
\end{aligned}
\tag{4.94}
$$

Interpreting the two-qubit state labels as binary numbers, we see that this implements the Fourier transform. As the first form consists of a combination of Hadamard transforms and phase gates, we can easily design the circuit implementing the operation (see Fig. 4.23). A little contemplation convinces one that the product form used in (4.94) can be used for any dimension 2^n.

Exercise 1   Show by direct evaluation that the expression

$$
\frac{\left(|0\rangle_1 + \omega_8^{4k}|1\rangle_1 \right) \left(|0\rangle_2 + \omega_8^{2k}|1\rangle_2 \right) \left(|0\rangle_3 + \omega_8^{k}|1\rangle_3 \right)}{\sqrt{8}}
$$

gives the Fourier transform on a three-qubit system. Here the states

$$
|a\rangle_1 |b\rangle_2 |c\rangle_3 = |abc\rangle
$$

are taken to code the binary number abc.

Exercise 2   Show that the matrix (4.89) consists of orthonormal column vectors that contain the various permutations of the nontrivial powers ω_N^k ($k < N$). Their orthogonality against the first column implies that

$$
\sum_{k=0}^{N-1} (\omega_N)^k = 0.
\tag{4.95}
$$

What is the interpretation of this relation in the complex plane?

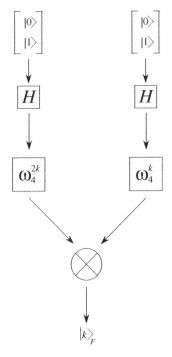

Figure 4.23 Circuit for a Fourier transform when $N = 4$.

Application: State Preparation   If we prepare the "zero" state, (4.87) tells us that it is the evenly weighted input state for quantum computations

$$|0\rangle_F = \frac{1}{\sqrt{N}} \sum_{k=0}^{N-1} |k\rangle. \tag{4.96}$$

Combining this with a CNOT, it can be used to perform the operation of creating a maximally entangled state [see (4.59)].

4.3 QUANTUM ALGORITHMS

The material above presents possible transformations that we hope to effect in a quantum information-processing device. The next question is what to do with such a system once it has been realized. There is a quantum computing software problem which asks how to utilize the large-scale parallelity offered in principle by quantum operations. It is not yet clear that there are many cases when such efficient use can be devised. The present great interest in quantum computing was started in 1994 when Peter Shor showed that, in principle, large numbers may be factored more efficiently than on a classical computer. To understand the progress offered in this field, we first need to present the classical background, which shows why the problem has attracted such wide interest.

4.3.1 Public Key Code

In both business and politics, how to communicate to one's partners without the danger of enemies being able to eavesdrop on the secret messages has always been a central problem. These can generally be assumed to consist of strings of numbers in a suitably chosen basis. The only provably fully secure method is that both parties know a random number as long as the message. This is added by the sender to the message, and the process is easily reversed by the receiver. As long as the random number is used only once, no deciphering method can be used by an outsider to read the message. The weak point here is obviously that the key has to be transmitted physically between the parties, which is always a point where interception or bribery can interfere. Thus, it created great interest when a system was devised that allows (nearly) secure communication without prior exchange of code sequences. This is the now famous *public key system* (RSA).

The use of the public key system is based on advanced number theory. It is not possible to go into the technical derivations of the results here, but we can easily demonstrate how the system is used in practice. It is based on the concept of numbers modulo some integer N. We say that two integers are equal modulo N, $x = y(\text{mod}N)$ if there exists an integer n such that

$$x = y + nN. \tag{4.97}$$

Modular arithmetics is very much like ordinary one because

$$(x + aN) + (y + bN) = x + y + (a + b)N,$$
$$(x + aN) * (y + bN) = x * y + (xb + ya + abN)N. \tag{4.98}$$

If $x + y$ or $x * y$ turn up larger than N, the appropriate factor has to be extracted and added to the multiplier of N on the right-hand side.

In its simplest form, the procedure to realize the RSA protocol is as follows:

1. Choose two primes p and q and set $N = p * q$.
2. Calculate the (Euler) function $\varphi(N) = (p - 1) * (q - 1)$.
3. Choose a number a with no factor common with $\varphi(N)$. There exists an easy (Euclid) algorithm to find common factors, if they exist.
4. Find integers $\{x, y\}$ such that

$$xa + y\varphi(N) = 1. \tag{4.99}$$

5. Make the pair of integers $\{N, a\}$ universally available by a suitable public channel.

6. Somebody, somewhere wants to send you the message string z without anybody being able to intercept the message. It is assumed that $z < p$ and $z < q$. The sender now calculates the number $m = z^a \pmod{N}$.

7. The number m is sent to you by any means available, not excluding publicly open channels.

8. Now you, as the receiver, know the number x, so you can use it to compute

$$z = m^x \pmod{N}, \tag{4.100}$$

which gives you access to the message that was transmitted.

We are not in a position here to prove that this method works, but we can demonstrate it by a simple example. Assume that $p = 3, q = 41$, giving $N = 123$. The calculations then proceed by

$$\varphi(N) = (3 - 1)(41 - 1) = 80,$$

$$a = 27 \text{ (no factor with 80)},$$

$$3 * 27 - 1 * 80 = 1 \Rightarrow \{x, y\} = \{3, -1\}.$$

Publish $\{123, 27\}$. If the sender has the message $z = 5$, we calculate

$$m = 5^{27} \pmod{123} = 125^9 = 2^9 = 128 * 4 = 4 * 5 = 20.$$

Note that in the intermediate steps we do not write (mod 123) down explicitly, for brevity. When the receiver obtains the number 20, he or she calculates

$$20^3 \pmod{123} = 200 * 40 = 77 * 2 * 20 = 154 * 20$$
$$= 31 * 4 * 5 = 124 * 5 = 1 * 5 = 5.$$

Thus, the original message is recovered.

The method above is based on the fact that finding the factors of large integers N is assumed to be a calculationally difficult problem requiring an exponentially large number of trials estimated to grow as $\sqrt{N} = 2^{(1/2)\log_2 N}$. All known factoring algorithms are of this type, even if there exists no proof excluding the existence of a factoring algorithm requiring only polynomial number of operations. In practice, the numbers p and q are on the order of 10^{100} to 10^{200}. Thus, even as it stands, the procedure requires extensive use of existing computing resources.

One should also note that the communication is one-sided. Anybody can send a secret message to a receiver who cannot send any information back without adding additional features to the procedure.

4.3.2   Quantum Factoring Algorithm

Theoretical Foundation   The quantum algorithm to factor large numbers is based on another sequence of operations derived from the classical theory of numbers. The procedure to factor an integer N is based on the following steps:

1. Find a number A such that

$$A^2 = 1 \,(\text{mod}\, N).$$

2. Write
$$(A - 1)(A + 1) = 0 \,(\text{mod}\, N).$$

   Thus, $(A - 1)$ or $(A + 1)$ must contain factors common with N.
3. This gives a factor of N. There is an easy algorithm (Euclid) to find the common factors of $\{(A - 1), (A + 1), N\}$.
4. The procedure is to choose a number y with no factor common with N and then to find a period r such that $y^{l+r} = y^l \,(\text{mod}\, N)$, which gives

$$y^r = 1 \,(\text{mod}\, N).$$

Thus, we may write

$$\left(y^{r/2} - 1\right)\left(y^{r/2} + 1\right) = 0 \,(\text{mod}\, N).$$

Then $\left(y^{r/2} \pm 1\right)$ must contain factors in common with N.

This procedure works if r is even and the y chosen gives an acceptable period. If it fails, one must start from the beginning, but it can be shown that the process is efficient enough to give acceptable results as the basis for a quantum algorithm.

It is evident that the procedure above gives a satisfactory result when it works. This is best seen in some simple examples.

Example 1   Assume that $N = 15$ and choose $y = 7$. The calculations to be performed are

n	0	1	2	3	4	5
y^n	1	7	49	343	2401	16,807
$y^n \,(\text{mod}\, 15)$	1	7	4	13	1	7

Thus, the period $r = 4$ and we have

$$y^{r/2} - 1 = 48 = 2^4 * 3,$$

$$y^{r/2} + 1 = 50 = 2 * 5^2.$$

From this it is easy to find the factors 3 and 5 of 15.

Example 2 Assume that $N = 35$ and choose $y = 13$. The calculations to be performed are

n	0	1	2	3	4	5
y^n	1	13	169	2197	28,561	371,293
$y^n \pmod{35}$	1	13	29	27	1	13

Thus, the period $r = 4$ and we have

$$y^{r/2} - 1 = 168,$$

$$y^{r/2} + 1 = 170.$$

From this it is not obvious what the factors of 35 are. Then the Euclid algorithm comes to one's aid: To find the common factor of two integers A and B, perform the division

$$\frac{A}{B} = \text{integer} + a.$$

Then replace A by B and B by a and continue until the rest of the division is zero. The last number A is then the common factor. The sequences give in this case

$$168/35 \Rightarrow 35/28 \Rightarrow 28/7 \Rightarrow 7/0,$$

$$170/35 \Rightarrow 35/30 \Rightarrow 30/5 \Rightarrow 5/0.$$

This uniquely picks out the factors 7 and 5. This example shows how rapidly the procedure leads to large numbers; consequently, only the recent emergence of powerful computers has made such methods practical.

Quantum Algorithm To start the application of the method from the preceding section to a quantum implementation, we assume that we have devised a black box (an oracle) that provides us with the following computational process:

$$\sum_x |x\rangle_1 |0\rangle_2 \Rightarrow \sum_x |x\rangle_1 |y^x (\text{mod } N)\rangle_2, \tag{4.101}$$

where N is the number to be factored and y is a number chosen as discussed above. To make the algorithm work, we must choose a dimension D of the state space such that $D > N$. Here we assume that $N = 15$ and let $x \in \{0, 1, \ldots, 15\}$. After consulting the oracle, we find the state (see above)

$$\begin{aligned} |\Psi_{\text{out}}\rangle = \frac{1}{\sqrt{16}} (&|0\rangle_1 |1\rangle_2 + |1\rangle_1 |7\rangle_2 + |2\rangle_1 |4\rangle_2 + |3\rangle_1 |13\rangle_2 \\ &+ |4\rangle_1 |1\rangle_2 + |5\rangle_1 |7\rangle_2 + |6\rangle_1 |4\rangle_2 + |7\rangle_1 |13\rangle_2 \\ &+ |8\rangle_1 |1\rangle_2 + |9\rangle_1 |7\rangle_2 + |10\rangle_1 |4\rangle_2 + |11\rangle_1 |13\rangle_2 \\ &+ |12\rangle_1 |1\rangle_2 + |13\rangle_1 |7\rangle_2 + |14\rangle_1 |4\rangle_2 + |15\rangle_1 |13\rangle_2). \end{aligned} \tag{4.102}$$

The period here is obviously $r = 4$, but this is not accessible to the quantum observer.

Now project this state on the second system without reading the outcome. The postmeasurement state of the first system is then of the form

$$|\varphi_l\rangle = \frac{1}{\sqrt{4}} (|l\rangle_1 + |l + r\rangle_1 + |l + 2r\rangle_1 + |l + 3r\rangle_1), \tag{4.103}$$

where $l \in \{0, 1, 2, 3\}$. This is called the *offset*, and it is not known after the measurement has been performed. The value observed in the second system is $y^l \pmod N$, but this cannot in itself be of any use.

We now perform the Fourier transform of the states to give

$$|y\rangle \Rightarrow \frac{1}{\sqrt{16}} \sum_{x=0}^{15} \omega_{16}^{xy} |x\rangle. \tag{4.104}$$

Applying this to (4.103) gives

$$|\varphi_l\rangle \Rightarrow \frac{1}{8} \sum_{x=0}^{15} \omega_{16}^{xl} |x\rangle \left(1 + \omega_{16}^{4x} + \omega_{16}^{8x} + \omega_{16}^{12x}\right). \tag{4.105}$$

The offset l has now moved to the prefactor, and the internal sum is written as

$$\left(1 + \omega_{16}^{4x} + \omega_{16}^{8x} + \omega_{16}^{12x}\right)$$
$$= \left\{1 + \exp\left[2\pi i \left(\frac{r}{16}x\right)\right] + \exp\left[2\pi i \left(\frac{r}{16}x\right)2\right] + \exp\left[2\pi i \left(\frac{r}{16}x\right)3\right]\right\}, \tag{4.106}$$

with $r = 4$. These are the powers $\{0, 1, 2, 3\}$ of the complex number $\omega^r = \exp\left[2\pi i \left(\frac{r}{16}x\right)\right] = i^x$, which for any x sum to zero unless x is a power of 4. In this case they add to the value 4, and the sum in (4.105) gives

$$|\varphi_l\rangle \Rightarrow \frac{1}{2} \left(|0\rangle + \omega_{16}^{4l}|4\rangle + \omega_{16}^{8l}|8\rangle + \omega_{16}^{12l}|12\rangle\right). \tag{4.107}$$

Now measuring the value of the state label, the result is of the form $m = k * 4$ ($k = 0, 1, 2, 3$). According to the construction it is also given by

$$m = k \frac{N + 1}{r}. \tag{4.108}$$

Here $N + 1$ and m are known and this makes it possible to find the integers k and r by trial and error. Thus, knowing the period r, we can proceed to find the factors of $N = 15$ in the present case. This example is, however, only for demonstration purposes. In the general case, N is huge and there is no guarantee that $(N + 1)/r \approx N/r$ is an integer. The method can, however, be made to work even in the more general case.

Actually, the first system need not be observed during the procedure. As we see from (4.102), the full quantum state can carry with it all the possible l-values, thanks to the superposition principle of quantum theory. After the Fourier transform (4.104) on the state (4.102), the sum over l appears only in the prefactor of state $|x\rangle$ in (4.106). Thus, the Fourier transform can be safely performed before the projective measurement. This possibility was suggested in the discussion of the measurement circuit in Sec. 4.2.6.

In the general case, the label of a state is of the form $|kr + l\rangle$. However, as there are r possible values of l (i.e., $l = 0$ to $l = r - 1$), we have to have

$$K = \frac{N+1}{r} \approx \frac{N}{r} \qquad (4.109)$$

values of k (i.e., $k \in \{0, K - 1\}$). To see the principle behind the method, let us assume that K is an integer. Then in the general case the normalized state after the projection on the second system is of the form

$$|\varphi_l\rangle = \sqrt{\frac{r}{N}} \sum_{k=0}^{K-1} |kr + l\rangle. \qquad (4.110)$$

We now perform the quantum Fourier transform

$$|kr + l\rangle \Rightarrow \frac{1}{\sqrt{N}} \sum_{x=0}^{N-1} \omega_N^{x(kr+l)} |x\rangle, \qquad (4.111)$$

where, as before,

$$\omega_N^N = 1. \qquad (4.112)$$

Rearranging the terms, we now find the result

$$|\varphi_l\rangle = \sqrt{r} \sum_{x=0}^{N-1} \left(\frac{1}{N} \sum_{k=0}^{K} \omega_N^{xkr} \right) \omega_N^{xl} |x\rangle. \qquad (4.113)$$

However, if r is a factor of N, we have

$$\frac{1}{N} \sum_{k=0}^{K} \omega_N^{xkr} = \frac{1}{r} \delta(xr|mN), \qquad (4.114)$$

where the $\delta(a|b)$ function is zero except if $a = b$. This again derives from the fact that the complex numbers ω_N^{xkr} form a symmetric star configuration of K unit vectors around the origin. Only if they all fall on the real axis do we get a nonvanishing result; and there are $K \approx N/r$ such terms altogether.

Now the sum in (4.113) becomes

$$|\varphi_l\rangle = \frac{1}{\sqrt{r}} \sum_{m=0}^{r-1} \left(\omega_N^l\right)^{mN/r} \left|m\frac{N}{r}\right\rangle. \tag{4.115}$$

Here again the unknown offset l affects the phases only. Now reading the state and observing a value M, we know that this must equal

$$M = m\frac{N}{r} \tag{4.116}$$

for some $m < r$. As we know M and N in this equation, we may again, by trial and error, find the integers m and r. If the process works, an even value of r allows the finding of the factors of N. If for some reason the procedure fails, we have to repeat it until we are successful. It can be shown that the total amount of time will grow only in a polynomial fashion. Thus, the method is, in principle, able to beat all presently known classical methods to find the factors.

As above, we point out that extraction of the separate l-states (4.110) need not be done actively. The quantum state can carry all possible offsets to the very end of the computation, and no intermediate measurements are necessary, as the value obtained is not actually utilized in the extraction of the desired information.

We have here assumed that the number defined in (4.109) is an integer. As the method really requires that $N + 1$ contains r as a factor, this assumption is not inconsistent. Thus in Example 2 we have $(35 + 1)/4 = 9$, and the quantum method will work as explained. If N is large enough, the method works approximately, even in the general case. However, the procedure then requires a more elaborate numerical evaluation to give the correct answer. This method is discussed in the references, and we will leave the subject by the presentation above, showing the basic principle.

4.3.3 Quantum Algorithms

General Considerations   A quantum algorithm must be able to utilize the large-scale parallelity implied by the computer transformation

$$\sum_x |x\rangle_1 |0\rangle_2 \Rightarrow \sum_x |x\rangle_1 |f(x)\rangle_2. \tag{4.117}$$

If we have to look at the states $|f(x)\rangle$ one by one, we are doing no better than the classical computer. The observables that we use to probe the ensuing state must somehow be of the form

$$M^{(2)} = \sum_\mu |\mu\rangle_2 \, M_\mu \, {}_2\langle\mu|, \tag{4.118}$$

where

$$|M_\mu| \approx \text{constant for } \forall\mu. \tag{4.119}$$

Because for reversible computations, the states $\{|f(x)\rangle_2\}$ span the full space, we have, from (4.117),

$$\langle M^{(2)}\rangle = \sum_x {}_2\langle f(x)|M^{(2)}|f(x)\rangle_2. \tag{4.120}$$

Only observables of the type (4.119) are expected to sample all the outcomes of the computation evenly. Thus, they may define the class of questions that can be fruitful in the context of quantum computations. This is highly speculative, but it may be significant that in the successful algorithms found so far, the Fourier transform and the Hadamard tend to play a central role; they are of the class defined here.

Example: Grover Search Algorithm   In addition to the Shor algorithm, the *Grover algorithm* appears as a nontrivial application of quantum processing. A detailed description of the Grover algorithm is too lengthy to give here, but we consider its basic aspects as an example. Consider a large database where items are labeled by integer numbers denoted by x, which ranges from 0 to $N - 1$. We wish to find, as fast as possible, the label x_0, which relates to the item we want to locate. For simplicity we assume that there is one-to-one correspondence between labels and items.

Normally, one would go through each label x and compare it with x_0, and the time it takes to find the right item scales proportional to N. The Grover algorithm promises a scaling with $\sqrt{N}$.

The first and very crucial step in the algorithm is to assume that we have a fast oracle, which is able to take any label state $|x\rangle$, compare it with the database, and return the state in the form $(-1)^{f(x)}|x\rangle$, where $f(x) = 1$ for $x = x_0$, and $f(x) = 0$ otherwise. The oracle is expected to work similarly for quantum superposition states as well.

To run the algorithm, we need a register of n quantum bits, with $N = 2^n$. The state of the register is denoted by $|\Psi\rangle$. We also assume that we can prepare an n-qubit state of equal superposition of all labels,

$$|X\rangle = \frac{1}{\sqrt{N}} \sum_{x=0}^{N-1} |x\rangle. \tag{4.121}$$

We initialize our register by setting $|\Psi\rangle = |X\rangle$. Note that for us x_0 is unknown; we supply to the oracle only the information that allows it to recognize x_0.

The second step is iterative. First we allow the oracle to operate on our register. It changes the sign of the term $|x_0\rangle$ in the superposition $|\Psi\rangle$. Then we apply to each qubit in our register the Hadamard transformation. Assuming a computational basis, we next multiply all states by -1, except the one standing for the number 0. The iteration step is completed with another Hadamard transformation for each qubit. The Hadamard–phase shift–Hadamard operation actually corresponds to $2|X\rangle\langle X| - I$ (note that the content of Ψ changes in each iterative step, but initially we have $|\Psi\rangle = |X\rangle$).

The interesting aspect here is that after about $(\pi/4)\sqrt{N}$ iterative steps, the content of our register has been reduced to a single number, x_0 (i.e., $|\Psi\rangle \rightarrow |x_0\rangle$). The action of each iterative step is to increase the weight of the state $|x_0\rangle$ in $|\Psi\rangle$ at the expense of other label states. The iteration process is actually cyclic; further repetition of iterations will again reduce the weight of $|x_0\rangle$. The result can be generalized to the case where one has M different labels corresponding to the item or items we want to locate, but then the number of iterations depends on M as well.

The speed of the Grover algorithm relies on the fact that the number of single- and two-qubit gates needed to perform the necessary Hadamard and phase-shift operations for each iterative step scale with n. Also, it is assumed that for each iterative step only one fast call to the oracle is needed. And here lies a serious or perhaps even a fatal problem with the Grover algorithm: how to device a working and efficient quantum oracle. Since there are no serious proposals in sight for performing the oracle action sufficiently fast, especially for databases of practical interest, the Grover algorithm remains a rather academic example with limited use.

Exercise 1 Show that the Hadamard–phase shift–Hadamard cycle of an iterative step in the Grover algorithm corresponds to the unitary operation $2|X\rangle\langle X| - I$.

Exercise 2 Rewrite the equal superposition state as

$$|X\rangle = \frac{1}{\sqrt{N}}|x_0\rangle + \frac{\sqrt{N-1}}{\sqrt{N}}|X'\rangle, \tag{4.122}$$

where $|X'\rangle$ stands for the equal superposition of all the "wrong" labels and $\langle x_0|X'\rangle = 0$. Define an angle α so that $\cos(\alpha/2) = \sqrt{(N-1)/N}$ and $\sin(\alpha/2) = 1/\sqrt{N}$. In the Grover algorithm m iteration cycles lead to the state

$$|\Psi\rangle = \sin\frac{2m+1}{2}\alpha|x_0\rangle + \cos\frac{2m+1}{2}\alpha|X'\rangle. \tag{4.123}$$

Use the result to derive the scaling condition for the algorithm in the limit of large N.

Entanglement Purification In connection with quantum computations, the issue of necessary resources arises. To carry through a definite computation we need to determine:

- How big a data space is required
- How many individual processing units (gates) are needed
- How many entangled subsystems are needed to perform the operations
- How many basic operations (clock cycles) are needed to reach the goal

As we see, the amount of entanglement is counted as an essential part of the resources. This derives from the fact that to be available when needed, entangled systems have to be prepared at some stage.

In general, entanglement is difficult to produce and maintain. Hence, procedures have been devised to extract entangled states from ensembles of systems with mixed states. They are called *entanglement purification* or *distillation*. We describe next one such procedure.

Purification provides a way to improve the degree of entanglement if this has been degraded by noise and perturbations. It works by assuming that an ensemble of systems is available, so that one may use a selection process to project out desired subensembles.

We consider the simple case of the entangled state

$$|I\rangle = \frac{1}{\sqrt{2}} \left(| - - \rangle + | + + \rangle\right). \tag{4.124}$$

We assume that this has become contaminated by random state flips, so that we have for some members of the ensemble the state

$$|II\rangle = \frac{1}{\sqrt{2}} \left(| - + \rangle + | + - \rangle\right). \tag{4.125}$$

If this has occurred with probability p, the ensemble of states is now described by the density matrix

$$\rho_1 = (1 - p)|I\rangle\langle I| + p|II\rangle\langle II|. \tag{4.126}$$

We next divide the ensemble into two halves and regard these as independent units; in the second half we relabel the states so that $|A\rangle = |I\rangle$ and $|B\rangle = |II\rangle$: The ensemble described by this part of the original ensemble is then described by

$$\rho_2 = (1 - p)|A\rangle\langle A| + p|B\rangle\langle B|. \tag{4.127}$$

The assembly consisting of these two ensembles is now described by the density matrix

$$\rho_1 \otimes \rho_2 = (1 - p)^2|IA\rangle\langle IA| + p^2|IIB\rangle\langle IIB|$$
$$+ (1 - p)p\left(|IB\rangle\langle IB| + |IIA\rangle\langle IIA|\right). \tag{4.128}$$

We now perform a local CNOT operation on the pairs from the two subensembles. This effects the transformations

$$|IA\rangle \Rightarrow |IA\rangle; \ |IB\rangle \Rightarrow |IB\rangle;$$
$$|IIA\rangle \Rightarrow |IIB\rangle; \ |IIB\rangle \Rightarrow |IIA\rangle. \tag{4.129}$$

Then we find that

$$\rho_1 \otimes \rho_2 \Rightarrow \left[(1-p)^2 \, |I\rangle\langle I| + p^2 |II\rangle\langle II|\right] |A\rangle\langle A|$$
$$+ (1-p)p \left(|I\rangle\langle I| + |II\rangle\langle II|\right) |B\rangle\langle B|. \qquad (4.130)$$

We now project the members of this ensemble on state $|A\rangle$ and normalize the result. In this procedure we lose half the members of the ensemble. The result is, however,

$$\rho = (1-p')|I\rangle\langle I| + p'|II\rangle\langle II|, \qquad (4.131)$$

where

$$p' = \frac{p^2}{p^2 + (1-p)^2},$$
$$1 - p' = \frac{(1-p)^2}{p^2 + (1-p)^2}. \qquad (4.132)$$

This is a mapping from p to p' which converges if $p < \frac{1}{2}$ initially. The shape of the function is given in Fig. 4.24. The dashed line shows an iteration starting from $p < \frac{1}{2}$ which converges toward $p = 0$. In that limit the density matrix is

$$\rho(\infty) = |I\rangle\langle I|, \qquad (4.133)$$

and the remaining members of the ensemble are in the desired pure state, constituting a resource for operations requiring entangled states.

We note that each application of the mapping loses half of the members of the original ensemble. After N applications we thus have a fraction of only 2^{-N} members surviving. If the ensemble really is inexhaustible, this does no harm. In realistic applications, such losses must, of course, be consider when implementing the processes.

There are additional aspects of purification of degraded ensembles, but this may suffice as an example of the types of operations that may be needed.

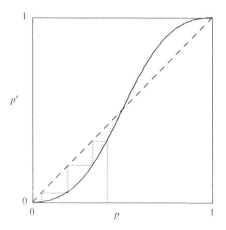

Figure 4.24 Purification process.

Nonlocal Information During the processing of quantum information, the original input data may be distributed over the various parts of the device in such a way that no local observation on any separate part can recover it. It has partly become transferred to the relations between the various parts, and its quantum character resides in the entanglement between several systems. Such a situation may also be used to one's advantage. The information is not generally available, but only those parties who can access the relevant subsystems can together decide what the information is.

Example 1 Consider an initial entangled state shared by two parties:

$$|\psi_1\rangle = \frac{i}{\sqrt{2}} \left(|0\rangle_1 |0\rangle_2 - |1\rangle_1 |1\rangle_2 \right). \tag{4.134}$$

We now apply a local transformation in system 1:

$$U^{(1)} = \exp\left(-i\frac{\theta}{2}\sigma_1^{(1)} \right) = \cos\frac{\theta}{2} - i\sigma_1^{(1)} \sin\frac{\theta}{2}. \tag{4.135}$$

The resulting state is

$$|\psi_2\rangle = U^{(1)}|\psi_1\rangle$$
$$= \frac{i}{\sqrt{2}} \left[\cos\frac{\theta}{2} \left(|0\rangle_1|0\rangle_2 - |1\rangle_1|1\rangle_2 \right) - i\sin\frac{\theta}{2} \left(|1\rangle_1|0\rangle_2 - |0\rangle_1|1\rangle_2 \right) \right]. \tag{4.136}$$

This can also be written as

$$|\psi_2\rangle = \frac{1}{\sqrt{2}} \left[\sin\frac{\theta}{2} \left(|1\rangle_1|0\rangle_2 - |0\rangle_1|1\rangle_2 \right) + i\cos\frac{\theta}{2} \left(|0\rangle_1|0\rangle_2 - |1\rangle_1|1\rangle_2 \right) \right]$$
$$= \exp\left(i\frac{\theta}{2}\sigma_1^{(2)} \right) |\psi_1\rangle. \tag{4.137}$$

Here the same state is seen to be obtained by a local operation in system 2. The same state can thus be reached by a local operation in either system.

But is the information about the angle θ locally accessible? To answer this question, we consider the state written in the following ways:

$$|\psi_2\rangle = \frac{i}{\sqrt{2}} \left[|0\rangle_1 \left(\cos\frac{\theta}{2}|0\rangle_2 + i\sin\frac{\theta}{2}|1\rangle_2 \right) \right.$$
$$\left. - |1\rangle_1 \left(\cos\frac{\theta}{2}|1\rangle_2 + i\sin\frac{\theta}{2}|0\rangle_2 \right) \right]$$
$$= \frac{1}{\sqrt{2}} \left[|0\rangle_2 \left(i\cos\frac{\theta}{2}|0\rangle_1 + \sin\frac{\theta}{2}|1\rangle_1 \right) \right.$$
$$\left. - |1\rangle_2 \left(i\cos\frac{\theta}{2}|1\rangle_1 + \sin\frac{\theta}{2}|0\rangle_1 \right) \right]. \tag{4.138}$$

These forms show that any projective measurement in either system 1 or 2 will send the information about the angle θ into the other system. Only by performing measurements in both systems and comparing notes can the observers in the two systems decide what the value of this angle is. Note, however, that even this combined operation requires an assembly of several systems.

Example 2   A second example of shared nonlocal information is given by a three-party system: In system 0, party A has the state

$$|\varphi\rangle_0 = \alpha|0\rangle + \beta|1\rangle. \tag{4.139}$$

She also has particle 1 in the entangled state

$$|\psi\rangle_{123} = \frac{1}{\sqrt{2}}\left(|000\rangle_{123} + |111\rangle_{123}\right). \tag{4.140}$$

Particle 2 is at the disposal of party B, and particle 3 is at the disposal of party C.
It is easy to show that the initial state can be written with Bell states $\{|\Psi_i\rangle\}$ as

$$|\Psi_{in}\rangle = |\varphi\rangle_0|\psi\rangle_{123}$$

$$= \frac{1}{2}\left[|\Psi_0\rangle_{01}\left(\alpha|00\rangle_{23} + \beta|11\rangle_{23}\right) + |\Psi_1\rangle_{01}\left(\alpha|11\rangle_{23} + \beta|00\rangle_{23}\right)\right.$$

$$\left.+ |\Psi_2\rangle_{01}\left(\alpha|00\rangle_{23} - \beta|11\rangle_{23}\right) + |\Psi_3\rangle_{01}\left(\alpha|11\rangle_{23} - \beta|00\rangle_{23}\right)\right] \tag{4.141}$$

(see Sec. 2.2.3). From this we see that if party A performs a Bell state measurement and openly declares the two-qubit result, everybody knows which state is shared by parties B and C.

However, even given an arbitrarily large ensemble, neither B nor C can access the quantum information $\{\alpha, \beta\}$. This is seen from the fact that they both have the reduced density matrix

$$\rho_2 = \rho_3 = \begin{bmatrix} \alpha^*\alpha & 0 \\ 0 & \beta^*\beta \end{bmatrix}; \tag{4.142}$$

thus, the phase information resides in the correlations between systems 2 and 3.
If we express the states in (4.141) in terms of the complementary basis, we find that

$$\left(\alpha|00\rangle_{23} + \beta|11\rangle_{23}\right) = \frac{1}{\sqrt{2}}\left[\frac{1}{\sqrt{2}}\left(|0\rangle_2 + |1\rangle_2\right)\left(\alpha|0\rangle_3 + \beta|1\rangle_3\right)\right.$$

$$\left.+ \frac{1}{\sqrt{2}}\left(|0\rangle_2 - |1\rangle_2\right)\left(\alpha|0\rangle_3 - \beta|1\rangle_3\right)\right]. \tag{4.143}$$

If party B now performs a measurement in the complementary basis and tells C the outcome, this can determine the information $\{\alpha, \beta\}$ from an ensemble of systems. The quantum information is now transferred to system 3. A similar argument works for the other terms in the result (4.141).

Example 3 Shared access can be demonstrated as follows. Party A has access to states $\{|1\rangle, |2\rangle, |3\rangle, |4\rangle\}$ and party B, to states $\{|\alpha\rangle, |\beta\rangle, |\gamma\rangle, |\delta\rangle\}$. The initial state is

$$|\psi_{\text{in}}\rangle = (a|1\rangle + b|2\rangle) \frac{1}{\sqrt{2}} (|\alpha\rangle + |\beta\rangle). \tag{4.144}$$

This implies that we have put the second system in a standard state. Such a reference state has been called *fiducial*.

We now apply two unitary transformations to this state. The first is given by

$$U_1 = \frac{1}{\sqrt{2}} [|4\rangle\langle 2| + |3\rangle\langle 1| + |2\rangle\langle 4| + |1\rangle\langle 3|$$

$$+ |1\rangle\langle 1| + |2\rangle\langle 2| - |3\rangle\langle 3| - |4\rangle\langle 4|]. \tag{4.145}$$

This duplicates the information in the first system:

$$U_1 (a|1\rangle + b|2\rangle) = \frac{1}{\sqrt{2}} (a|1\rangle + b|2\rangle + a|3\rangle + b|4\rangle). \tag{4.146}$$

The second transformation is given by

$$U_2 = \frac{1}{2} (|1\rangle\langle 1| + |2\rangle\langle 2|) \otimes \left[(|\alpha\rangle + |\beta\rangle) (\langle\gamma| + \langle\delta|) \right.$$

$$+ (|\gamma\rangle + |\delta\rangle) (\langle\alpha| + \langle\beta|) \Big] + |3\rangle\langle 3| \otimes |\alpha\rangle\langle\alpha|$$

$$+ |4\rangle\langle 4| \otimes |\beta\rangle\langle\beta| + |4\rangle\langle 3| \otimes |\alpha\rangle\langle\beta| + |3\rangle\langle 4| \otimes |\beta\rangle\langle\alpha| + W, \tag{4.147}$$

where the part denoted by W is needed to make the transformation unitary, but it is not needed in the present calculation.

With these definitions, we now find that

$$|\psi_{\text{fin}}\rangle = U_2 U_1 |\psi_{\text{in}}\rangle$$

$$= \frac{1}{\sqrt{2}} \left[(a|1\rangle + b|2\rangle) \frac{|\gamma\rangle + |\delta\rangle}{\sqrt{2}} + \frac{|3\rangle + |4\rangle}{\sqrt{2}} (a|\alpha\rangle + b|\beta\rangle) \right]. \tag{4.148}$$

This shows that a successful projection on the state $(|3\rangle + |4\rangle)/\sqrt{2}$ transfers the state to the other party. Similarly, a successful projection on $(|\gamma\rangle + |\delta\rangle)/\sqrt{2}$ retains the information with the first party. This procedure combines a teleportation process with a delayed choice of whom the information should be given to.

The procedure is, however, not fully efficient. The observation may fail, but we may assume that the measurement is perfect; for example, failing to obtain the state

$$|+\rangle = \frac{1}{\sqrt{2}} \left(|3\rangle + |4\rangle \right), \tag{4.149}$$

projects the system on the subspace selected by

$$P_+ = 1 - |+\rangle\langle+|. \tag{4.150}$$

But this is the subspace where the initial information state $(a|1\rangle + b|2\rangle)$ resides, and hence the procedure can be repeated. A similar argument holds if we want to retain the state with the first party; a failed measurement has transferred the state, which may then be returned by a second application of the same method.

Before any observation is carried out, both parties have access to the same amount of information because each can access the reduced density matrix

$$\rho_{\text{reduced}} = \frac{1}{2} \begin{bmatrix} aa^* & ab^* & 0 & 0 \\ a^*b & bb^* & 0 & 0 \\ 0 & 0 & \dfrac{1}{2} & \dfrac{1}{2} \\ 0 & 0 & \dfrac{1}{2} & \dfrac{1}{2} \end{bmatrix}. \tag{4.151}$$

At this point, consequently, both parties have the same amount of information available. The procedure to extract it is outlined above.

4.4 ERRORS IN QUANTUM COMPUTING

All technical devices introduce errors. In classical computers, there is an extensive theory of how to guard against them and correct them when they appear. This is based on advanced computational methods beyond the range of questions discussed here. Ironically enough, the state of the art of electronic computation is such that these methods play only a minor role. It is, however, of the utmost importance to look into the possible errors appearing in quantum computations and how to guard against them such that it is possible to correct them.

4.4.1 Types of Errors in Quantum States

Error Operators   Errors are introduced by interaction of the computing element with an environment outside our control. In Secs. 2.3.3 and 2.4.2, we showed how to describe the environment-induced perturbations on a density matrix. This was done in terms of a set of operators $\{A_\mu\}$ affecting the state vectors and density matrices as

$$|\psi\rangle \Rightarrow A_\mu |\psi\rangle,$$
$$\rho \Rightarrow A_\mu \rho A_\mu^\dagger. \tag{4.152}$$

Each such process is supposed to occur with the probability p_μ. If the state of the environment is not monitored, the change of a density matrix describing an ensemble can then be written as

$$\rho \Rightarrow \sum_\mu p_\mu A_\mu \rho A_\mu^\dagger = \sum_\mu \tilde{A}_\mu \rho \tilde{A}_\mu^\dagger, \tag{4.153}$$

where we set $\tilde{A}_\mu = \sqrt{p_\mu} A_\mu$.

The probability interpretation of the density matrix requires the normalization

$$\mathrm{Tr} \sum_\mu p_\mu A_\mu \rho A_\mu^\dagger = \sum_\mu \mathrm{Tr}\left(\tilde{A}_\mu^\dagger \tilde{A}_\mu \rho\right) = \mathrm{Tr}\rho = 1. \tag{4.154}$$

The general condition for this is that

$$\sum_\mu \tilde{A}_\mu^\dagger \tilde{A}_\mu = 1; \tag{4.155}$$

the operators $\tilde{A}_\mu$ thus define a set of POVMs.

After these preliminary considerations, we can introduce the various errors by describing their operators $\tilde{A}_\mu$.

Types of Errors

Bit-Flip Error   This error changes the state according to

$$c_0|0\rangle + c_1|1\rangle \Rightarrow c_0|1\rangle + c_1|0\rangle, \tag{4.156}$$

which occurs with probability $1 - p$. The corresponding operators are

$$A_0 = \begin{bmatrix} 1 & 0 \\ 0 & 1 \end{bmatrix}; \quad A_1 = \begin{bmatrix} 0 & 1 \\ 1 & 0 \end{bmatrix}. \tag{4.157}$$

The density matrix

$$\rho = \begin{bmatrix} \rho_{00} & \rho_{01} \\ \rho_{10} & \rho_{11} \end{bmatrix} \tag{4.158}$$

goes over into

$$\rho \Rightarrow p A_0 \rho A_0^\dagger + (1 - p) A_1 \rho A_1^\dagger$$
$$= \begin{bmatrix} \rho_{00} & \rho_{01} \\ \rho_{10} & \rho_{11} \end{bmatrix} + (1 - p) \begin{bmatrix} \rho_{11} - \rho_{00} & \rho_{10} - \rho_{01} \\ \rho_{01} - \rho_{10} & \rho_{00} - \rho_{11} \end{bmatrix}. \tag{4.159}$$

Phase-Flip Error   This type of error changes the sign of the state $|1\rangle$ with probability $1 - p$. The corresponding operators are

$$A_0 = \begin{bmatrix} 1 & 0 \\ 0 & 1 \end{bmatrix}; \quad A_1 = \begin{bmatrix} 1 & 0 \\ 0 & -1 \end{bmatrix}. \tag{4.160}$$

The density matrix is transformed according to

$$\rho \Rightarrow p \begin{bmatrix} \rho_{00} & \rho_{01} \\ \rho_{10} & \rho_{11} \end{bmatrix} + (1 - p) \begin{bmatrix} \rho_{00} & -\rho_{01} \\ -\rho_{10} & \rho_{11} \end{bmatrix}$$

$$= \begin{bmatrix} \rho_{00} & (2p - 1)\rho_{01} \\ (2p - 1)\rho_{10} & \rho_{11} \end{bmatrix}. \tag{4.161}$$

For $p = 0.5$, we lose all information about coherences.

It is easily seen that it does not matter in which state the sign change has occurred; for the density matrix we get the same result.

Depolarization   The density matrix describing a uniform ensemble carrying no information is

$$\mathbf{1} = \frac{1}{2} \begin{bmatrix} 1 & 0 \\ 0 & 1 \end{bmatrix}. \tag{4.162}$$

If the environment wipes out all information with probability $1 - p$, the density matrix is transformed according to

$$\rho \Rightarrow p\rho + (1 - p)\mathbf{1}. \tag{4.163}$$

We notice that this transformation cannot be effected by an operator of the type given above.

Phase Diffusion   We described above the process of a phase flip; one may, however, claim that the phase degrading of a qubit will be of the more gentle type described by the transformation

$$c_0|0\rangle + c_1|1\rangle \Rightarrow c_0|0\rangle + c_1 \exp(i\varphi)|1\rangle, \tag{4.164}$$

where φ is a random variable. The density matrix is transformed according to

$$\rho \Rightarrow \begin{bmatrix} \rho_{00} & \exp(-i\varphi)\rho_{01} \\ \exp(i\varphi)\rho_{10} & \rho_{11} \end{bmatrix}. \tag{4.165}$$

For a distribution of the random phases, we must average this to obtain the result

$$\overline{\exp(i\varphi)} \equiv \alpha. \tag{4.166}$$

For a Gaussian distribution of phases we have

$$\alpha = 1 + i\overline{\varphi} - \frac{1}{2}\overline{\varphi^2} + \cdots \sim \exp\left(-\frac{\overline{\varphi^2}}{2}\right), \tag{4.167}$$

because we expect all odd moments to vanish, and the parameter α is real. We show below that this expression is exact for a phase diffusion process. The phase relaxation parameter γ in Sec. 2.4.1 gives rise to this kind of process.

This transformation can now be described by the normalized operators

$$\tilde{A}_0 = \begin{bmatrix} 1 & 0 \\ 0 & \alpha \end{bmatrix},$$

$$\tilde{A}_1 = \begin{bmatrix} 0 & 0 \\ 0 & \sqrt{1 - \alpha^2} \end{bmatrix}. \tag{4.168}$$

These are easily seen to satisfy the normalization condition

$$\tilde{A}_0^\dagger \tilde{A}_0 + \tilde{A}_1^\dagger \tilde{A}_1 = \begin{bmatrix} 1 & 0 \\ 0 & 1 \end{bmatrix}. \tag{4.169}$$

They give the transformation

$$\rho \Rightarrow \tilde{A}_0 \rho \tilde{A}_0^\dagger + \tilde{A}_1 \rho \tilde{A}_1^\dagger = \begin{bmatrix} \rho_{00} & \alpha\rho_{01} \\ \alpha\rho_{10} & \rho_{11} \end{bmatrix}, \tag{4.170}$$

which is indeed the average of (4.165).

One may think that the phase diffusion process would be very different from the phase flip described above. However, as the only effect we are interested in here is the deterioration of the density matrix describing the qubit, it turns out that there are no discernible differences between these two cases.

If we compare the results (4.161) and (4.170), we find that they are identical for

$$2p - 1 = \alpha. \tag{4.171}$$

Thus, we may try the operator

$$A_0 = \begin{bmatrix} 1 & 0 \\ 0 & 1 \end{bmatrix} \tag{4.172}$$

with probability

$$p = \frac{1 + \alpha}{2}, \tag{4.173}$$

and the operator

$$A_1 = \begin{bmatrix} 1 & 0 \\ 0 & -1 \end{bmatrix} \tag{4.174}$$

with probability

$$1 - p = \frac{1 - \alpha}{2}.$$ (4.175)

We find that

$$\rho \Rightarrow \frac{1 + \alpha}{2} A_0 \rho A_0 + \frac{1 - \alpha}{2} A_1 \rho A_1 = \begin{bmatrix} \rho_{00} & \alpha \rho_{01} \\ \alpha \rho_{10} & \rho_{11} \end{bmatrix}.$$ (4.176)

Thus, we have found that from the point of view of the computing system, the phase diffusion can be replaced by a phase flip.

Phase Diffusion Process   The distribution function $W(\varphi, t)$ for the classical diffusion process is governed by the differential equation

$$\frac{\partial W(\varphi, t)}{\partial t} = D \frac{\partial^2 W(\varphi, t)}{\partial \varphi^2}.$$ (4.177)

It can be verified directly that the normalized solution is

$$W(\varphi, t) = \frac{1}{\sqrt{4 \pi D t}} \exp \left(-\frac{\varphi^2}{4Dt} \right).$$ (4.178)

We can calculate directly that this describes the standard diffusion behavior,

$$\overline{\varphi^2} = \int_{-\infty}^{\infty} \varphi^2 W(\varphi, t) \, d\varphi = 2Dt,$$ (4.179)

and D is identified as the diffusion constant.

In the same way we can calculate the average

$$\overline{\exp(i\varphi)} = \int_{-\infty}^{\infty} \exp(i\varphi) W(\varphi, t) \, d\varphi.$$ (4.180)

By writing

$$i\varphi - \frac{\varphi^2}{4Dt} = -\frac{(\varphi - 2i Dt)^2}{4Dt} - Dt$$ (4.181)

and carrying out the integral in the complex coordinate, we find that

$$\overline{\exp(i\varphi)} = \exp(-Dt) = \exp \left(-\frac{\overline{\varphi^2}}{2} \right),$$ (4.182)

as we used in (4.166). Thus, the expression for α is obtained easily in this case. However, in the general case when all odd moments of φ vanish, the result of the average can always be described by one real number.

Remark: In fact, the phase is really confined to the interval $\varphi \in [0, 2\pi]$, but for simplicity we have presented the derivation over the infinite interval. To carry out the calculation over the bounded region is much more demanding.

4.4.2 Quantum Error Correction

General Considerations Classical computers can secure the information against deterioration by using redundancy, that is, by storing the same information as multiple bits:

$$\{0, 1\} \Rightarrow \{\{0, 1\}, \{0, 1\}, \{0, 1\}\}. \tag{4.183}$$

Because arbitrary quantum states cannot be cloned, we cannot effect the transformation

$$(\alpha|0\rangle + \beta|1\rangle) \Rightarrow (\alpha|0\rangle + \beta|1\rangle) \otimes (\alpha|0\rangle + \beta|1\rangle) \otimes (\alpha|0\rangle + \beta|1\rangle). \tag{4.184}$$

However, as the computational basis is fixed, we can perform the mapping

$$\alpha|0\rangle + \beta|1\rangle \Rightarrow \alpha|000\rangle + \beta|111\rangle. \tag{4.185}$$

This duplicates the information, but it still does not solve the problem. Even if one of the three qubits involved flips, we cannot verify this with an observation, because by measuring any of the qubits we destroy the entanglement between the constituents of the state, and the quantum information $\{\alpha, \beta\}$ is lost.

The ability to perform error correction on quantum informational processes has encouraged researchers to believe in the possibility of realizing quantum computing. Quantum states are rather fragile to perturbations, and without error correction, nothing could guarantee the reliability of the computations. In the following we introduce a few simple examples of how such schemes may be devised. For the full range of possibilities and the current state of the art, the reader should consult the references.

If we can perform measurements on an arbitrary pair of constituents, we can check if the first two qubits are in the same state by measuring the operator $\sigma_3^{(1)}\sigma_3^{(2)}$; we assume that this can be done without distorting the state. We thus find that

$$\begin{aligned}
\sigma_3^{(1)}\sigma_3^{(2)}|000\rangle &= |000\rangle, \\
\sigma_3^{(1)}\sigma_3^{(2)}|111\rangle &= (-1)^2|111\rangle.
\end{aligned} \tag{4.186}$$

If one of these qubits has flipped,

$$|0\rangle \Leftrightarrow |1\rangle, \tag{4.187}$$

we get minus the original state. In neither case have we changed the state by the measurement. By measuring the operator $\sigma_3^{(2)}\sigma_3^{(3)}$ subsequently, we get another result. From these two results we can easily determine where spin flip has occurred. We assume that we are now able to correct this by inducing the appropriate spin flip on one of the constituents only. The procedure is as follows:

Observe $\sigma_3^{(1)}\sigma_3^{(2)}$	Observe $\sigma_3^{(2)}\sigma_3^{(3)}$	Correct
-1	1	bit 1
-1	-1	bit 2
1	-1	bit 3

Thus, the procedure allows us to correct all errors if *at most one bit flip* has occurred. If bit flips take place with probability p, this happens with probability

$$P_{\leq 1} = (1-p)^3 + 3p(1-p)^2 = 1 - 3p^2 + 2p^3. \tag{4.188}$$

The procedure fails if more than one bit flip error has occurred, which takes place with probability

$$1 - P_{\leq 1} = (3 - 2p)p^2. \tag{4.189}$$

If no error correction has been carried out, the probability of an incorrect performance is given by p, and hence the correction scheme described above gives an advantage when

$$(3 - 2p)p^2 < p. \tag{4.190}$$

This holds if $p < \frac{1}{2}$, which indicates that even the rather primitive scheme above is surprisingly efficient.

Can we make this procedure more systematic? Look at the states ensuing if the single bit error occurs in the various bits:

Error in Bit:	Original State	Replaced by:
1	$\alpha\lvert 000\rangle + \beta\lvert 111\rangle$	$\alpha\lvert 100\rangle + \beta\lvert 011\rangle$
2	$\alpha\lvert 000\rangle + \beta\lvert 111\rangle$	$\alpha\lvert 010\rangle + \beta\lvert 101\rangle$
3	$\alpha\lvert 000\rangle + \beta\lvert 111\rangle$	$\alpha\lvert 001\rangle + \beta\lvert 110\rangle$

We now define a complete set of orthogonal projectors on the three-qubit states by writing

$$\begin{aligned}
P_0 &= \lvert 000\rangle\langle 000\rvert + \lvert 111\rangle\langle 111\rvert, \\
P_1 &= \lvert 100\rangle\langle 100\rvert + \lvert 011\rangle\langle 011\rvert, \\
P_2 &= \lvert 010\rangle\langle 010\rvert + \lvert 101\rangle\langle 101\rvert, \\
P_3 &= \lvert 001\rangle\langle 001\rvert + \lvert 110\rangle\langle 110\rvert.
\end{aligned} \tag{4.191}$$

It is obvious that these span the entire state space, so if we can perform ideal projection measurements on these and find out which one is the case, we know in which bit the error has occurred. We assume that we can then correct this bit by applying a local operation. A measurement that shows us where the error is to be found is called an *error syndrome*.

The entire procedure rests, of course, on the assumption that ideal von Neumann measurements can be performed and that the required error-correcting operation can be carried out.

Phase-Flip Error   In the preceding section we devised a system that could correct an arbitrary bit-flip error. As another illustration we present a scheme that can detect phase errors. As we saw above, it suffices to consider a case in which the sign of one state is flipped.

To devise the phase-flip corrector, we decode the "0" and "1" by the orthogonal three-qubit states

$$|``0"\rangle = \frac{1}{2}(|---\rangle + |-++\rangle + |+-+\rangle + |++-\rangle),$$
$$|``1"\rangle = \frac{1}{2}(|+++\rangle + |+--\rangle + |-+-\rangle + |--+\rangle), \tag{4.192}$$

where to avoid confusion we have designated the basis states by $|\pm\rangle$.

Now if we have a single phase flip in one of the qubits, the ensuing states are as follows:

State	$|``0"\rangle$	$|``1"\rangle$
Bit 1	$\frac{1}{2}(\|---\rangle + \|-++\rangle$	$\frac{1}{2}(-\|+++\rangle - \|+--\rangle$
	$-\|+-+\rangle - \|++-\rangle)$	$+\|-+-\rangle + \|--+\rangle)$
Bit 2	$\frac{1}{2}(\|---\rangle - \|-++\rangle$	$\frac{1}{2}(-\|+++\rangle + \|+--\rangle$
	$+\|+-+\rangle - \|++-\rangle)$	$-\|-+-\rangle + \|--+\rangle)$
Bit 3	$\frac{1}{2}(\|---\rangle - \|-++\rangle$	$\frac{1}{2}(-\|+++\rangle + \|+--\rangle$
	$-\|+-+\rangle + \|++-\rangle)$	$+\|-+-\rangle - \|--+\rangle)$

It is easy to check that these states are orthogonal to each other and to the two original states, so that one can devise an ideal measurement that distinguishes between them. Together with the unaffected states, there are altogether eight orthogonal states, defining eight orthogonal projectors. This guarantees that an ideal measurement observing these projectors always gives an outcome. Consequently, the table above tells us directly which phase flip has to be performed to correct the error. As the present method also corrects states with at most one error, the probability analysis carried out above is valid.

There are simple codes giving syndromes for both bit flips and phase flips. One is given by the Shor code:

$$|``0"\rangle = \frac{(|---\rangle + |+++\rangle)\,(|---\rangle + |+++\rangle)\,(|---\rangle + |+++\rangle)}{2\sqrt{2}},$$
$$|``1"\rangle = \frac{(|---\rangle - |+++\rangle)\,(|---\rangle - |+++\rangle)\,(|---\rangle - |+++\rangle)}{2\sqrt{2}}. \tag{4.193}$$

It is a straightforward but somewhat tedious exercise to combine the methods used above to find an error syndrome for these states.

As we see, the Shor code is a nine-qubit system, which illustrates one feature of error-correcting codes; they require the use of more computer resources. The safer they are, the more demanding they become. This overhead has to be taken into account when one wants to estimate the resources that a quantum computation will require.

We do not, however, go deeper into the field of error correction here; the examples given may serve as illustrations of the issues involved. To construct a more complicated scheme assumes familiarity with the classical theory of error corrections.

4.5 ENERGETICS OF QUANTUM COMPUTATIONS

4.5.1 Energy Used by a Classical Computer

Present-day computers are extremely wasteful of energy. They heat up the circuitry independent of whether or not they perform calculations. However, it is not without interest to investigate the question of necessary energy consumption required to carry out a given computation. The fundamental question is whether or not there exist fundamental physical limitations on the energy requirements.

The processing of information is often taken to change the informational entropy, defined as

$$S = -\sum_k p_k \log p_k. \tag{4.194}$$

If we vary this, we obtain the relation

$$\Delta S = -\sum_k \Delta p_k \log p_k - \Delta \sum_k p_k. \tag{4.195}$$

The second term is zero because of normalization. If we have a system in thermal equilibrium, the probabilities are given by

$$p_k = N \exp\left(-\frac{E_k}{k_B T}\right). \tag{4.196}$$

Then we have

$$\log p_k = -\frac{E_k}{k_B T} + \log N. \tag{4.197}$$

Inserted into (4.195), this gives

$$\Delta S = \sum_k \Delta p_k \frac{E_k}{k_B T} = \frac{1}{k_B T} \Delta \sum_k p_k E_k = \frac{\Delta \overline{E}}{k_B T}. \tag{4.198}$$

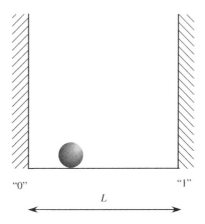

Figure 4.25 Particle in a box.

If we define the thermodynamic entropy as $k_B S = S_T$, we find the ordinary thermal relation

$$\Delta S_T = \frac{\Delta \overline{E}}{T}. \tag{4.199}$$

This us tells that if we increase the energy of a system in thermal equilibrium, we increase its entropy. Does this imply that if we change the informational entropy of an information-processing system, we must change its energy? The derivation above assumes thermal equilibrium, and computing systems are not operating close to equilibrium. So the question remains open.

Let us consider next a highly simplified classical computing device. A particle is situated in a one-dimensional box with flat bottom (Fig. 4.25). Sitting in the left-side corner it signifies "0"; sitting in the right-side corner it signifies "1." This system is, however, not a very reliable coding; the particle will move over and give an error at the slightest perturbation. To overcome this disadvantage, we assume the box to be filled with a highly viscous fluid which prevents the particle from straying.

A computational process consists in a purposeful transfer of the particle from one corner to the other. This implies applying to it a constant force F. As the fluid is highly viscous, this gives the particle a steady velocity, determined by

$$M\dot{v} = F - \gamma v = 0, \tag{4.200}$$

where γ is the coefficient of friction. If the size of the box is L, we find that the transfer takes the time

$$t_c = \frac{L}{v} = \frac{L\gamma}{F}; \tag{4.201}$$

this is the time required for a single computational step.

But the damping medium also reacts on the particle by a random force. This is an inevitable consequence of the physics of random environments. This means that left to itself, the particle will eventually drift to the other side of the box. This is described by a diffusion coefficient D, which determines how the particle deviates from any initial position. If we use this to estimate a diffusion time scale by setting

$$L^2 \sim 2Dt_d, \tag{4.202}$$

we assume this to set a time limit on how long the computation can use this particle. After the time t_d, we have lost the information it carries. Thus, if we ask how many computational steps this device can take, we get the result

$$N_c = \frac{t_d}{t_c} \sim \frac{FL}{2D\gamma}. \tag{4.203}$$

But the Einstein relation in a thermal environment gives

$$D\gamma = k_B T \tag{4.204}$$

and $FL = \Delta E$ is the work done by a single computational step. Thus, we find the relation

$$N_c = \frac{1}{2}\left(\frac{\Delta E}{k_B T}\right) \propto \Delta S. \tag{4.205}$$

This seems to suggest that the computer is most efficient if we change the entropy as much as possible and/or work at as low an ambient temperature as is possible. An interpretation of this is not easy. It seems to say that it pays to use a lot of force to effect a computational transition as fast as possible. In any case, it suggests that entropy may play a role in determining computational efficiency.

Interlude: Einstein Relation   For completeness, we indicate a derivation of the result (4.204). Let the particle be a constituent in a matter flowing with density function W. When it is subjected to a force F, its velocity will be given by

$$v = \frac{F}{\gamma}. \tag{4.206}$$

The diffusive flow of the medium is given by the current $-D\nabla W$, which has to be counteracted by the flow vW of the medium. In equilibrium these two currents must compensate each other and we find that

$$-D\frac{d}{dx}W = vW = \frac{F}{\gamma}W. \tag{4.207}$$

The solution of this equation is

$$W \sim \exp\left(-\frac{F}{D\gamma}x\right). \tag{4.208}$$

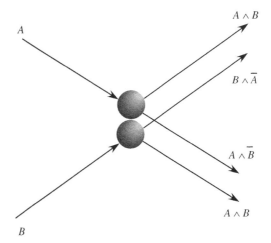

Figure 4.26   Classical billiard logic.

The force, however, supplies the potential energy $E = Fx$ and in thermal equilibrium, we know that this must correspond to the distribution function

$$W \sim \exp\left(-\frac{E}{k_B T}\right). \tag{4.209}$$

Comparing this with (4.208), we find that the relation (4.204) follows.

But is it necessary to use force at all to carry out a logical operation? A priori this seems not to be so, and another simple model calculation suggests that this is not needed. Assume that we carry out a logical operation with ideal billiard balls. They undergo fully elastic collisions, and we assume that we can launch them precisely along selected trajectories. The presence of a ball on a trajectory is given by the proposition A, and the absence of a ball on the same trajectory is given by $\overline{A}$. Then Fig. 4.26 shows how the presence or absence of two balls on their trajectories can be taken to symbolize various logical relations. As our balls are assumed to undergo ideal elastic collisions, the operation to obtain these functions costs no energy. The example is highly idealized, but it has been used to indicate that classical computations require no energy. It is difficult to judge how seriously we should take this example.

4.5.2   Resetting Energy

What about the energy required in a quantum logic operation? We have assumed that the computations are reversible and thus effected by unitary transformations. These conserve the energy, and whatever operations we perform, no exchange of energy is assumed to take place.

But what happens after a long series of computations? We have read in information, we have written this to scratchpad systems, ancillas, and used these to extract final results which are then read and utilized in various ways. But what happened to the scratchpad systems? After a lengthy computation we will be left with a huge assembly of systems in random quantum states. When they were taken into use, they had to be in a well-known state, an initial fiducial state corresponding to the classical blank state. In quantum systems we may assume arbitrarily that this is the state $|0\rangle$ of the computational basis.

The ancillas used in a computation go into a reservoir of used qubits with their states

$$|\psi\rangle = c_0|0\rangle + c_1|1\rangle \tag{4.210}$$

occurring with totally random coefficients $\{c_0, c_1\}$; this is an ensemble with the entropy $\log 2$ per qubit. To transfer these to the reservoir of qubits ready to be used in the next computation, they have to be reset to the state $|0\rangle$. The ensuing ensemble has zero entropy. Thus, an irreversible act of processing has to be used; no unitary process can take an arbitrary state (4.210) to the single state $|0\rangle$.

One way to achieve this is to raise the energy of the state $|1\rangle$ by an amount ΔE and put the ancillas in contact with a heat bath at temperature T. If the energy difference is large enough, all systems will eventually end up in the lower state $|0\rangle$. On average, half the systems started out in the upper level, and hence the systems have to give up an average energy of $\frac{1}{2}\Delta E$ to the heat bath. The change of entropy in this process is given by

$$\Delta S = \frac{1}{2}\left(\frac{\Delta E}{k_B T}\right), \tag{4.211}$$

which, remarkably, agrees with the result (4.205) even if the physical contexts are very different. But this may suggest that the energy cost one has to invest in resetting the ancillas is related to their disorder of $\log 2$ per qubit. Similar considerations led Rolf Landauer to present his *erasure principle*.

Proposition   After a quantum computation, the resetting of all the states used will require an energy use equal to

$$\Delta E = Nk_B T \log 2,$$

when N qubits have been affected.

Notice that this involves the use of a temperature T; thus, some part of the system must be in such an equilibrium that it may be described by a temperature. If this is not the case, it is far from obvious how to implement this proposition. When, however, the resetting is carried out by introducing a heat bath, the heuristic investigations above can be put on a firmer basis. Let us have a look at the thermodynamics of resetting from a computational point of view.

Assume that the assembly of used ancillas can be represented by an ensemble described by the initial density matrix ρ_{in}. Then the initial entropy of the system is calculated as

$$S_{in} = -\text{Tr}\left(\rho_{in} \log \rho_{in}\right). \tag{4.212}$$

Here we scale the entropy as an informational one; the Boltzmann constant is introduced explicitly later. After the system of ancillas has been allowed to reach thermal equilibrium with the heat bath, it has reached a final state described by

$$\rho_{fin} = \frac{1}{Z} \exp\left(-\frac{H}{k_B T}\right), \tag{4.213}$$

where Z is the partition function and H is the Hamiltonian introduced to separate the energies of the two systems. If we solve (4.213) for the Hamiltonian, we find that

$$H = -k_B T \log \rho_{fin} - k_B T \log Z. \tag{4.214}$$

The energy that has to be supplied when the Hamiltonian is introduced is

$$E_{in} = \text{Tr}\left(\rho_{in} H\right) = -k_B T \text{ Tr}\left(\rho_{in} \log \rho_{fin}\right) - k_B T \log Z. \tag{4.215}$$

In the same way, the energy of the system after thermal equilibrium has been reached is

$$E_{fin} = \text{Tr}\left(\rho_{fin} H\right) = -k_B T \text{ Tr}\left(\rho_{fin} \log \rho_{fin}\right) - k_B T \log Z. \tag{4.216}$$

After the process, the Hamiltonian can be removed and this energy can be recovered. If we calculate this change of energy, we find that

$$E_{in} - E_{fin} = -k_B T \text{ Tr}\left(\rho_{in} \log \rho_{fin}\right) + k_B T \text{ Tr}\left(\rho_{fin} \log \rho_{fin}\right). \tag{4.217}$$

Using (4.212), we can write this as

$$\begin{aligned} E_{in} - E_{fin} = &-k_B T \ Tr\left(\rho_{in} \log \rho_{fin}\right) + k_B T \text{ Tr}\left(\rho_{in} \log \rho_{in}\right) \\ &- k_B T S_{fin} + k_B T S_{in}. \end{aligned} \tag{4.218}$$

This can be written further as

$$\begin{aligned} E_{in} - E_{fin} &+ k_B T S_{fin} - k_B T S_{in} \\ &= k_B T \text{ Tr}\left[\rho_{in}\left(\log \rho_{in} - \log \rho_{fin}\right)\right] \geq 0, \end{aligned} \tag{4.219}$$

which gives

$$E_{in} - k_B T S_{in} \geq E_{fin} - k_B T S_{fin}. \tag{4.220}$$

Thus, the free energy must decrease during the resetting process. If the resetting is effected by a thermal contact, this seems to be an unavoidable result.

Now let us look at the energy balance of the process; we have to supply the energy E_{in}, and we can ideally regain the energy E_{fin} after the resetting process is finished. The energy needed is thus given by

$$E_{in} - E_{fin} \geq k_B T \left(S_{in} - S_{fin}\right). \tag{4.221}$$

If the ancilla ensemble is fully random, we have initially $\log 2$ of entropy per qubit, and having succeeded in resetting almost all ancillas to the fiducial state, the final entropy is zero. Hence we find that we need to supply an energy

$$E_{in} - E_{fin} \geq k_B T \log 2 \tag{4.222}$$

per qubit to reset the ancillas. This is indeed the *Landauer principle*, following from the thermodynamics of resetting.

The derivation above does, however, rest on the assumption that the resetting is achieved by the heat bath. It is indisputable that the resetting must be an irreversible process in order to reset all possible states to the state desired. However, there seems to be no general proof that only a thermal bath will do the trick: It remains an open question whether there exist irreversible processes effecting the transformation $\log 2 \Rightarrow 0$ with less use of energy than that in (4.222).

Alternative Resetting Mechanics   After a series of computing operations, we have an ensemble of used ancillas, which is described by the density matrix

$$\rho_i = \frac{1}{2} \left(|0\rangle\langle 0| + |1\rangle\langle 1|\right). \tag{4.223}$$

Its entropy is $\log 2$ per qubit, and we want to reset all to the state $|0\rangle$, say. Instead of using a thermal bath, we choose to separate the states by an energy $E = \hbar\omega$; if the states are coupled by a dipole transition, spontaneous processes will take them all to the desired state, $|0\rangle$. The energy is carried away by the state, and it is thus lost. But the process can be carried out at a temperature such that

$$\hbar\omega \gg k_B T \tag{4.224}$$

and no entropy considerations are needed. Thus, the Landauer limit loses its relevance.

One may ask where the entropy of the initial ensemble is going. By using the Schmidt decomposition of the two-level system coupled to the radiation in the form

$$|\Psi\rangle = |0\rangle|\varphi_{rad}^{(0)}\rangle + |1\rangle|\varphi_{rad}^{(1)}\rangle, \tag{4.225}$$

we find that the radiation field is only involved in two states $\left\{|\varphi_{rad}^{(0)}\rangle, |\varphi_{rad}^{(1)}\rangle\right\}$ at any one time; at the eventual final time, only one state, $|\varphi_{rad}^{(0)}\rangle$, survives. Thus, the entropy $\log 2$ is transferred to the outgoing state. If the radiation is detected by a coarse-graining device, the uncertainty of the state of the radiation will exceed this.

The spontaneous emission rate $\Gamma \propto \omega^3$, and consequently, we need to achieve some considerable energy separations to effect the resetting in a reasonably short time; optical frequencies are presumably needed. Thus, we find the process to be significantly more costly in terms of energy than the use of a thermal reservoir. However, the resetting time will also need to be considered when thermal processes are utilized.

The issue of qubit resetting is still far from clear; novel and detailed investigations may still change our view on this aspect of quantum information processing.

4.6 REFERENCES

The elements of mathematical logic are presented in many texts. For the purposes of information considerations, the book by Humphreys and Prest [49] is highly useful. It presents the material in a formal, yet practically oriented manner. As a curiosity it may be mentioned that it is usually stated that truth tables were introduced by Wittgenstein [106]. The relation of logic to information processing and the carry-over to quantum processes is standard material in the texts [43] and [72]. Most of the material presented in this section is explored in greater detail in these books.

It is usually claimed that Feynman initiated the present interest in quantum aspects of computing. His seminal articles and some works exposing their relevance are found in the collection [46], which gives an excellent background to the entire field. As usual, Feynman's own description of computing [36] is highly enjoyable. A popular but still technical description of Turing's work is given by Penrose in [77]. A more popular presentation by Milburn is given in [68]. As in all cases, the complementary aspect of popularization is here at work: The more readable a presentation is, the less informative it becomes. The interplay between mathematical ideas and logical implications is presented informatively in a text by Kneebone [54].

A mathematically oriented presentation of the public key code and error corrections is given in [49]. The use of number theory and the Hadamard transformation is presented by Schroeder [87]. The quantum factorization algorithm is described by Peter Shor in [90]. For details of the process, the book by Nielsen and Chuang [72] should be consulted. Introductions and surveys of the theory are given in the books [2] and [17]. The field is reviewed in [46] (p. 191) and [39] (p. 141).

The Grover algorithm was proposed originally by Grover in [42], but again, a detailed presentation is given by Nielsen and Chuang [72] (beware, though, of the notation that occasionally confuses the states $|X\rangle$ and $|\Psi\rangle$). These presentations, however, tend to seriously overestimate the usefulness of the algorithm, downplaying the difficulty in constructing the required oracle. In addition, other problems arise on the path of efficient quantum search (see, e.g., [100, 108]).

The concept of purification was formalized by Bennett et al. in [12]. Example 3 in Sec. 4.3.3 is taken from [95], where some further details are given.

The treatment of quantum errors in computing is reviewed in [17] (p. 221). A book by Humphreys and Prest [49] presents the use of symmetry arguments to build classical error-correcting codes. The most recent developments of quantum error correction are built on this, but the quantum features introduce essential modifications; consult [72].

The energetics of computation have been discussed extensively. Many of the earlier contributions are collected in [59]. Some elementary discussions are given by Feynman [36]. The quantum point of view is summarized by Plenio and Vitelli in [83]. It seems that the last word has not been said about this question, which posed some debatable enigmas already at the classical level.

CHAPTER 5

PHYSICAL REALIZATION OF QUANTUM INFORMATION PROCESSING

5.1 GENERAL CONSIDERATIONS

Quantum information processing is unique within the field of physics. Despite its rapid growth and the wide interest it has created, its early development has not been driven by any major breakthroughs in experimental science. It arose mainly from an effort to take quantum mechanics seriously. Researchers started to explore the possibilities offered even by the more esoteric nonclassical features of the theory. The entire enterprise may be seen as a systematic exploration of specifically quantum mechanical features, relating human knowledge to the description of measurements as an information-gathering process. Coupled to the contemporary interest in coding, communication, and computing, physics saw a totally new field emerge.

The development should perhaps not have been entirely unexpected. It is a natural direction of exploration when a field of research reaches maturity. After having created the theory to achieve understanding of observed phenomena, the practitioners turn to exploiting the possibilities offered by the newly gained understanding. They start to enquire about which new problems may be solved with the theory and under which experimental circumstances these can be realized. One moves from the stage of analysis to that of synthesis. We have seen the same happen before; the physics of the steering of free electrons and the specialities offered by semiconductor devices have both had their heydays in electronics. In molecular spectroscopy the emphasis has lately moved toward active control of chemical reactions with ultrashort pulses, away from the mere passive observation

Quantum Approach to Informatics, by Stig Stenholm and Kalle-Antti Suominen
Copyright © 2005 John Wiley & Sons, Inc.

of the molecular spectra and other properties. Similarly, it is apparently now time for quantum physics to turn into quantum technology.

The statement that the development of quantum information processing has not been brought forward by breakthroughs in experimental physics can naturally be questioned. This development has always been mixed with studies of basic or "fundamental" quantum mechanics. Before the emergence of quantum information processing in its current form, these studies were limited to a small group of researchers. They stubbornly continued to work on ideas that arose in the 1920s and 1930s, when the structure and consistency of quantum mechanics was tested with thought experiments and important concepts such as entanglement and quantum jumps were brought forward. At the same time, our experimental ability to observe and manipulate matter and radiation on the level of single atoms and photons reached new levels, manifested by photon correlation measurements, studies in cavity quantum electrodynamics, the development of tunneling and atomic force microscopes, and laser cooling and trapping of ions and neutral atoms.

Experimental studies of fundamental issues started in the field of quantum optics and atomic physics, and their success clearly helped to make quantum information processing more palatable to the larger community of physicists. From this perspective it is not surprising that the first physical realizations were proposed within the quantum optics community, although researchers in other fields quickly grasped the basics. Clearly, experimental development in precision control of matter and radiation has fanned the flames, but the fire itself was nevertheless started independently.

To demonstrate the late arrival of experimental work, there are as yet few cases where practical quantum technology matches the vast progress in theory. Quantum coding in communications has been convincingly demonstrated and proved to be technically feasible. As to quantum computing components, only the most elementary circuits have been demonstrated in the laboratory. The field is, however, developing rapidly, and technical understanding has been progressing well. Still, today only the most elementary schemes have been realized, and we are very far from even an elementary quantum computing device. It is far from clear whether we will ever see a useful quantum computer, but as so often before, novel and presently unfathomed applications may eventually emerge from this effort.

What has already become clear are the benefits the research activities have brought to quantum physics. By exploring its scope and possibilities and analyzing the strategies and effects of quantum measurements, we have gained new insights into the structure and workings of the theory as we know it presently. In the end, the entire enterprise of quantum information processing may serve the physics community best in this role.

In this part of the present book we summarize the physical properties of some of the basic systems considered for quantum components. This is already a vast field, and we can only give the outlines of proposed realizations of quantum logical operations. Many groups today are involved in this endeavor, and we cannot hope to review their progress adequately. In addition, any such attempt would rapidly become obsolete anyway. The examples that we outline here, however, serve the important purpose of demonstrating the conditions that any serious attempt at building a quantum computer must meet.

5.2   REQUIREMENTS FOR QUANTUM COMPUTERS

Any physically realistic proposal for a quantum computer must satisfy some general requirements. The list of these requirements can take different shapes depending on the emphasis chosen, as the various aspects involved are somewhat entangled. We have chosen to identify the requirements as follows:

1. *Well-identifiable qubits.* Quantum information is encoded in the quantum degrees of freedom of the system, but these must be carried by systems behaving classically. We need to know which system represents the nth bit in an encoded binary number. We also need a definite and reliable way to write a desired quantum state onto a preassigned system and need to be able to read the information by selective interrogation of any qubit. This requirement can be called *addressability*.

2. *The quantum states must not be destroyed.* The main obstacle to realizing quantum information processes is the fragility of quantum states due to influence from the environment. This changes the dynamic time dependence from the unitary evolution implied by the Schrödinger equation to that of an open dissipative system. In Sec. 2.4 we have described in detail how interaction with the environment leads to irreversibility, and how such systems can be treated with the master equation of Lindblad form. The various forms of resulting errors were presented in Sec. 4.4. Let us summarize briefly the basics.

The general state of a single two-state quantum system is

$$|\psi\rangle = c_1|1\rangle + e^{i\varphi}c_2|2\rangle \tag{5.1}$$

and it can be perturbed irreversibly in two ways:

- The absolute values of the coefficients $|c_1|$, $|c_2|$ change (bit-flip error). If we use for quantum information storage the electronic ground and excited states of an atom, spontaneous emission becomes a clear example of an environmental effect. Here the excited atomic states are coupled to the vacuum of electromagnetic modes, which form the environment. Writing $n_1 = |c_1|^2$ and $n_2 = |c_2|^2$, and choosing state 2 as the ground state and state 1 as the excited state, we have

$$\begin{aligned}
\frac{d}{dt}n_1 &= -\frac{n_1}{T_1}, \\
\frac{d}{dt}n_2 &= \frac{n_1}{T_1}.
\end{aligned} \tag{5.2}$$

As this changes the energy content of the system, it is called *energy relaxation* or *longitudinal relaxation*. The corresponding rate is given by the relaxation time T_1. The process evidently destroys any quantum information coding utilizing either one or both of the states in (5.1).

- There may be random movement of the relative phase φ due to the perturbations of the environment. This erodes the coherence between the two quantum states, thus affecting the off-diagonal elements of the density matrix

$$\frac{d}{dt}\rho_{21} = -\frac{\rho_{21}}{T_2}. \tag{5.3}$$

The corresponding relaxation time T_2 is called the *transverse* or *phase relaxation time*. Such a process was described by a phase diffusion model in Sec. 4.4.1.

The situation with two types of relaxation rates can be illuminated by the Bloch equation treatment offered in Sec. 2.4.1. The relaxation processes pose the ultimate obstacle to the experimental realization of quantum information circuits. Because the phase is usually more easily disturbed than the level populations, we have $T_2 < T_1$. This provides the fundamental limit in most experiments and is often called *decoherence time* T_{decoh}.

Unfortunately, in quantum information processing, phase relaxation is not limited to the level of a single quantum bit. The phase relations between different bits are also important to the success of information processing. In the example of a single two-state system above, we have in addition to the relative phase φ a global phase that is usually ignored by selecting c_1 and c_2 to be real. Let us consider a quantum system formed by two such systems:

$$\begin{aligned}
|\psi\rangle &= (a_1 e^{i\alpha}|1\rangle_1 + e^{i\beta}a_2|2\rangle_1) \times (b_1 e^{i\gamma}|1\rangle_2 + e^{i\delta}b_2|2\rangle_2) \\
&= e^{i(\alpha+\gamma)}a_1 b_1|1\rangle_1|1\rangle_2 + e^{i(\alpha+\delta)}a_1 b_2|1\rangle_1|2\rangle_2 \\
&\quad + e^{i(\beta+\gamma)}a_2 b_1|2\rangle_1|1\rangle_2 + e^{i(\beta+\delta)}a_2 b_2|2\rangle_1|2\rangle_2.
\end{aligned} \tag{5.4}$$

Here a_1, a_2, b_1, b_2 are real. Clearly, we can remove the global phase (e.g., by setting $\alpha + \gamma = 0$), but this fixes only one of the four independent phases, leaving us with three relative phases instead of two.

The number of independent phases increases rapidly as more quantum bits are added to the system. If the system has L quantum bits and it is in a nonentangled pure state, as in the example above, we have $2L - 1$ independent phases. As for entangled quantum bits, we can describe the complete register of L bits more generally by a $2^L \times 2^L$ density matrix, which at worst has $2^L(2^L - 1)$ independent parameters stored in the complex-valued off-diagonal elements. This scaling reflects partly the difficulty of realizing macroscopic quantum objects. If each qubit interacts independently with the environment, it can be shown that the fastest-eroding density matrix element has the relaxation time $T_{\text{decoh}} \sim T_2/L$, where T_2 refers to the longitudinal relaxation time of a single quantum bit as in Eq. (5.3).

The appearance of decoherence is not an automatic killer of quantum computing, as now it becomes a matter of time scales. The strength of the interaction determines how fast a single cycle of the logical processing can be carried out. Assume that this is characterized by a computing cycle time T_c. If the fastest relaxation time scale of the physical degrees of freedom is T_{relax}, we define the number of computing steps possible by the ratio

$$N_c = \frac{T_{relax}}{T_c};$$ (5.5)

a useful system should have this ratio as large as possible. Usually, $T_{relax} = T_{decoh}$. We can define N_c as the *computing capability*. Of course, this is only a crude estimate, as the sensitivity of various computations to phase errors may vary significantly.

3. *Interaction needed*. To perform conditioned logical operations, we have to let systems carrying the information interact. Thus, they must be able to sustain such interactions in a controlled way. The problem here is that entities that are not easily perturbed by the environment also do not interact efficiently with each other. Thus, photons are ideal carriers of information; they travel long distances without being perturbed and retain quantum coherence over these long distances. However, their ability to interact is weak, so the effects of nonlinear optics are usually minute. Electrons, on the other hand, have strong interactions, as their electrostatic repulsion makes them highly aware of each other. But by the same token, they pick up perturbations from even minute stray fields in the environment. The situation with electrons in solids tends to be even worse. Neutral atoms are in between; when cooled they can retain coherence over rather long distances, but they interact strongly only when their electron clouds start to overlap. At longer separations one is then limited to using photons or phonons as mediators, or rely on the weaker dipole–dipole interactions. Collective phenomena such as superconductivity or Bose–Einstein condensation tend to improve the situation (see below).

The formulation of quantum information processes with circuits of quantum gates implies that one should be able to make controlled interactions between *any* two quantum bits. Especially in solid-state systems, physical representations of quantum bits are fixed in position so that the representations cannot be moved with respect to each other, and each of them can interact only with its nearest neighbors. Even if this may seem a serious limitation, it can actually be bypassed with the swap gate shown in Fig. 4.16. Although the physical representations cannot be moved, we can alternatively move the state of the quantum bit from one representation to another with a sequence of swap actions each involving only nearest neighbors. A swap operation between two quantum bits can be realized with three controlled-NOT gates. Obviously, all this increases the number of gate operations required, but not seriously. At worst one needs $(L - 2)$ swaps per 2-bit gate operation in a system of L quantum bits (assuming that a return trip afterward is not required). If the number of 2-bit operations required scales as $f(L)$, the new scaling is at worst $\sim f(L)L$. In general, the inclusion of swapping opens a new dimension in circuit optimization. One may also envisage teleportation schemes for moving quantum information between distant and perhaps even physically different representation units.

4. *Universality and scalability*. Ultimately, we want to combine the single quantum components into quantum computing circuits. This demands that the physical character of the system carrying the output qubit must coincide with the character of the input qubits. Only in this way is it possible to use the components to cascade them and design networks that are of arbitrary size and complexity. Any output should be able to serve as an input for the next stage. This requirement is not satisfied in some of the realizations suggested. They may thus serve as illustrations of the principles, but they can never lead to a useful computing device. When this requirement is met, however, the number of possible computing steps N_c still limits the complexity of the system. Applied to the individual qubit, it tells us how many times this may be able to perform. However, as discussed earlier, the coherence between the coupled components may dephase much faster, allowing far smaller devices only. The ability of a realization to build up ever-larger networks is called its *scalability*.

5.3 LOGIC IN ELECTROMAGNETIC CAVITIES

5.3.1 Cavity Quantum Electrodynamics

Quantization of Cavity Fields We have pointed out that the photons of electromagnetic fields are eminent carriers of quantum bits. Because of their nature, they travel easily, they do not perturb each other, and they can be made rather insensitive to environmental perturbations. In addition, they can occur in linear combinations of two polarization states, thus manifesting the basic feature of qubits directly. However, in order to make them interact, they have to impinge on matter, and hence they need an atomic medium to effect conditional operations.

In free space the energy spectrum of photons forms a continuum. Consequently, it is difficult to identify the individual modes carrying the various qubits in an encoded message. In addition, interaction of the field with atomic matter will not be easily controlled. This situation changes radically if we confine the electromagnetic field to a finite cavity. The boundary conditions this imposes cause the spectrum to consist of separated discrete modes, which can be made to interact selectively with the quantum states of atomic matter. The cavity approach is well known from laser and maser technology. In a laser, the cavity is in practice a Fabry–Perot interferometer, and in the microwave regime it is a closed volume with metallic confining walls. When we quantize these modes, we obtain photons capable of serving as carriers of qubits. This field of research is called *cavity quantum electrodynamics* (cavity QED).

If we assume the inside of the cavity to be empty, the field is described by the Maxwell equations

$$\nabla \times \mathbf{H} = \varepsilon_0 \frac{\partial \mathbf{E}}{\partial t},$$
$$\nabla \times \mathbf{E} = -\mu_0 \frac{\partial \mathbf{H}}{\partial t}. \tag{5.6}$$

In addition to the boundary conditions at the edges of the cavity, the fields must satisfy the relations

$$\nabla \cdot \mathbf{E} = 0,$$
$$\nabla \cdot \mathbf{H} = 0. \tag{5.7}$$

From these equations we obtain directly the wave equation

$$\left(\nabla^2 - \varepsilon_0 \mu_0 \frac{\partial^2}{\partial t^2} \right) \mathbf{E} = 0. \tag{5.8}$$

This describes waves propagating with velocity

$$c^2 = \frac{1}{\varepsilon_0 \mu_0}. \tag{5.9}$$

Combined with the boundary conditions, this serves to define the eigenmodes of the cavity; after quantization the photons will reside in these modes.

To simplify treatment, we make a one-dimensional model of the cavity and require the field modes to stay coherent with themselves after a round trip through a cavity of length L (Fig. 5.1). We thus demand that the radiation wavelength λ satisfy

$$2L = n\lambda, \tag{5.10}$$

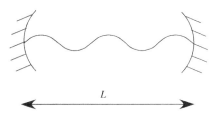

Figure 5.1   Fabry–Perot cavity of length L.

where n is an integer. This leads to eigenmodes with the wavenumbers and eigenfrequencies given by

$$k_n = \frac{2\pi}{\lambda} = \frac{\pi}{L}n,$$
$$\omega_n = ck_n = \frac{\pi c}{L}n. \tag{5.11}$$

The frequency separation between the modes is

$$\Delta f = \frac{\Delta \omega_n}{2\pi} = \frac{c}{2L}. \tag{5.12}$$

For a length of 1 cm, this is a separation of 15 GHz. The corresponding eigenmodes are given by

$$u_n(z) = \sqrt{\frac{2}{L}} \sin k_n z, \tag{5.13}$$

which are normalized as

$$\int_0^L u_n(z)u_m(z)\, dz = \delta_{nm}. \tag{5.14}$$

We look at the situation where only one mode is involved, and hence its label may be omitted. If we now write the electromagnetic field in the form

$$E_x(z) = E_0 q(t)u(z), \quad E_y(z) = 0, \tag{5.15}$$

the first of the equations (5.6) is satisfied if we take

$$H_y(z) = \sqrt{\frac{\varepsilon_0}{\mu_0}} E_0 \frac{\dot{q}(t)}{\omega} \sqrt{\frac{2}{L}} \cos kz. \tag{5.16}$$

The energy of the field is now given by the expression

$$E = \frac{1}{2} \int_0^L \left[\varepsilon_0 E_x^2(z) + \mu_0 H_y^2(z) \right] dz = \frac{\varepsilon_0 E_0^2}{\omega^2} \left(\frac{1}{2}\dot{q}^2(t) + \frac{1}{2}\omega^2 q^2(t) \right). \tag{5.17}$$

We recognize here the Hamiltonian of the harmonic oscillator as discussed in Sec. 1.2, and after identifying q with Q and $\dot{q}$ with P, we introduce a change of variables to creation and annihilation operators as defined in Eq. (1.20).

The eigenstates of the energy are given by the photon number states $|n\rangle$, again following Sec. 1.2. These states can be used further to define *coherent states*, which are as close to classical fields as can be constructed within the quantized system (see Sec. 2.3.3). For a small amplitude $|\alpha| \ll 1$, we may write a coherent state as

$$|\alpha\rangle = \frac{|0\rangle + \alpha|1\rangle}{1 + \frac{1}{2}|\alpha|^2}. \tag{5.18}$$

Because of the restriction on α, this is unfortunately not a good representation of a qubit.

We have discussed the case of a single mode only, but the extension to several modes is straightforward. The Hamiltonian may be written as

$$H = \sum_k \hbar\omega_k a_k^\dagger a_k, \tag{5.19}$$

the modes are labeled by k, and $\left[a_k, a_n^\dagger\right] = \delta_{kn}$. Here we have omitted the vacuum energies $\hbar\omega_k/2$ of the photons. The quantum states are now given by

$$|\Psi\rangle = |n_1, n_2, \ldots\rangle. \tag{5.20}$$

Interaction with Matter   According to the quantum description of matter, the energy eigenstates are discrete and we denote them by $|i\rangle$ with the corresponding eigenenergy $E_i = \hbar\omega_i$. The photons can effect the following transformations: With $E_i > E_j$, the photon absorption $|j\rangle \to |i\rangle$ is described by the term

$$a|i\rangle\langle j|$$

and shown in Fig. 5.2a. The corresponding emission $|i\rangle \to |j\rangle$, described by the term

$$a^\dagger|j\rangle\langle i| = (a|i\rangle\langle j|)^\dagger,$$

is shown in Fig. 5.2b. We note that the terms $a^\dagger|i\rangle\langle j|$ and $a|j\rangle\langle i|$ do not conserve energy and may be omitted. The Hamiltonian including the interactions is

$$H = \sum_k \hbar\omega_k a_k^\dagger a_k + \sum_i E_i|i\rangle\langle i| + \hbar \sum_{k,i>j} g_{ij}\left(a_k|i\rangle\langle j| + a_k^\dagger|j\rangle\langle i|\right). \tag{5.21}$$

Two-Level System   Much of quantum dynamics can be described in terms of level pairs coupled by a single mode. The Hamiltonian (5.21) can then be written as

$$H = \hbar\omega a^\dagger a + \frac{\hbar\Omega}{2}(1 + \sigma_3) + \hbar g\left(a\sigma^+ + a^\dagger\sigma^-\right), \tag{5.22}$$

where we have again introduced the Pauli operators (1.12) acting on the space $\{|0\rangle, |1\rangle\}$, and $\sigma^\pm = \frac{1}{2}(\sigma_1 \pm i\sigma_2)$ as in Eq. (2.214). This is the much used *Jaynes–Cummings model*. It is solved by the ansatz

$$|\psi_n\rangle = \exp(-i\omega n t)\left(c_0|n, 0\rangle + c_1|n - 1, 1\rangle\right). \tag{5.23}$$

(a)

(b)

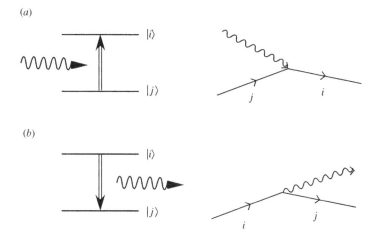

Figure 5.2 Diagrams for absorption and emission.

The coefficients are determined from the equations

$$i\frac{d}{dt}\begin{bmatrix} c_0 \\ c_1 \end{bmatrix} = \begin{bmatrix} 0 & g\sqrt{n} \\ g\sqrt{n} & \Delta \end{bmatrix}\begin{bmatrix} c_0 \\ c_1 \end{bmatrix},$$

(5.24)

where the detuning is written as

$$\Delta = \Omega - \omega.$$

(5.25)

The eigenvalues are clearly given by

$$\lambda_\pm = \frac{1}{2}\left(\Delta \pm \Omega_n\right),$$

(5.26)

where

$$\Omega_n^2 = \Delta^2 + 4g^2 n.$$

(5.27)

With the initial state defined by

$$c_0(0) = 1; \quad c_1(0) = 0,$$

(5.28)

we find the solution

$$c_0(t) = \exp\left(-i\frac{\Delta t}{2}\right)\left(\cos\frac{\Omega_n t}{2} + i\frac{\Delta}{\Omega_n}\sin\frac{\Omega_n t}{2}\right),$$

$$c_1(t) = -\frac{2ig\sqrt{n}}{\Omega_n}\exp\left(-i\frac{\Delta t}{2}\right)\sin\frac{\Omega_n t}{2}.$$

(5.29)

This looks like a classical solution, with the oscillations given by the effective Rabi frequency $\Omega_n = \sqrt{\Delta^2 + 4g^2 n}$. Because the total state space factors into uncoupled blocks for different values of n, all problems can be solved fully in this model.

Special Cases.

π *Pulse*   If we select the time such that

$$\Omega_n t_\pi = \pi, \tag{5.30}$$

we find that

$$
\begin{aligned}
c_0(t_\pi) &= i\frac{\Delta}{\Omega_n}\exp\left(-i\frac{\Delta t_\pi}{2}\right) \to 0, \\
c_1(t_\pi) &= -\frac{2ig\sqrt{n}}{\Omega_n}\exp\left(-i\frac{\Delta t_\pi}{2}\right) \to -i,
\end{aligned}
\tag{5.31}
$$

where the limit emerges when $\Delta \to 0$. This pulse inverts the population in the two-level system.

2π *Pulse*   If we select the time such that

$$\Omega_n t_{2\pi} = 2\pi, \tag{5.32}$$

we find that

$$
\begin{aligned}
c_0(t_{2\pi}) &= -\exp\left(-i\frac{\Delta t_{2\pi}}{2}\right) \to -1, \\
c_1(t_{2\pi}) &= 0.
\end{aligned}
\tag{5.33}
$$

This pulse thus returns the population to the original state. Note, however, that the phase has become -1 in the limit $\Delta \to 0$. This is a special property of the two-level system, which requires a phase change of 4π to restore the original state completely. Also, here we have $c_1 = 0$, independent of the value for Δ, and we can use Δ to set the phase change in c_0 to any value desired.

Another useful case is the $\pi/2$ pulse that for $\Delta = 0$ distributes the population evenly between the two states [see Eq. (5.29)]. Note that the special conditions given for $\Omega_n t$ can be fixed for only one value of n at a time; indeed, for superpositions of photon states the Rabi oscillations are quickly lost by dephasing. If we assume a semiclassical model, where the quantum states of an atom (or any qubit representation) are coupled by a classical oscillating field, the Rabi oscillations occur, but the photon number–dependent term in Eq. (5.27) is replaced by the classical Rabi frequency, which is proportional to the classical field intensity.

5.3.2 Conditional Logic

Interactions between photons can be achieved only with some material object being the intermediator. Atoms can be chosen for this purpose. We can, for instance, consider sending individual atoms through cavities where the photonic qubits are stored. Next we present two possible schemes that utilize the atomic structure and selection rules for electronic transitions. These two schemes serve as examples of how to proceed after one has determined the physical representation of information.

Scheme I We consider a four-level system where the ground state $|0\rangle$ is coupled to a doublet intermediate state $|1\pm\rangle$, which in its turn is coupled to a singlet $|2\rangle$. The intermediate state could be an $\ell = 1$ atomic state, where one of the Zeeman states ($m_\ell = 0$) is not used. This can be achieved by choosing the photon polarization appropriately, and fixing the atomic quantization axis with a weak magnetic field (which leaves the states more or less degenerate in energy). We have two field modes involved, described by the operators $a_\pm$ and $b_\pm$. The subscripts denote the two polarization states, which are taken to encode the two qubits involved.

The interaction Hamiltonian is taken to be

$$H_I = \hbar g \left(a_+^\dagger |1+\rangle\langle 0| + a_-^\dagger |1-\rangle\langle 0| + b_+^\dagger |2\rangle\langle 1 - | + b_-^\dagger |2\rangle\langle 1 + | + \text{h.c.} \right).$$
(5.34)

The level scheme is shown in Fig. 5.3. The two-qubit quantum state is taken to be

$$|\Psi\rangle_{\text{in}} = \left(\alpha_+ a_+^\dagger + \alpha_- a_-^\dagger \right) \left(\beta_+ b_+^\dagger + \beta_- b_-^\dagger \right) |0\rangle.$$
(5.35)

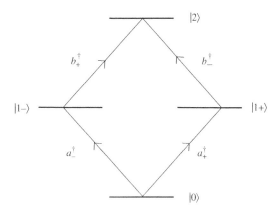

Figure 5.3 Four-level scheme for conditional logic.

The coding is set here as

$$
\begin{aligned}
a_+^\dagger |0\rangle &= |0\rangle_a; \ a_-^\dagger |0\rangle = |1\rangle_a; \\
b_+^\dagger |0\rangle &= |0\rangle_b; \ b_-^\dagger |0\rangle = |1\rangle_b,
\end{aligned}
\tag{5.36}
$$

where a and b are now the qubit labels.

Without carrying out a full analysis, we indicate how this system may be used to effect a conditional logic operation:

1. Let the detuning on the lower transition be at resonance $\Delta_{10} = 0$. Then applying a π pulse, we populate the levels $|1\pm\rangle$ in a proportion determined by the coefficients $\{\alpha_+, \alpha_-\}$. We choose the interaction time such that a single photon can transfer the population efficiently to the upper level:

$$
\Omega_{10} t = \pi.
\tag{5.37}
$$

2. We assume the second transition to be well detuned, $\Delta_{21} \gg g$. Then we have for the states involved in the transition

$$
\begin{aligned}
c_1(t) &\approx O\left(\frac{g}{\Delta}\right) \sim 0, \\
c_0(t) &\approx \exp\left(-i\frac{\Delta t}{2}\right)\left(\cos\frac{\Omega_n t}{2} + i\sin\frac{\Omega_n t}{2}\right) \\
&= \exp\left(i\frac{\Omega_n - \Delta}{2}t\right).
\end{aligned}
\tag{5.38}
$$

The rate of change of the phase of the lower state is now

$$
\frac{\Omega_n - \Delta}{2} = \frac{\sqrt{\Delta^2 + 4g^2 n} - \Delta}{2} \sim \frac{g^2}{\Delta}.
\tag{5.39}
$$

If we denote the phase by $\Phi = (g^2/\Delta)t$, we find that the presence of population on the levels $|1\pm\rangle$ shifts selectively the phases of the states $b_\pm^\dagger |0\rangle$. The action becomes

$$
\begin{aligned}
&\left(\alpha_+\beta_+ a_+^\dagger b_+^\dagger + \alpha_+\beta_- a_+^\dagger b_-^\dagger + \alpha_-\beta_+ a_-^\dagger b_+^\dagger + \alpha_-\beta_- a_-^\dagger b_-^\dagger\right)|0\rangle \\
&\Rightarrow \alpha_+\beta_+ b_+^\dagger |1+\rangle + \alpha_+\beta_- e^{i\Phi} b_-^\dagger |1+\rangle + \alpha_-\beta_+ e^{i\Phi} b_+^\dagger |1-\rangle + \alpha_-\beta_- b_-^\dagger |1-\rangle \\
&= \alpha_+\left(\beta_+ b_+^\dagger + e^{i\Phi}\beta_- b_-^\dagger\right)|1+\rangle + \alpha_-\left(e^{i\Phi}\beta_+ b_+^\dagger + \beta_- b_-^\dagger\right)|1-\rangle.
\end{aligned}
\tag{5.40}
$$

Thus, the polarization direction of the b-photons is shifted by the phases $\pm\Phi$, depending on the state of the a-photon. This amounts to conditional dynamics. Both inputs are photons and the state manipulated is a photon state. The atomic state and the control photon are destroyed in the process, but they may be restored by applying a suitably chosen second π pulse. There remains, however, the asymmetry between the detunings. This may be compensated by various technical means. The main drawback with the scheme is the requirement that a single photon is influential enough to produce a phase shift of π in times compatible with the restrictions imposed by relaxation rates of the system.

Scheme II Now we deal with a three-level system where the photon a couples $|0\rangle \rightarrow |1\rangle$ and the photon b couples $|0\rangle \rightarrow |2\rangle$ (Fig. 5.4). The presence of a photon codes 1 and its absence 0. There is a hazard in letting the absence of a photon carry information; this makes a failed detection convey information even if it is spurious. The initial state is given by

$$|\Psi\rangle_{\text{in}} = \left(\alpha_0 + \alpha_1 a^\dagger\right)\left(\beta_0 + \beta_1 b^\dagger\right)|0\rangle \tag{5.41}$$

and the interaction is taken as

$$H_I = \hbar g\left(a|1\rangle\langle 0| + b|2\rangle\langle 0| + \text{h.c.}\right). \tag{5.42}$$

The computational process now goes as follows:

1. If the a photon is not present, we have the two-level system $\{|0\rangle, |2\rangle\}$. Applying a 2π pulse now transforms the state as

$$\left(\beta_0 + \beta_1 b^\dagger\right)|0\rangle \Rightarrow \left(\beta_0 - \beta_1 b^\dagger\right)|0\rangle. \tag{5.43}$$

2. If the photon b now is not present, a similar situation applies, and we obtain the transformation

$$\left(\alpha_0 + \alpha_1 a^\dagger\right)|0\rangle \Rightarrow \left(\alpha_0 - \alpha_1 a^\dagger\right)|0\rangle. \tag{5.44}$$

3. If, however, both photons are present, the dynamic situation is more complicated, and we expect a phase shift given by $e^{i\Phi}$. To obtain this phase,

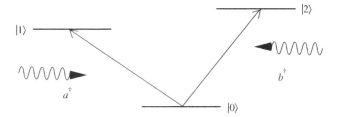

Figure 5.4 Three-level scheme for conditional logic.

we need to carry out the calculation in some detail. However, on the space of the states $\{|00\rangle, |01\rangle, |10\rangle, |11\rangle\}$, the transformation is

$$
\begin{bmatrix}
1 & 0 & 0 & 0 \\
0 & -1 & 0 & 0 \\
0 & 0 & -1 & 0 \\
0 & 0 & 0 & e^{i\Phi}
\end{bmatrix}.
$$

This is conditional logic of a simple kind.

The discussion above is highly simplified, but it indicates how three levels can be used to achieve a coupling between photon states. As above, the weakness is the fact that usually a single photon can be made to effect a small phase shift only.

5.3.3 Dissipative Processes in Cavity QED

In the discussions above, we have assumed that all dissipative processes may be neglected. This puts restrictions on the computing cycle time T_c that can be used. Thus, efficient computing requires large coupling constants, which allow one to reduce T_c accordingly. In real experiments, there are two types of relaxation processes:

1. Cavity decay, characterized by a rate parameter κ.
2. Atomic decay, characterized by a rate parameter γ.

If the coupling dipole moment for one atom is given by μ, the total atomic dipole is proportional to μN when we have N atoms involved. For an electromagnetic field E, the interaction time scale is determined by μE. Let us scale μ so that it corresponds to the coupling induced by the field of one photon, so for quantized fields, $\mu E = \mu \sqrt{n}$. This rescaled dipole moment in frequency units is equal in fact to the coupling term g in Eq. (5.22). It characterizes the interaction strengths generating the coherent processes and can be compared with the relaxation rates. One can consider two limiting situations:

1. *Weak coupling.* The relaxation processes dominate the dynamics

$$
\mu < \kappa; \ \ \mu < \gamma. \tag{5.45}
$$

In this regime, coherent processes are difficult, and the transitions induced can be calculated in perturbation theory.

2. *Strong coupling.* Here we have

$$
\mu^2 \gtrsim \kappa\gamma \tag{5.46}
$$

and we may estimate the dynamical behavior of the system:

a. First the field is driven by the atomic polarization P and damped by κ. In suitable scaled units, its evolution is given by

$$\dot{E} \sim P - \kappa E, \tag{5.47}$$

which allows us to estimate the field as

$$E \sim \frac{P}{\kappa} \sim \frac{\mu N}{\kappa}. \tag{5.48}$$

b. The polarization is driven by the field

$$\dot{P} \sim (\mu E)\, P \sim \frac{\mu^2 N}{\kappa} P \equiv \frac{P}{T}, \tag{5.49}$$

thus defining a time scale given by T.

c. For strong coupling to hold, we need to have

$$\gamma T = \frac{\gamma \kappa}{\mu^2 N} < 1. \tag{5.50}$$

This defines a critical atom number above which the strong coupling holds:

$$N > N_{\text{crit}} = \frac{\gamma \kappa}{\mu^2}. \tag{5.51}$$

If we require this critical value to be one atom, we find the condition (5.46).

On the other hand, $\mu E = \mu \sqrt{n}$ leads to

$$\mu \sqrt{n} \geq \gamma; \tag{5.52}$$

the field drives the atoms faster than the decay progresses. This requires

$$n_{\text{crit}} > \frac{\gamma^2}{\mu^2}. \tag{5.53}$$

If this critical value is 1, even a single photon can make a significant change of the state in the cavity. This is the extreme quantum limit of cavity QED.

In typical experiments, the parameters can be estimated to be:

	Microwave Experiments	Optical Experiments
$\gamma/2\pi$	1 Hz–1 MHz	1–100 MHz
$\kappa/2\pi$	0.5–500 Hz	100 kHz–0.5 MHz
$\mu/2\pi$	50 kHz	10–500 MHz

These rough estimates show that it is possible to achieve strong coupling in both frequency regimes. For actual experiments, the reader must consult the recent literature, because the field is developing rapidly.

5.4   LOGIC WITH IONS IN TRAPS

5.4.1   Trapping Cool Ions

It is possible to cool atoms using the exchange of momentum between atoms and light interacting with them. These schemes are based on the internal level structure of the particles, and thus the method can equally well be applied to ionized systems (i.e., we can produce cold ions). Here *cold* obviously only means having low energy. The trapping of only a few particles makes the assignment of a temperature more a metaphor than a thermodynamic statement.

The advantage in using ions is that their motion can be strongly affected by external fields. In particular, they can be confined to a bounded region by trapping potentials. The *Earnshaw theorem* states that static potentials alone cannot trap charged objects in all three dimensions. The reason is that any potential configuration $V(r)$ must in empty space obey the potential condition

$$\nabla^2 V(r) = 0, \tag{5.54}$$

which implies that extreme values cannot occur inside the region. Extremes at the edges are given by the electrodes, and thus trapping is not achieved.

It is, however, possible to trap particles in a rapidly varying electric field. To see this, we look at the one-dimensional equation of motion

$$m\ddot{x} = \lambda x \cos \omega t. \tag{5.55}$$

There seems to be no stable solution because the force averages to zero with time. In the limit of large frequency ω, we can separate the rapid following of the field from the slow drift over long times. This *micromotion* $\xi(t)$ is superimposed on a smooth average motion $X(t)$,

$$x(t) = X(t) + \xi(t), \tag{5.56}$$

to give

$$m\ddot{X} + m\ddot{\xi} = \lambda X \cos \omega t + \lambda \xi \cos \omega t. \tag{5.57}$$

We now assume that $\xi \ll X$ and $\ddot{\xi} \gg \ddot{X}$, giving in lowest order

$$m\ddot{\xi} = \lambda X \cos \omega t, \tag{5.58}$$

with the solution

$$\xi(t) = -\frac{\lambda X(t)}{m\omega^2} \cos \omega t. \tag{5.59}$$

Inserting this into the remaining part of (5.57) gives

$$m\ddot{X} = \lambda\xi\cos\omega t = -\frac{\lambda^2 X}{m\omega^2}\cos^2\omega t, \tag{5.60}$$

which determines the smooth motion. Replacing the trigonometric term by its time average, we obtain the equation

$$\ddot{X} = -\Omega^2 X, \tag{5.61}$$

which describes bound harmonic motion with the frequency

$$\Omega = \frac{\lambda}{\sqrt{2}\,m\omega}. \tag{5.62}$$

This demonstrates how stable motion can emerge from rapidly varying forces with a vanishing average. Traps of this kind are called *Paul traps*.

In general, the mode of operation described by (5.62) is not the most advantageous. The full equation of motion is an example of the Mathieu equation, which has got several regimes of stable bounded motion. In fact, laboratory traps are set on an operating point differing from the one above.

To achieve trapping in real three-dimensional systems, experimentalists use a quadrupole field of the type

$$V(x, y, z) = V_0\left(x^2 + y^2 - 2z^2\right)\cos\omega t, \tag{5.63}$$

which is seen to satisfy (5.54) and gives an equation of motion like (5.61) in each direction. An electrode configuration giving this potential is shown in Fig. 5.5. The resulting trapping of ions is quite stable, the binding energy is on the order of electron volts and the oscillational frequencies are in the range 100 kHz to 10 MHz. As the fast-driving field has a frequency on the order of a few times 100 Mz, the separation of the micromotion is well justified.

Even if the micromotion makes the dynamical trapping differ from the genuine harmonic motion, in many aspects we may utilize the harmonic oscillator as its model. This has the advantage that we may apply well-known theoretical results from quantum mechanics. If we consider the level scheme in Fig. 5.6, we can write rate equations for the laser-induced transitions as

$$\frac{dP(n)}{dt} = (n+1)A_-P(n+1) + nA_+P(n-1) - nA_-P(n) - (n+1)A_+P(n). \tag{5.64}$$

Here $P(n)$ is the occupation probability of the harmonic oscillator level n, and $A_\pm$ are the transition rates, up and down, induced by the external laser fields. If $A_- > A_+$, cooling ensues. The steady-state solution of (5.64) is given by

$$P(n+1) = \frac{A_+}{A_-}P(n), \tag{5.65}$$

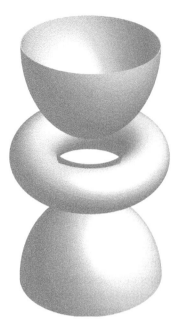

Figure 5.5 Electrode setup for ion trapping.

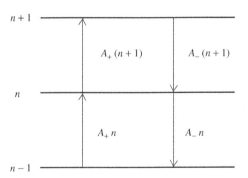

Figure 5.6 Schematics for the rate processes.

which also indicates a detailed balance between each level pair (Fig. 5.6). The normalized solution of the recurrence relation (5.65) is

$$P(n) = \left(1 - \frac{A_+}{A_-}\right)\left(\frac{A_+}{A_-}\right)^n. \tag{5.66}$$

If we introduce an effective temperature by writing

$$\frac{A_+}{A_-} = \exp\left(-\frac{\hbar\Omega}{k_B T}\right), \tag{5.67}$$

we find the solution to correspond to the Planck distribution with final energy

$$E_f = \hbar\Omega \left(\langle n \rangle + \frac{1}{2} \right) = \hbar\Omega \left(\frac{1}{\exp(\hbar\Omega/k_BT) - 1} + \frac{1}{2} \right). \qquad (5.68)$$

In the theory of laser cooling, the rate coefficients $A_\pm$ are calculated from quantum theory. Once known, they determine the final energy of the cooling process. If the cooling is very efficient, $A_- \gg A_+$, we find that

$$k_BT = \frac{\hbar\Omega}{\log(A_-/A_+)} \ll \hbar\Omega; \qquad (5.69)$$

then the ions can be cooled to their vibrational ground state.

Many Ions and Collective Motions When many ions are introduced into an ion trap, they experience a strong repulsive Coulombic force between them. Then they tend to order in regular latticelike structures. The distance between the ions is rather large, but they still have collective modes of oscillations, due to their strong repulsion.

In a highly elongated trap the ions tend to form regular strings (Fig. 5.7). If the trapping in transversal directions is very efficient, the simplest collective motion is a uniform vibration of the center of mass in the longitudinal direction, which occurs at the longitudinal trap frequency Ω. Another mode is one where the interparticle distances increase and decrease periodically: the breathing mode. This corresponds to a stretch oscillation in a molecule, and its frequency is higher than that of the center of mass oscillation. These modes are shown in Fig. 5.8.

This discussion omits the influence of the micromotion. This is imposed on the harmonic dynamics and makes the ions jitter. With several ions in the trap, this motion may induce collisionlike interactions between them and they may heat up. Thus, energy can leak from the fast driving frequency to the smooth motion, which will tend to heat the system. The actual operation of this mechanism is still not fully understood.

Combining the existence of collective modes with the rather large ionic distances, one may utilize an ion trap for quantum logic operations. The collective motion acts to couple the individual ions; it serves as a data bus, and the distances allow the focusing of light on an arbitrary individual in the chain. Thus, by encoding quantum information in the internal states of the ions, we have the raw material for a computing circuit.

Without the external couplings, we may write the Hamiltonian in the form

$$H = \hbar \left(\omega_e |e\rangle\langle e| + \omega_g |g\rangle\langle g| + \Omega a^\dagger a \right); \qquad (5.70)$$

here a and $a^\dagger$ act on the vibrational level of the collective oscillation. Resonant transitions are induced between the ground and excited motional level whenever the laser frequency is given by

$$\omega_0 = \omega_e - \omega_g + \Omega \left(n_f - n_i \right), \qquad (5.71)$$

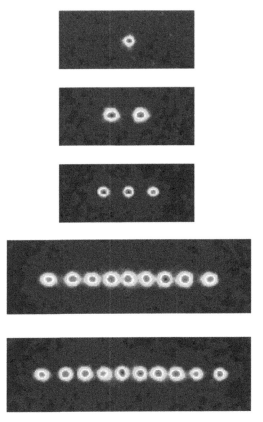

Figure 5.7   Ions in a string in a linear trap. (From Ref. [70]; with permission of Rainer Blatt.).

where the transition is between the levels $|g, n_i\rangle \longleftrightarrow |e, n_f\rangle$. If we assume that no off-resonant driving needs to be taken into account, this allows us to address each ion separately, but with a transition frequency depending on the collective motion of the ionic assembly. The corresponding level scheme is shown in Fig. 5.9.

5.4.2 Quantum Logic in an Ion Trap

Coupling by a resonant laser acting on the two-level system $\{|g\rangle, |e\rangle\}$ is assumed to effect the coupling

$$\Sigma = a|e\rangle\langle g| + a^\dagger|g\rangle\langle e|. \tag{5.72}$$

Note here that the operators a act on the oscillational states of the motion. This generates the transformation

$$U_\theta = \exp(-i\theta\Sigma), \tag{5.73}$$

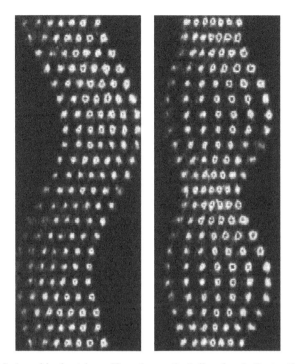

Figure 5.8 Modes of ionic strings. Here the vertical direction indicates time. As can be seen from the right-hand figure, there is an admixture of the center of mass oscillation in the breathing mode. (From Ref. [16]; with permission of Rainer Blatt.).

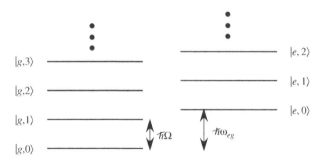

Figure 5.9 Level scheme for ionic states. Here $\omega_{eg} \equiv \omega_e - \omega_g$, and typically, $\omega_{eg} \gg \Omega$.

where the parameter θ is proportional to the coupling strength times the interaction time. We have

$$U_\theta |g, 0\rangle = |g, 0\rangle. \tag{5.74}$$

We also have

$$\Sigma^2 = aa^\dagger |e\rangle\langle e| + a^\dagger a |g\rangle\langle g|. \tag{5.75}$$

Acting on the states $\{|e, 0\rangle, |g, 1\rangle\}$ we have

$$\Sigma^2|e, 0\rangle = |e, 0\rangle; \quad \Sigma|e, 0\rangle = |g, 1\rangle;$$
$$\Sigma^2|g, 1\rangle = |g, 1\rangle; \quad \Sigma|g, 1\rangle = |e, 0\rangle. \tag{5.76}$$

We expand:

$$\exp(-i\theta\Sigma) = \sum_{k=0}^{\infty} \frac{(-i\theta)^k}{k!} \Sigma^k$$
$$= \sum_{\nu=0}^{\infty} \frac{(-i\theta)^{2\nu}}{(2\nu)!} \Sigma^{2\nu} + \sum_{\nu=0}^{\infty} \frac{(-i\theta)^{2\nu+1}}{(2\nu+1)!} \Sigma^{2\nu+1}. \tag{5.77}$$

Using the relations (5.76), we obtain

$$U_\theta|g, 1\rangle = \cos\theta|g, 1\rangle - i\sin\theta|e, 0\rangle \tag{5.78}$$

and

$$U_\theta|e, 0\rangle = \cos\theta|e, 0\rangle - i\sin\theta|g, 1\rangle. \tag{5.79}$$

Thus, a π pulse, $2\theta = \pi$, effects the transformations

$$|g, 1\rangle \Rightarrow -i|e, 0\rangle,$$
$$|e, 0\rangle \Rightarrow -i|g, 1\rangle, \tag{5.80}$$

and a 2π pulse, $2\theta = 2\pi$, effects the transformations

$$|g, 1\rangle \rightarrow -|g, 1\rangle,$$
$$|e, 0\rangle \Rightarrow -|e, 0\rangle. \tag{5.81}$$

See also the discussion at the end of Sec. 5.3.1.

We are now ready to present a two-qubit logical gate. We assume two arbitrary ions in an ion trap, denoted as 1 and 2. Two internal levels are used to encode two binary numbers in the manner

$$\{|g\rangle_1|g\rangle_2, |g\rangle_1|e\rangle_2, |e\rangle_1|g\rangle_2, |e\rangle_1|e\rangle_2\} \Longleftrightarrow \{|00\rangle, |01\rangle, |10\rangle, |11\rangle\}. \tag{5.82}$$

We denote by U_π^k a π pulse applied to ion $k(= 1, 2)$ and $U_{2\pi}^k$ the corresponding 2π pulse. We also need an additional 2π pulse $\tilde{U}_{2\pi}^2$ coupling the state $|g\rangle_2$ to an auxiliary state $|\tilde{e}\rangle_2$ without affecting anything else. This thus transforms $|g\rangle_2 \Rightarrow -|g\rangle_2$. We assume that the collective oscillational mode has been cooled to its ground state. We now perform the following sequence of steps, displaying their effect on the basis states:

	$|g\rangle_1|g\rangle_2|0\rangle$	$|g\rangle_1|e\rangle_2|0\rangle$	$|e\rangle_1|g\rangle_2|0\rangle$	$|e\rangle_1|e\rangle_2|0\rangle$
U_π^1	$\downarrow$	$\downarrow$	$\downarrow$	$\downarrow$
	$|g\rangle_1|g\rangle_2|0\rangle$	$|g\rangle_1|e\rangle_2|0\rangle$	$-i|g\rangle_1|g\rangle_2|1\rangle$	$-i|g\rangle_1|e\rangle_2|1\rangle$
$\tilde{U}_{2\pi}^2$	$\downarrow$	$\downarrow$	$\downarrow$	$\downarrow$
	$|g\rangle_1|g\rangle_2|0\rangle$	$|g\rangle_1|e\rangle_2|0\rangle$	$i|g\rangle_1|g\rangle_2|1\rangle$	$-i|g\rangle_1|e\rangle_2|1\rangle$
$U_{2\pi}^1$	$\downarrow$	$\downarrow$	$\downarrow$	$\downarrow$
	$|g\rangle_1|g\rangle_2|0\rangle$	$|g\rangle_1|e\rangle_2|0\rangle$	$|e\rangle_1|g\rangle_2|0\rangle$	$-|e\rangle_1|e\rangle_2|0\rangle$

As a transformation matrix on the basis states (5.82), this is the transformation

$$U = \begin{bmatrix} 1 & 0 & 0 & 0 \\ 0 & 1 & 0 & 0 \\ 0 & 0 & 1 & 0 \\ 0 & 0 & 0 & -1 \end{bmatrix}. \tag{5.83}$$

In Sec. 4.1.3 we showed that this is equivalent to a controlled-not (CNOT) logical operation. Thus, we can realize an arbitrary two-qubit operation on the ion system. This seems to be a most promising way to implement quantum logic on a real laboratory system.

Evaluation of an Ion Trap Computer Referring to the criteria proposed in Sec. 5.2, we can give an evaluation of the prospects offered by a trapped ion system:

1. Single qubits can be stored in a reliable way. The decoherence times in ion traps are shown to be up to the order of minutes.

2. Due to the large separation between ions, individual qubits can be addressed by external laser beams. The ions retain their place (i.e., they behave as classical storage locations).

3. The common vibrational modes act as data buses coupling the individual qubits. This allows us to perform reliable two-qubit operations. The rate of a single logical step depends on the intensity of the external light. But increasing this will eventually induce too much harmful off-resonant excitation.

4. There exist reliable methods to read the value of a qubit. These are based on quantum jump techniques (e.g., an ion in its internal ground state can be excited externally to another state, which fluoresces rapidly back to the original state). The photons emitted signal the presence of the ground state, assuming that the other computational state is not affected by the interrogating light. The reading process obviously destroys the coherence between the computational states.

5. There are atomic ions that can easily be combined with existing laser wavelengths. Experiments have been carried out with Be^+, Ca^+, and Ba^+ ions, for example.

The methods also offers some disadvantages:

1. Good cooling is required to get the proper initial state well prepared. Cooling a single ion down to its motional ground state is no longer very difficult, but cooling a chainlike structure with laser light is complicated even for a chain of two ions. This has prompted researchers to propose schemes where it is not necessary to reach the lowest motional states.
2. The method is not too scalable. It may not be easy to go beyond a dozen atoms. This already gives a rather larger trap, as the ion separation has to be considerably larger than the optical wavelength used in addressing the qubits. The requirement to focus on a single ion imposes this limitation.

5.4.3 Computing with Hot Ions

We are still considering a chain of trapped ions that have collective vibrational states labeled with the phonon quantum number n. For effecting conditional logic between any two ions, one now uses off-resonant lasers with two different frequencies. Regarding the four possible state of a two-ion system, we use the notation of Eq. (5.82), with the phonon quantum number as an additional quantum label. The idea for the two-ion *bichromatic gate* proceeds roughly as follows.

When a laser with frequency ω_1 targets the first ion, it is detuned by the amount $\delta > 0$ above the $|00, n\rangle \longleftrightarrow |10, n\rangle$ transition. The other laser, with frequency ω_2 and targeting the second ion, is detuned below $|00, n\rangle \longleftrightarrow |01, n\rangle$ by the amount $-\delta$. This arrangement means that in a two-ion system, we have a two-photon resonance between the states $|00, n\rangle \longleftrightarrow |11, n\rangle$ for any value of n, as shown in Fig. 5.10.

If δ is suitably large, the lasers are off-resonant with any of the intermediate states, and these are not populated. However, for two-photon transitions we can, in second-order perturbation theory, assign intermediate states. Depending on the order of applying the lasers, we find that there are two possible intermediate states, $|10, n + 1\rangle$ and $|01, n - 1\rangle$. This being a quantum mechanical system, the two paths interfere and it turns out that any n-dependence is canceled. Thus, the ionic chain can be in any pure or mixed (e.g., thermal) state without affecting the coherent, controllable transitions between states $|00\rangle$ and $|11\rangle$. There are n-sensitive light-induced frequency shifts that affect states $|01\rangle$ and $|10\rangle$, but these can be eliminated by applying the two lasers simultaneously on both ions. A similar two-photon connection is also established between states $|01, n\rangle$ and $|10, n\rangle$. The ability to effect n-independent Rabi oscillations between the two sets of two-ion states can be combined with various single-ion operations to produce a CNOT gate.

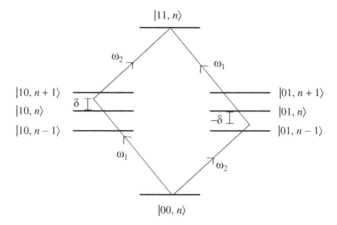

Figure 5.10 Level scheme for a bichromatic gate.

It should be noted that although in this scheme, the laser beams play an important role in effecting the conditional logic, it is still made possible only by the existence of the states of collective motion. The problem with the scheme above is that as we again rely on a perturbative effect, it takes considerable time to perform gate operations. For example, if the frequency difference for the vibrations of collective motion is about 200 kHz and detuning is of the same order, gate operation times are measured in milliseconds. This time scale is too long, considering, for example, the fluctuating magnetic fields that affect the experiments. The method can, however, be improved by allowing some sensitivity to heating. This improvement is too complicated to be presented here, but it is expected to reduce T_c into the microsecond region.

5.5 SOLID-STATE SYSTEMS

5.5.1 General Considerations

From many instances in laser physics, we know that most of the fundamental progress emerges from experiments on atoms or molecules. The reasons are obvious: These entities have well-defined spectra, they can be isolated from each other, and their relevant parameters can be manipulated easily. Their number can be controlled by pressure and their motion by cooling; the internal structure can be tuned by electric and magnetic fields. However, when reliable operation and compact realizations are needed in commercial applications, one must eventually turn to solid-state devices. These have to be manufactured to given specifications, which assumes that the mode of operation is well understood physically. The advantage is that the parameters do not drift and usually deteriorate slowly. Also, small assemblies of components become realizable; integrated devices have many advantages.

This holds also with quantum information-processing devices; when the physics becomes manageable, any commercial device should preferably be based on solid matter. Quantum cavities and ion traps are too bulky and mechanically fragile to be reliable components.

To learn which solid-state systems are promising, we should consider the ways we can store energy in solids. The imprinting of information on any physical system must necessarily bring it out of its thermal equilibrium state. As this is one of minimum entropy, the writing must increase its entropy. This is considered by many to be a measure of the amount of information encoded in the system; see the discussion in Sec. 4.5.2.

We list below the main elementary excitation modes of bulk solids.

- *Band electrons*: Conduction-carrying charges in solids and semiconductors.
- *Excitons*: Bound electron–hole compounds in semiconductors.
- *Polarons*: Electrons redressed by their corresponding lattice distortion.
- *Polaritons*: Collective excitations combining the electromagnetic photons with lattice vibrational quanta.
- *Spin waves*: The elementary excitations in magnetically ordered solids.

All these react rapidly and faithfully to external guiding fields, and thus they can be manipulated easily. However, they are obviously poor candidates for quantum information processing. Despite the fact that quantization makes them into individual countable entities, they do not retain their identity, and they travel freely along the volume of the sample. Thus, they violate one of the basic requirements for carriers of qubits: We cannot be sure which entity carries which bit. A similar problem will be encountered by all methods to store digital information in any continuous degree of freedom. This also applies to electromagnetic field propagation in open space. Uniquely definable carriers of discrete quantum information are far from trivially found.

Thus, we need to look into human-made solid circuits. Here the local character of the fundamental system guarantees that they form an assembly of classically identifiable units. The existence of nanostructure technology makes this a promising enterprise. Next we consider two widely investigated candidates.

5.5.2 Special Examples

Quantum Dots   The modern technology of epitaxial growth allows scientists to build up spatial structures of preassigned geometry. The accuracy is so good that essentially single-atom precision can be achieved. Such structures usually have the spatial sizes given in terms of nanometers (10^{-9} m), giving the resulting technology its name *nanophysics*.

One type of structure much investigated is islands of material where individual electrons can be confined. These are called *quantum dots* because the confining potentials are so localized that the electrons find themselves in the ideal quantum well described by elementary exercises in textbooks; the dots act like artificial atoms. The material can be of different types: We may have metal dots on insulating templates or semiconductor materials embedded in insulators. The latter offers the usual semiconductor advantage of allowing bandgap engineering by alloying and doping. The primary substances are still gallium (Ga) and arsenic (As).

The typical length scale of a quantum dot array is $x = 10$ nm $= 10^{-8}$ m, making the energy scale equal to

$$E \sim \frac{\hbar^2}{mx^2} \sim 0.76 \text{ meV}, \tag{5.84}$$

which corresponds to frequencies in the microwave region. Each dot is assumed to carry one qubit in the form of quantum states based on two of its discrete electronic states:

$$|\psi\rangle = c_0|E_0\rangle + c_1|E_1\rangle. \tag{5.85}$$

The internal states can usually be coupled by radiation-induced dipole transitions, which makes single-qubit operations possible.

As the lattice constant in GaAs is on the order of $a \sim 0.6$ nm, the dots are well separated. The packing density of qubits is, however, rather impressive: 1 cm^3 of the material can carry

$$\left(\frac{10^{-2}}{10^{-8}} \right)^3 = 10^{18} \tag{5.86}$$

qubits. Thus, even well-separated units can provide huge numbers of computational units.

The possibilities of achieving two-qubit logic are, however, limited. When acted upon by radiation, the units develop induced dipoles. These convey information between each other by dipole–dipole interaction, which depends on the dot-to-dot distance R as

$$V_{\text{dipole}} \sim \frac{1}{R^3}. \tag{5.87}$$

As this decreases rather rapidly with distance, it seems reasonable to assume that only the neighboring dots can perform logic operations. As discussed in Sec. 5.2, this restriction can be lifted with swap operations, although the number of operations required then increases to some extent.

The huge obstacle to using quantum dots is their sensitivity to dephasing, destroying the quantum coherence between the carriers of the individual qubits. As the information-carrying entities are charged, the sensitivity to stray fields is large, but in this case we have an additional complication. The dots are deposited on a solid template, which has its own stochastic fluctuations and provides excellent coupling from mechanical disturbances in the entire setup. It is not clear at present if and how these difficulties will be overcome.

Superconducting Junctions   Modern nanotechnology has introduced a novel device termed a *single-electron transistor*. The geometry is depicted in Fig. 5.11, where we see a well-isolated island of conducting material weakly coupled to two electron reservoirs through tunneling junctions. As in the case of quantum dots, the island has a set of internal electronic bound states. However, the minute size of the island makes it have an exceedingly small capacitance C to the common ground of the device. Thus, if the island is occupied by a single electron, it costs the energy

$$E_{\text{charge}} = \frac{e^2}{2C} \tag{5.88}$$

to introduce the second electron (Fig. 5.12). If this is large enough not to be available, the first electron efficiently blocks transmission through the circuit (Coulomb blockade). Thus, the experiments have shown conclusively that charges pass the island one at a time only. This possibility to control the flow has justified the term *single-electron transistor*.

As any solid-state device, the one described above is highly sensitive to dephasing. This may, however, be improved if the metallic conductors are replaced by superconductors. They have much more coherent quantum states and are very robust against perturbations by the environment. Their elementary charge carrier is the Cooper pair of charge $2e$; with this replacement the argument above goes through directly. A single Cooper pair confined to an island may then serve as the

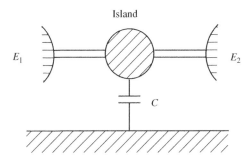

Figure 5.11   Metallic island surrounded by two tunneling junctions.

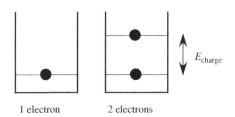

Figure 5.12   Energy states of a metallic island.

carrier of the qubit. It has also been shown experimentally that coherent single-qubit manipulations are feasible.

The difficulty with superconducting islands as information carriers is how to retain coherence between two different units. The very construction of the device leads to rather large distances between them, and then the possibility of effecting coherently driven conditional logic operations becomes more difficult. On the other hand, action on one island by voltage manipulation affects the energy states of the other islands as well, despite the seemingly long distances. The individual pairs of units will also be fragile to decoherence induced by the environment. If and how these difficulties can be overcome is still an open question.

As an alternative to using the individual Cooper pairs as carriers of quantum information, we may consider another discrete variable in a superconducting device: the magnetic flux. A closed superconducting circuit of the type shown in Fig. 5.13 has to have a gauge-invariant state function. The quantum state of a Cooper pair feels the vector potential through a prefactor of the type

$$\exp\left(i\frac{2e}{\hbar}\oint \mathbf{A}\cdot d\mathbf{r}\right) = \exp\left(i\frac{2e}{\hbar}\oint \nabla \times \mathbf{A}\cdot d\mathbf{a}\right). \tag{5.89}$$

In order to give a unique phase, we must have

$$\frac{2e}{\hbar}\oint \nabla \times \mathbf{A}\cdot d\mathbf{a} = \frac{2e}{\hbar}\oint \mathbf{B}\cdot d\mathbf{a} = \frac{2e}{\hbar}\Phi = 2\pi n, \tag{5.90}$$

where n is an integer. This demands the magnetic flux to be quantized in units of

$$\Phi_0 = \frac{2\pi\hbar}{2e}. \tag{5.91}$$

Because of the quantum nature of the system, it is possible to achieve a coherent superposition of the states of a circuit like the one in Fig. 5.14. We may have

$$|\psi\rangle = c_0|\Phi_0\rangle + c_1|-\Phi_0\rangle. \tag{5.92}$$

As these two states correspond to the current circulating in opposite directions, their coupling involves changing the motional state of a huge number of electrons $\sim 10^6$. Consequently, the two states are difficult to couple to each other and the

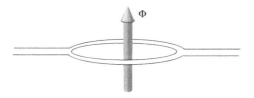

Figure 5.13   Closed superconducting circuit in a magnetic flux Φ.

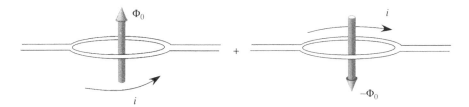

Figure 5.14 Superposition of superconducting currents.

qubit becomes highly robust against dephasing. To what extent this phenomenon can be used as the basis for quantum information processing is not clear for the moment. When networks are to be formed from several individual units, the difficulties are the same as listed above for the case of devices based on Cooper pairs.

5.6 MACROMOLECULES AND OPTICAL LATTICES

5.6.1 Nuclear Spin in Molecules

The spin of an elementary particle would be a rather invisible quantity without its contribution to the magnetic moment of the particle and thus its interaction with magnetic fields. Turning the tables, we can picture the spin as a qubit, magnetic fields as tools for control, and spin–spin interaction as a mediator for conditional logic. Here we will, in particular, be concerned with the spin of the atomic nucleus given by the physical entity $\mathbf{I}$, which carries with it a magnetic moment $\mu = \gamma \mathbf{I}$, where γ is called the *gyromagnetic ratio*. (From its definition, it should be called the *magnetogyric ratio*.) In an external magnetic field, the nucleus thus experiences the interaction

$$H = -\mu \cdot \mathbf{B} = -\gamma \mathbf{I} \cdot \mathbf{B} \sim \hbar \omega_{\text{Larmor}}. \tag{5.93}$$

For standard laboratory magnetic fields, the Larmor frequency is of the order

$$\frac{\omega_{\text{Larmor}}}{2\pi} \sim 500 \text{ MHz}, \tag{5.94}$$

which is a very manageable value for modern electronics. Wide use of the nuclear magnetic resonance (NMR) in materials research and medical investigations (MRI) implies that reliable and flexible commercial apparatuses are easily available. Thus, quantum information manipulations based on nuclear spins offer a promising possibility.

The nuclear spins are located on the individual atoms. At molecular sites, the spins interact with the local environment and their resonance frequencies are displaced by what is called a *chemical shift*. These are often of the order 100 to 1000 Hz, which allows even the individual nuclei of identical atoms to be addressed separately by varying the frequency. Thus, the two hydrogen atoms in

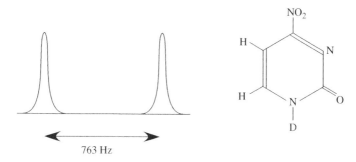

Figure 5.15 Hydrogen atom lines and position in deuterated cytosine.

the partially deuterated cytosine unit occurring in DNA are separated by 763 Hz (Fig. 5.15). One may also use different nuclei. As an example, replacing an individual hydrogen atom by another atom may lead to shifts up to 100 MHz. This gives excellent selectivity in the addressing process.

If we ask how many different nuclei one may be able to access, we have to know their frequency separations. If we combine this with the frequency tunability of our apparatus, we can deduce the potentialities of our system. By applying the proper radiation pulse to a selected nucleus, we can achieve an arbitrary single-qubit operation.

To achieve conditional logic manipulations, the qubits have to interact. Inside a molecule they do this by their magnetic dipole–dipole interaction, also known as *spin–spin interaction*. This is of long range, so many qubits can be affected by the manipulations, but on the other hand, the interactions are badly controlled. This problem has got a surprising solution; in a room-temperature liquid, the molecules are constantly disturbed by the thermal motion and the strongly anisotropic dipole–dipole interaction averages to zero.

The remaining interaction is the valence electron–transmitted interaction, which leads to isotropic and local interaction between the spins of the nuclei. This is of the type

$$H = J\mathbf{I}_1 \cdot \mathbf{I}_2 = J(I_1^x I_2^x + I_1^y I_2^y + I_1^z I_2^z). \tag{5.95}$$

This is the same mechanism that gives rise to the Heisenberg interaction in magnetic insulators. In the thermal environment, the molecules still rotate rapidly around the axis parallel with the external field, and from the expansion

$$I_1^y I_2^y + I_1^x I_2^x = \frac{1}{2}\left(I_1^+ I_2^- + I_1^- I_2^+\right) \tag{5.96}$$

we find that this part also averages to zero. Thus, the remaining interaction is

$$\overline{H} = J I_1^z I_2^z = J \begin{bmatrix} 1 & 0 & 0 & 0 \\ 0 & -1 & 0 & 0 \\ 0 & 0 & -1 & 0 \\ 0 & 0 & 0 & 1 \end{bmatrix}, \tag{5.97}$$

where the basis $\{|00\rangle, |01\rangle, |10\rangle, |11\rangle\}$ is used. This can be utilized to effect conditional logic.

Left to itself, the system will evolve with the operator $\exp(-i\overline{H}t/\hbar)$, which can carry out any operation on the state space when the interaction time is suitably chosen. The time scale over which this takes place is given by $\hbar J^{-1} \sim 0.1 - 0.01$ s. This time scale allows easy control, but it makes the process rather slow. In addition, all qubits will evolve together, and the result depends sensitively on the control of the time variable.

A major problem with nuclear spin systems is that their energy scales are such that the system cannot be prepared in its ground state. In fact, the frequency 500 MHz corresponds to 10^{-5} of the room-temperature energy. Thus, nearly all levels are occupied initially. However, surprisingly enough, the smallness of the energies involved may again be utilized to facilitate the process. We may, namely, expand the density matrix of the system

$$\rho = Z^{-1} \exp\left(-\frac{H}{k_B T}\right) \simeq Z^{-1}\left(1 - \frac{H}{k_B T}\right). \tag{5.98}$$

Carrying out quantum manipulations on this system, we observe spin components I^α when reading the system. As they are represented by traceless operators, the unity term in the expansion of the density matrix gives no contribution:

$$\langle I^\alpha \rangle = \text{Tr}(I^\alpha \rho) = 0 + \mathcal{O}\left(\frac{H}{k_B T}\right). \tag{5.99}$$

Thus, even if only a minute fraction (10^{-5}) of all nuclei contribute to the signal, they are the only ones observed.

We still need to be able to prepare the initial ensemble of the spins in the liquid. This can be done by pulses. According to the basic interactions (5.93) and (5.95), we have terms of the form $I_1 + I_2$ and $I_1 \cdot I_2$. By combining these, suitably we may realize the interaction

$$\frac{1}{4}(1 + 2I_1)(1 + 2I_2) = \frac{1}{4} + \frac{1}{2}(I_1 + I_2) + I_1 \cdot I_2. \tag{5.100}$$

Letting this act on the basis states $\{|--\rangle, |-+\rangle, |+-\rangle, |++\rangle\}$, we find the representation

$$\frac{1}{4}(1 + 2I_1)(1 + 2I_2) = \begin{bmatrix} 0 & 0 & 0 & 0 \\ 0 & 0 & 0 & 0 \\ 0 & 0 & 0 & 0 \\ 0 & 0 & 0 & 1 \end{bmatrix}. \tag{5.101}$$

This projects out the state $|++\rangle$, which serves as an effective state coding $|\text{"0"}, \text{"0"}\rangle$. Addressing the individual spins, we may then prepare the other three states of the two-qubit system by single-qubit operations.

When reading the outcome of a computational sequence, we note that the signal from one individual spin is not observable; its contribution to the dipole moment is too small. However, despite the fact that only a minute fraction of all nuclei contribute, there are enough of them in a bulk sample to give an easily observable effect. Thus, quantum computation is simultaneously performed on an entire ensemble of systems. This has the benefit that we get classically measurable signals, as the observation automatically provides the ensemble average. The drawback is, however, that we lose the possibility of utilizing specifically quantum mechanical features. Thus, the reduction of the quantum state by the observation loses its relevance in the nuclear spin method. Any scheme based on the measurement-induced state projection cannot be applied directly to the present case.

The advantage is, on the other hand, that the possibility to design various molecular systems offers great variety. So far it has been shown that up to seven-qubit systems can be utilized to perform quantum computations; this is more than any other method has achieved so far. The problem is, however, its scalability. All the nuclei involved have to be part of the same molecule, and this sets a practical limit on what can be achieved. With huge molecules it may prove difficult to maintain coherence over the molecule, and restrictions on the addressability of the individual spins determined by the range of chemical shifts may be severe.

The future of this method depends on its internal prospects and limitations:

1. Only simple algorithms are possible. The molecular architecture puts strict limitations on the possibilities.
2. When the number of qubits is increased, the fact that only a fraction of the nuclei contributes will set its own limitations. If N qubits are involved, the projection algorithm makes their number decrease at least as 2^{-N}. This seems to limit the number of qubits to about 10.
3. Dephasing destroys coherences in times that can be no longer than seconds. As the processing rate given above may be no better than 0.1 s, we cannot hope to perform much more than 10 computational steps coherently.
4. The addressability of individual qubits forces one to use ever more complex molecules. The disadvantage is that this also creates more complex internal couplings. Thus, it becomes harder to perform the conditional operations in a well-controlled manner.

The case of quantum computations utilizing nuclear spins is an odd situation: In most cases the thermal fluctuations of the environment are harmful to the quantum processes. In this case they are used to achieve the operations desired. The method works at its best in a liquid with large thermal motions. Thus, it has been called "computing in a cup of coffee." Whether the method can be extended efficiently to nuclear spins localized in solid matrices is still a question under investigation.

5.6.2 Optical Lattices

The concept of spins localized in solid matrices brings forward another possibility provided by cold atoms. With laser cooling one can reach very low temperatures with gaseous neutral atoms, down to the milli- or even microkelvin range. These slow atoms can be transferred to magnetic traps, which are based on spin-polarizing the atoms, or confined nondissipatively with focused, far off-resonant laser beams. By controlled reduction of the depth of the trapping potential, one lets hot atoms escape while the rest thermalize to increasingly lower temperatures. Atoms can be, as composite particles, bosons or fermions, and at sufficiently low temperatures, we see in experiments either Bose–Einstein condensation or incompressibility due to Fermi pressure, respectively.

By combining several off-resonant laser beams, instead of basic traps, one can produce, more elaborate structures. Taking advantage of the connection between atomic Zeeman states and light polarization, one can prepare optical lattices where the atoms see the spatial periodicity in light polarization as a lattice potential. In such a lattice, bosonic atoms, in the condensed state, can undergo a further phase transition into a Mott insulator, in which the atoms have settled into the lattice sites with equal, fixed numbers of atoms per site. This has been achieved experimentally, and it naturally opens many possibilities for quantum computing.

Since the lattice constant is typically smaller than the wavelength of the trapping laser, individual addressing is a serious problem. A suitable candidate for inducing conditional logic is again dipole–dipole coupling, typically involving induced electronic dipoles. Other possibilities exist, such as using chromium atoms that have permanent electric dipoles. One can also associate atoms into molecules using magnetic fields (Feshbach resonances) or laser light. For instance, one can prepare heteronuclear polar molecules from atoms localized at lattice sites. One can also superpose various lattices and move them with respect to each other. As an alternative to optical lattices, one can consider magnetic microtraps with more tunable separation of local minima. All in all, the field of atomic quantum gases is currently a very rich and rapidly moving field.

5.7   CONCLUSIONS

Here we conclude our survey of the possible physical realizations of devices performing quantum information processing. The presentations have by necessity been sketchy and incomplete. They are introduced merely to give the reader a feeling for the exciting and multifarious physical considerations entering the present experimental effort to bring quantum information manipulations into reality.

The main obstacle to realizing all schemes of information processing at the quantum level is decoherence and scalability. We summarize the properties of the

TABLE 5.1   Properties of the Systems Proposed

System	$T_{\text{relax}}s^{-1}$	$T_c s^{-1}$	N_c	N_0
Microwave cavity	10^0	10^{-4}	10^4	~ 10
Optical cavity	10^{-5}	10^{-14}	10^9	~ 10
Ion trap	10^{-1}	10^{-14}	10^{13}	~ 10
Quantum dots	10^{-6}	10^{-9}	10^3	~ 1
Nuclear spins	10^{-1}	10^{-6}	10^5	~ 10
Superconducting flux	10^{-6}	10^{-8}	10^2	~ 1
Cooper pairs in junctions	10^{-4}	10^{-8}	10^4	~ 1

systems proposed in the form of Table 5.1. In fact, most of the entries are highly speculative; in practice, the parameters needed are only imperfectly known:

- The relaxation times T_{relax} are difficult to measure. In addition, it is not clear that the rates observed so far are really those relevant for computing applications.
- The time T_c of the individual computing cycle is mostly an estimate only; in practice this will be limited by technical details such as the magnitude of coupling fields and the interaction times allowed.
- The number of computing steps, $N_c = T_{\text{relax}}/T_c$, is obviously affected by the uncertainties in both previous parameters.
- The scalability N_0 is telling how many qubits may reasonably be combined. This estimate is based on the understanding of today. Novel ideas may improve this, or new experimental information on dephasing may decrease this.

Recently suggested uses of atomic Bose–Einstein condensates are too preliminary even to warrant any estimates. The results in the table give a rather pessimistic view of the potentialities of all known systems. However, the many groups and individuals involved and the wide range of physical processes utilized suggests that novel and challenging physics will emerge eventually. Thus even if we never will see a practically useful quantum computer, the effort may provide insights into quantum physics with accompanying ability to manipulate quantum states. What unfathomed feats of physics and technology this will promote is for the future to decide. The fact remains, however, that the quantum information movement has motivated us to ask new questions and to apply our quantum theories in new ways. This may be the ultimate benefit brought by the present lively activity.

5.8   REFERENCES

The technical evolution of laboratory quantum information is rapid and multifarious. Thus, we can only touch on the main directions of the research. Much progress is taking place, and entirely new ideas will probably emerge. Thus, the following presentation is neither exhaustive nor complete. Most of the topics treated here are also discussed in [72]. Section 6 of [39] reviews the situation.

The field of cavity quantum electrodynamics is covered in considerable detail in [13]. The special considerations relating to information processing are presented in [17] (p. 133), concentrating on the microwave region. The optical region is discussed, for example, by Turchette and co-workers in [99]. As mentioned in Sec. 1.5, the field quantization procedure used in the nonrelativistic energy range is presented in detail in [29]. The special conditions in cavity geometries makes many of the standard texts on QED useless for the present purpose. The special aspects related to quantum optics are covered in, for example, [64]. Many other texts on quantum optics, such as Refs. [62, 88, 102], contain equivalent material.

Ion traps are discussed in the monograph by Ghosh [37], and a good compact review, including applications in problems of fundamental quantum mechanics, is given by Horvath and co-workers in [47]. The methods of the ion trap information processing is reviewed in [17] (p. 163). The physics of the situation is discussed in [101]. Cirac and Zoller were the first to suggest the implementation of a quantum gate on trapped ions [27]. This has subsequently been demonstrated experimentally, (see [17]). For a short review of the two-ion experiments, see [60]. There are several proposals for quantum computing with hot ions, and we have chosen the one suggested by Sørensen and Mølmer in [92]. A fast version of the bichromatic gate is described in [93].

The various solid-state implementations are surveyed in [65]. The superconducting tunneling junction systems and the use of the charge or flux degrees of freedom as qubits are reviewed in [63]. One of the latest work in superconducting flux qubits is [26], which has served as a basis for estimates on the related relaxation and computing time scales. The specific aspects relating to nuclear resonance manipulations are reviewed in [17] (p. 177). A more detailed exposition is found in [85]. The many aspects of atomic Bose–Einstein condensates are described in [80], and the first experimental realization of a phase transition into a Mott insulator in optical lattices is reported in [41].

A large number of relevant references on physical realizations may be found in [72]. For the most recent experimental advances, the topical literature should be consulted.

In Sec. 5.2 we present criteria for evaluating potential candidates for the realization of quantum computers. Such requirements were offered in a systematic fashion first by DiVincenzo [32]; our presentation is somewhat more elaborate but essentially equivalent.

REFERENCES

1. Akhieser, N. I., and I. M. Glazman, *Theory of Linear Operators in Hilbert Space*, Vol. 2, Ungar, New York, 1963.

2. Alber, G., T. Beth, M. Horodecki, P. Horodecki, R. Horodecki, M. Rötteler, H. Weinfurter, R. Werner, and A. Zeilinger, *Quantum Information: An Introduction to Basic Theoretical Concepts and Experiments*, Springer-Verlag, Heidelberg, Germany, 2001.

3. Alicki, R., and M. Fannes, *Quantum Dynamical Systems*, Oxford University Press, Oxford, 2001.

4. Alicki, R., and K. Lendi, *Dynamical Semigroups and Applications*, Lecture Notes in Physics 286, Springer-Verlag, Berlin, 1987.

5. Allen, L., and J. H. Eberly, *Optical Resonance and Two-Level Atoms*, Dover, New York, 1987.

6. Ash, R. B., *Information Theory*, Dover, New York, 1965.

7. Aspect, A., Bell's theorem: the naive view of an experimentalist, in [14], p. 119.

8. Belinfante, F. J., *Measurement and Time Reversal in Objective Quantum Theory*, Pergamon Press, Oxford, 1975.

9. Bell, J. S., On the Einstein–Podolsky–Rosen paradox, *Physics* **1**, 195 (1964).

10. Bennett, C. H., and G. Brassard, Quantum cryptography: public key distribution and coin tossing, in *Proceedings of the IEEE International Conference on Computers, Systems and Signal Processing*, IEEE, New York, 1984, p. 175.

11. Bennett, C. H., G. Brassard, C. Crépeau, R. Jozsa, A. Peres, and W. K. Wootters, Teleporting an unknown quantum state via dual classical and Einstein–Podolsky–Rosen channels, *Phys. Rev. Lett.* **70**, 1895 (1993).

12. Bennett, C. H., G. Brassard, S. Popescu, B. W. Schumacher, J. A. Smolin, and W. K. Wootters, Purification of noisy entanglement and faithful teleportation via noisy channels, *Phys. Rev. Lett.* **76**, 722 (1996).

13. Berman, P. R. (Ed.), *Cavity Quantum Electrodynamics*, Academic Press, New York, 1994.

14. Bertlmann, R. A., and A. Zeilinger (Eds.), *Quantum [Un]speakables: From Bell to Quantum Information*, Springer-Verlag, Berlin, 2002.

15. Born, M., and E. Wolf, *Principles of Optics*, 7th ed., Cambridge University Press, Cambridge, 1999.

16. Bouwmeester, D., J. W. Pan, M. Daniell, H. Weinfurter, and A. Zeilinger, Observation of three-photon Greenberger–Horne–Zeilinger entanglement, *Phys. Rev. Lett.* **82**, 1345 (1999).

17. Bouwmeester, D., A. Ekert, and A. Zeilinger (Eds.), *The Physics of Quantum Information*, Springer-Verlag, Berlin, 2000.

18. Bouwmeester, D., H. Weinfurter, and A. Zeilinger, Quantum dense coding and quantum teleportation, in [17], p. 49.

19. Breuer, H.-P., and F. Petruccione, *The Theory of Open Quantum Systems*, Oxford University Press, Oxford, 2002.

20. Busch, P., M. Grabowski, and P. J. Lahti, *Operational Quantum Physics*, Springer-Verlag, Berlin, 1997.

21. Bužek, V., and D. DiVincenzo (Eds.), Physics of quantum information, special issue of *J. Mod. Phys.* **47**, 125 (2000).

22. Bužek, V., and M. Hillery, Quantum copying: beyond the no-cloning theorem, *Phys. Rev. A* **54**, 1844 (1996).

23. Carmichael, H., *An Open Systems Approach to Quantum Optics*, Springer-Verlag, Berlin, 1993.

24. Carmichael, H., *Statistical Methods in Quantum Optics 1: Master Equations and Fokker–Planck Equations*, Springer-Verlag, Berlin, 1999.

25. Chefles, A., Quantum state discrimination, *Contemp. Phys.* **41**, 401 (2000).

26. Chiorescu, I., Y. Nakamura, C. J. Harmans, and J. E. Mooij, Coherent quantum dynamics of a superconducting flux qubit, *Science* **299**, 1869 (2003).

27. Cirac, J. I., and P. Zoller, Quantum computations with cold trapped ions, *Phys. Rev. Lett.* **74**, 4091 (1995).

28. Clauser, J. F., Early history of Bell's theorem, in [14], p. 61.

29. Cohen-Tannoudji, C., J. Dupont-Roc, and G. Grynberg, *Photons and Atoms; Introduction to Quantum Electrodynamics*, Wiley, New York, 1989.

30. Davies, E. B., *Quantum Theory of Open Systems*, Academic Press, London, 1976.

31. Dieks, D., Communication by EPR devices, *Phys. Lett. A* **96**, 271 (1982).

32. DiVincenzo, D. P., The physical implementation of quantum computation, *Fortschr. Phys.* **48**, 771 (2000); special issue on experimental proposals for quantum computation.

33. Ekert, A., Secret sides of Bell's theorem, in [14], p. 209.

34. Ekert, A., N. Gisin, B. Huttner, H. Inamori, and H. Weinfurter, Quantum cryptography, in [17], p. 15.

35. Fano, U., Description of states in quantum mechanics by density matrix and operator techniques, *Rev. Mod. Phys.* **29**, 74 (1957).

36. Feynman, R. P., *Lectures on Computation*, Addison-Wesley, Reading, MA, 1996.

37. Ghosh, P. K., *Ion Traps*, Oxford University Press, Oxford, 1995.

38. Gorini, V., A. Kossakowski, and E. C. G. Sudarshan, Completely positive dynamical semigroups of n-level systems, *J. Math. Phys.* **17**, 821 (1976).

39. Gramss, T., S. Bornholdt, M. Gross, M. Mitchell, and T. Pellizzari, *Non-standard Computations*, Wiley-VCD, Weinheim, Germany, 1998.

40. Greenberger, D. M., M. A. Horne, A. Shimony, and A. Zeilinger, Bell's theorem without inequalities, *Am. J. Phys.* **58**, 1131 (1990).

41. Greiner, M., O. Mandel, T. Esslinger, T. W. Hänsch, and I. Bloch, Quantum phase transition from a superfluid to a Mott insulator in a gas of ultracold atoms, *Nature* **415**, 39 (2002).

42. Grover, L. K., Quantum mechanics helps in searching for a needle in a haystack, *Phys. Rev. Lett.* **79**, 325 (1997).

43. Gruska, J., *Quantum Computing*, McGraw-Hill, Maidenhead, Berkshire, England, 1999.

44. ter Haar, D., Theory and applications of the density matrix, *Rep. Prog. Phys.* **24**, 304 (1961).

45. Helstrom, C. W., *Quantum Detection and Estimation Theory*, Academic Press, New York, 1976.

46. Hey, A. J. G. (Ed.), *Feynman and Computation: Exploring the Limits of Computers*, Perseus Books, New York, 1999.

47. Horvath, G. Z. K., R. C. Thompson, and P. L. Knight, Fundamental physics with trapped ions, *Contemp. Phys.* **38**, 25 (1997).

48. Hughston, L. P., R. Jozsa, and W. K. Wootters, A complete classification of quantum ensembles having a given density matrix, *Phys. Lett. A* **183**, 14 (1993).

49. Humphreys, J. F., and M. Y. Prest, *Numbers, Groups and Codes*, Cambridge University Press, Cambridge, 1989.

50. Isham, C. J., *Lectures on Quantum Theory*, Imperial College Press, London, 1995.

51. Jammer, M., *The Philosophy of Quantum Mechanics; The Interpretation of Quantum Mechanics in Historical Perspective*, Wiley, New York, 1974.

52. Jones, G. A., and J. M. Jones, *Information and Coding Theory*, Springer-Verlag, London, 2000.

53. Khinchin, A., *Mathematical Foundations of Information Theory*, Dover, New York, 1957.

54. Kneebone, G. T., *Mathematical Logic and the Foundations of Mathematics*, Van Nostrand, Princeton, NJ, 1963.

55. Knight, P. L., Quantum fluctuations in optical systems, in *Les Houches Session LXIII, 1995*, Elsevier, Amsterdam, 1997, p. 1.

56. Kraus, K., General state changes in quantum theory, *Ann. Phys.* **64**, 311 (1971).

57. Kraus, K., *States, Effects and Operations: Fundamental Notions of Quantum Theory*, Lecture Notes in Physics, Vol. 190, Springer-Verlag, Heidelberg, Germany, 1983.

58. Landau, L. D., and R. Peierls, Extension of the uncertainty principle to relativistic quantum theory, *Z. Phys.* **69**, 56 (1931); also in [105], p. 465.

59. Leff, H. S., and A. F. Rex, *Maxwell's Demon 2*, IOP Publishing, Bristol, Gloucestershire, England, 2003.

60. Levi, B. G., Two-ion logic gates open the way to further advances in quantum computing, *Phys. Today* **56**(5), 17 (2003).

61. Lindblad, G., On the generators of quantum dynamical semigroups, *Commun. Math. Phys.* **48**, 119 (1976).

62. Loudon, R., *The Quantum Theory of Light*, 3rd ed., Oxford University Press, Oxford, 2000.

63. Makhlin, Y., G. Schön, and A. Shnirman, Quantum-state engineering with Josephson junction devices, *Rev. Mod. Phys.* **73**, 357 (2001).

64. Mandel, L., and E. Wolf, *Optical Coherence and Quantum Optics*, Cambridge University Press, Cambridge, 1995.

65. Matsueda, H., Solid-state quantum computations, in [79], p. 422.

66. Meijer, P. H. E. (Ed.), *Views of a Physicist: Selected Papers of N. G. van Kampen*, World Scientific, Singapore, 2000.

67. Mensky, M. B., *Quantum Measurements and Decoherence: Models and Phenomenology*, Kluwer Academic, Dordrecht, The Netherlands, 2000.

68. Milburn, G. J., *The Feynman Processor*, Perseus Books, Cambridge, 1998.

69. Mølmer, K., Y. Castin, and J. Dalibard, Monte-Carlo wave function method in quantum optics, *J. Opt. Soc. Am. B* **10**, 527 (1993).

70. Nägerl, H. C., W. Bechter, J. Eschner, F. Schmidt-Kaler, and R. Blatt, *Appl. Phys. B* **66**, 603 (1998).

71. Neumann, J. von, *Mathematical Foundations of Quantum Mechanics*, Princeton University Press, Princeton, NJ, 1955.

72. Nielsen, M. A., and I. L. Chuang, *Quantum Computation and Quantum Information*, Cambridge University Press, Cambridge, 2000.

73. Pan, J. W., and A. Zeilinger, Multi-particle entanglement and quantum non-locality, in [14], p. 225.

74. Pan, J. W., D. Bouwmeester, H. Weinfurter, and A. Zeilinger, Experimental test of quantum nonlocality in three-photon Greenberger–Horne–Zeilinger entanglement, *Nature* **403**, 515 (2000).

75. Pauli, W., *General Principles of Quantum Mechanics*, Springer-Verlag, Berlin, 1980.

76. Pegg, D. T., and S. M. Barnett, Retrodiction in quantum optics, *J. Opt. B: Quantum Semiclass. Opt.* **1**, 442 (1999).

77. Penrose, R., *The Emperor's New Mind: Concerning Computers, Minds, and the Laws of Physics*, Oxford University Press, Oxford, 1989.

78. Peres, A., *Quantum Theory: Concepts and Methods*, Kluwer Academic, Dordrecht, The Netherlands, 1995.

79. Peřina, J. (Ed.), *Coherence and Statistics of Photons and Atoms*, Wiley, New York, 2001.

80. Pethick, C. J., and H. Smith, *Bose–Einstein Condensation in Dilute Gases*, Cambridge University Press, Cambridge, 2002.

81. Plenio, M. B., and P. L. Knight, The quantum jump approach to dissipative dynamics in quantum optics, *Rev. Mod. Phys.* **70**, 101 (1998).

82. Plenio, M. B., and V. Vedral, Teleportation, entanglement and thermodynamics in the quantum world, *Contemp. Phys.* **39**, 431 (1998).

83. Plenio, M. B., and V. Vitelli, The physics of forgetting: Landauer's erasure principle and information theory, *Contemp. Phys.* **42**, 25 (2001).

84. Preskill, J., Quantum information and physics: some future directions, in [21], p. 127.

85. Sakaguchi, U., H. Ozawa, and T. Fukumi, NMR quantum computations, in [79], p. 470.

86. Schrödinger, E., Discussion of probability relations between separated systems, *Proc. Cambridge Philos. Soc.* **31**, 555 (1935).

87. Schroeder, M. R., *Number Theory in Science and Communication*, Springer-Verlag, Berlin, 1990.

88. Scully, M. O., and M. S. Zubairy, *Quantum Optics*, Cambridge University Press, Cambridge, 1997.

89. Shannon, C. E., A mathematical theory of communication, *Bell System Tech. J.* **27**, 379 and 623 (1948).

90. Shor, P. W., Polynomial-time algorithms for prime factorization and discrete logarithms on a quantum computer, *SIAM J. Comput.* **26**, 1484 (1997).

91. Silverman, R. A., *Introductory Complex Analysis*, Dover, New York, 1972.

92. Sørensen, A., and K. Mølmer, Quantum computation with ions in thermal motion, *Phys. Rev. Lett.* **82**, 1971 (1999).

93. Sørensen, A., and K. Mølmer, Entanglement and quantum computation with ions in thermal motion, *Phys. Rev. A* **62**, 022311 (2000).

94. Stenholm, S., Occurrences, observations and measurements in quantum mechanics, *Phys. Scr.* **47**, 724 (1993).

95. Stenholm, S., and E. Andersson, Shared access to quantum information, *Phys. Rev. A* **62**, 044301 (2000).

96. Stenholm, S., and M. Wilkens, Jumps in quantum theory, *Contemp. Phys.* **38**, 257 (1997).

97. Stinespring, W. F., Positive function on C^* algebras, *Proc. Am. Math. Soc.* **6**, 233 (1955).

98. Sudarshan, E. C. G., Quantum dynamics, metastable states and contractive semi-groups, *Phys. Rev. A* **46**, 37 (1992).

99. Turchette, Q. A., C. J. Hood, W. Lange, H. Mabuchi, and H. J. Kimble, Measurement of conditional phase shifts for quantum logic, *Phys. Rev. Lett.* **75**, 4710 (1995).

100. Viamontes, G. F., I. L. Markov, and J. P. Hayes, *Is Quantum Search Practical*, LANL database article quant-ph/0405001 (2004).

101. Vogel, W., and S. Wallentowitz, Manipulation of the quantum state of a trapped ion, in [79], p. 333.

102. Walls, D. F., and G. J. Milburn, *Quantum Optics*, Springer-Verlag, Berlin, 1994.

103. Wehrl, A., General properties of entropy, *Rev. Mod. Phys.* **50**, 221 (1978).

104. Werner, R. F., Quantum information theory: an invitation, in [2], p. 14.

105. Wheeler, J. A., and W. H. Zurek, *Quantum Theory and Measurements*, Princeton University Press, Princeton, NJ, 1983.

106. Wittgenstein, L., *Tractatus Logico-Philosophicus*, Routledge & Kegan Paul, London, 1961.

107. Wootters, W. K., and W. H. Zurek, A single quantum cannot be cloned, *Nature* **299**, 802 (1982).

108. Zalka, C., Using Grover's quantum algorithm for searching actual databases, *Phys. Rev. A* **62**, 052305 (2000).

109. Zurek, W. H. (Ed.), *Complexity, Entropy and the Physics of Information*, Santa Fe Institute, Vol. VIII, Addison-Wesley, Redwood City, CA, 1990.

INDEX

Quantum Approach to Informatics, by Stig Stenholm and Kalle-Antti Suominen
Copyright © 2005 John Wiley & Sons, Inc.

Printed and bound by CPI Group (UK) Ltd, Croydon, CR0 4YY

Printed and bound by CPI Group (UK) Ltd, Croydon, CR0 4YY

27/10/2024

14580261-0001